Introduction to Organizational Behaviour

Introduction to
Organizational Behaviour

Steve Ellis and Penny Dick

McGraw-Hill Publishing Company
London · Burr Ridge IL · New York · St Louis · San Francisco · Auckland
Bogotá · Caracas · Lisbon · Madrid · Mexico · Milan · Montreal
New Delhi · Panama · Paris · San Juan · São Paulo · Singapore · Sydney
Tokyo · Toronto

Published by
McGraw-Hill Publishing Company
Shoppenhangers Road, Maidenhead, Berkshire SL6 2QL, UK
Telephone 01628 502500
Facsimile 01628 770224

Cataloguing in Publication Data is available from the British Library

Cataloguing-in-publication Data is available from the Library of Congress

**Further information on this title is to be found at
http://www.mcgraw-hill.co.uk/ellis**

Publisher: Andy Goss
Sponsoring Editor: Dominic Recaldin
Senior Marketing Manager: Jackie Harbor
Editorial Assistant: Caroline Howell
Desk Editor: Alastair Lindsay

Printed and bound in Malta by Interprint Limited

ISBN 007 709535 9

McGraw-Hill

A Division of The McGraw·Hill Companies

Brief table of contents

Contents

Preface and Guided Tour

This text is aimed at those who are new to the study of organizational behaviour (OB). Our purpose in writing this book was to provide you with a concise grounding in the major areas that comprise the field of OB, and so give you the conceptual and practical foundations on which to build further knowledge.

As an introductory text, it is more concerned with building sound pillars of understanding than developing a grand philosophical approach to the issues that face organizations and people who work in them at this time. In studying with this text you will quickly gain an appreciation of how much OB theory underpins today's business practices and how, if correctly applied, it can help managers turn poor business results into better ones. Many texts offer exhaustive coverage of the topics you will find here but our concern is to make this book a useful tool for those who need a concise and sharply focused guide to the central issues.

The book is therefore intended for use by all students on first-level degree or diploma OB modules at college or university. It should also be valuable for students preparing for papers or assignments in the organizational behaviour subjects of numerous professional bodies.

The underlying concepts that comprise much of what OB is are increasing in significance as the study of organizations continues to be one of the most vigorous research areas of the social sciences. A direct consequence of this vigour is the fact that some areas within the field remain subject to much conjecture and dispute. We have tried to reflect this in our treatment by highlighting the areas of contention rather than offer 'cast in stone' conclusions.

One of the key themes in the text is that of the organization's need to interact with the external environment. The penetration of the world outside the organization has, by any recognized measure, increased significantly in recent times and the requirement for organizations to interact more with their rapidly changing environments, rather than operate in isolation, presents many organizations with a major challenge. The move toward globalization of many marketplaces has further increased this impact as organizations seek to operate effectively in culturally diverse environments.

Despite the all-pervasive intervention of technology into organizations, they remain, in their many forms, a fundamentally human experience. The richness that this affords those of us who work in or study organizations in vast. Organizations, which comprise human beings after all, display the same degrees of divergence that we can see in individuals. The ideas and concepts that underpin all aspects of human behaviour presented in this book will give you a lens though which you will see more clearly the fascinating way that organizations operate and develop.

Organizations, as you know, are capable of creating great feats of human achievement and equally capable of fantastic failures and mistakes. We hope that the understanding you develop through working through this book will help you to see the reasons for both.

To familiarize yourself with the learning features, illustrative examples and assessment material that you will encounter as you work through each chapter, please take a few minutes to go through the Guided Tour (pp. xii–xiii). These elements include learning objectives, highlighted key terms, 'reflection' boxes, a chapter summary, 'discussion' and 'self-test' questions, and a comprehensive reference and bibliography listing.

Case studies

The final section of the book comprises six case studies drawn from real organizations. These are designed to illustrate the practical application and implications of the concepts covered in the text, and how OB integrates ideas and knowledge from a variety of disciplines to tackle its unique and challenging problems. Each case study, which is followed by some questions for you to consider, also serves to highlight how the broad concepts and ideas contained in the field of OB apply to organizations. The section begins with an outline of how you should approach a case study.

Website

Additional material for lecturers and students including website links, self-test questions, analysis of the case studies and lecture slides and notes can be found at the following web address:

www.mcgraw-hill.co.uk/textbooks/ellis

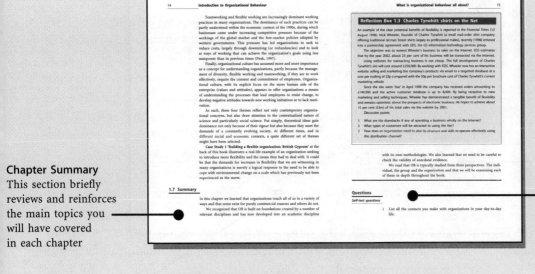

Chapter Summary
This section briefly reviews and reinforces the main topics you will have covered in each chapter

Self-test Questions
These short questions enable you to put your understanding of the main topics and issues to the test – brief suggested answers are given in a section at the end of the text

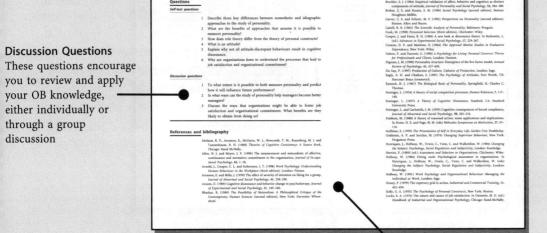

Discussion Questions
These questions encourage you to review and apply your OB knowledge, either individually or through a group discussion

References/Bibliography
A full listing of the books and other sources referred to closes each chapter, providing you with an opportunity to undertake further study and research into OB topics

Learning Objectives
These bullet-points identify the primary topics in terms of the learning outcomes you should acquire after studying each chapter

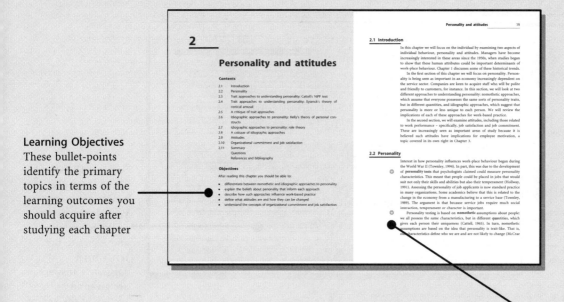

Key Terms
Alerting you to a core concept or technique, these colour-highlighted terms appear throughout the text with an adjacent icon; key terms are also highlighted in the index to assist revision

Figures/Tables
Each chapter includes a number of figures and tables to explain and summarize important concepts

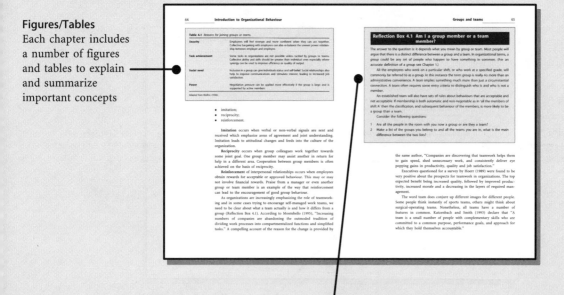

Reflection Boxes
These boxes provide additional illustrative examples and linked questions to highlight the practical application of OB concepts, and to encourage you to analyse and discuss the issues

Acknowledgements

Our thanks go to the following reviewers for their comments at various stages in the text's development:

Trevor Bolton, Anglia Polytechnic University
Brian Stone, Manchester Metropolitan University
Beryl Sanders, London Guildhall University
Stephen Gourlay, University of Kingston
Jean Kellie, University of Lincolnshire and Humberside
Val Finnigan, Leeds Metropolitan University
Rupert Leathes, Bournemouth University
Sue Simpson, University of Derby
Martin Gammell, Luton University
Tara Fleming, Southampton Institute

Dedication

For Kathryn – my reason.

1

What is organizational behaviour all about?

Contents

Objectives

At the end of the chapter you should be able to:

- acknowledge the importance of OB to commercial society
- appreciate that OB draws on a number of disciplines to create a legitimate field of study in its own right
- recognize the methodologies and techniques commonly used in OB research
- comprehend the contexts in which the study of OB operates

1.1 Introduction

We come into contact with organizations from the cradle to the grave. Indeed, organizations regulate and dictate so many aspects of our lives – giving many of us somewhere to work, entertaining us when we are at leisure and developing new products and services for our enjoyment – that even if you do not work in one, you can rarely escape their influence.

Organizations are responsible for your education and training, health and welfare, and security. In most economies, the government will take responsibility for organizing a country's infrastructure. Infrastructure includes motorways, air and rail networks, communication systems, emergency services and even legal and regulatory authorities. All are maintained by some form of organization.

We can make a distinction between commercial organizations, on the one hand, whose chief intention is to provide financial returns to their owners and **not-for-profit** and public sector organizations, on the other, whose objectives are based on a broader set of outcomes, such as the provision of a social service. Many OB issues apply equally to both but some are more significant in one sector than the other. It is crucially important to be aware of an organization's objectives before attempting to apply what you have learned.

Whether an organization is privately owned or not, demands for ever-increasing efficiency and effectiveness lead us to look for responses to previously unconsidered issues. For example, until the mid-1990s many organizations believed they could offer employees long-term job security, and an important personnel function was to plan the long-term development of their employees' careers.

The current uncertainty of the business world has caused some organizations to shy away from offering these long-term agreements to employees, resulting in a reassessment of the unwritten understanding between the employee and the organization (the so-called **psychological contract**) (Stredwick and Ellis, 1998; Herriot and Pemberton, 1995; Makin, Cooper and Cox, 1996). The position today, according to Pascale (1995) and Kissler (1994), is very different. An offer of long-term job security is no longer seen as an effective way of building a flexible and competitive organization. Employees find it equally hard to keep their side of the bargain. Indeed, for some professions a career can be built more effectively by moving from one organization to another.

At a more sociological or psychological level organizations also have significant effects on our lives. They offer a source of identity to those who wish to be associated with them, a sense of continuity between generations and opportunities for social interaction with other members of society.

As a new student in the field you need to be aware of the effects of many of the major changes currently being experienced in organizations and the people who work there. As you progress through this book you will encounter a number of OB concepts and theories which attempt to explain and describe what we can all see going on in organizations.

1.2 What is OB?

OB is the study of human behaviour in the workplace. As an academic discipline its concern is to gain an understanding of those factors, both individual and organizational, that influence people's behaviour. Ultimately, through this understanding there is an over-arching interest in the control and direction of people at work. Basically, finding out how people can best be utilized to maximize the effectiveness of the organization in whatever it is trying to achieve. After all, people are often referred to as an organization's greatest asset but they are also its greatest cost. Salaries and associated employment costs can make up 75 per cent of the operating costs of a business. The darker side of employee control could be seen as manipulative or, even worse, bullying if managers try to take control too far.

As your studies progress you will recognize the elements that make up the field of OB. Typically, you will need to understand something of psychology, sociology, management science, social anthropology and, some would argue, economics, law and politics. As an area of study, therefore, OB is a very broad church. But it is the way in which OB borrows ideas from relevant disciplines and shapes and integrates them to tackle practical issues at work that gives the OB discipline its particular style and flavour.

According to George and Jones (1996), OB is the study of the many factors that have an impact on how individuals and groups respond to and act in organizations and how organizations manage their environments. The study of OB provides guidelines for managers and employees to understand and appreciate the many forces that effect behaviour and to make better decisions about how to motivate and coordinate resources (including people) to achieve organizational goals. OB provides a set of tools – in terms of concepts and theories – that help people to understand, analyse and describe what goes on in organizations.

Reflection Box 1.1 Typical OB problems

Businesses bring together very diverse groups of people who might have widely differing interests, attitudes, abilities, beliefs and values. The effective organization has a set of practices and policies that weld diverse groups into a workforce that contributes to the organization's goals and objectives. What kinds of issues must an organization or its managers confront when it attempts to mould its workforce?

1   How can an organization allocate people to specific roles that make the best use of their personalities, beliefs or attitudes? What would be the benefits of this approach and how practical is it?

2   What is the best way to manage and develop the culture of the organization?

3   What is more important to an organization: achieving employee job satisfaction or getting results? How far can you justify achieving results as the number one priority regardless of employee satisfaction?

4   Who will be responsible for managing employee performance: the individual's manager, the personnel department or the employee? What tools would each group require to manage performance?

5   How should the organization develop and change over time to take account of market shifts and new technology?

6   Work groups can provide opportunities for enhanced performance, but they can also go wrong. What techniques or strategies can the organization employ to capture the best and eliminate the worst aspects of team working?

OB may have borrowed much from other disciplines, but it has a full complement of theories of its own. One of the principal aims of this book is to get you to think critically about the OB theories and concepts and to use your judgement to weigh evidence in an informed way.

You can see that the issues in Reflection Box 1.1 are not solely about the people side of business but also involve the consideration of organization structures, organizational culture and organization development.

1.3 How do you measure behaviour?

Social science research, of which OB is a part, inevitably involves the study of people, either in groups or in isolation. The richness available to researchers, in looking at the variety of behaviours that people display, is also a source of frustration, as what is observed in one situation is not repeated elsewhere when other people are observed. To research into OB we have to find ways of measuring and interpreting such things as behaviour, attitudes, actions and beliefs, in order to give meaning which may be understood by others and sometimes generalized to other similar situations.

In order to understand the way humans behave in organizations we must rely on rigorous investigations into the aspects of behaviour that we can see – the actions and decisions that humans take in a variety of situations. The research tools that OB has at its disposal are not the same as those used by scientific researchers in other disciplines, but the evidence presented in OB must be subjected to the same standards of criticism and testability if it is to maintain credibility. The complexity of collecting data from a range of sources and interpreting the multiple drivers that cause behaviours makes research, leading to sound evidence, a necessarily complicated process. As OB researchers attempt to develop a framework for the interpretation of current behaviour and prediction of future outcomes, they have to take care to avoid misinterpretation of results and look out for situationally specific characteristics which might influence the research outcomes.

Research findings are more acceptable if others can prove them too. As recently as the late 1800s it was believed that the Universe was embedded in a colourless odourless substance called the ether, through which light waves passed on their way to Earth. It took an experiment designed by two American physicists, Michelson and Morley, in 1887 to prove that the ether did not exist (cited in Zukav, 1979). Furthermore, their experiment could be **replicated**; that is, other scientists produced the same result using the same experimental technique.

Valid research is not only replicable but is also *predictable*. In the so-called 'hard' sciences (e.g. chemistry or physics) it is possible to predict what will happen to a physical object if it is subjected to known and measurable forces. For example, a length of copper wire of a certain gauge, under normal conditions of temperature and pressure, will break if it is subjected to loads of a certain predictable mass. The value of research is also enhanced by its general *applicability*. We can say that because the wire breaks under a certain load, all copper wires of that gauge wherever they are will do the same.

Unfortunately, for the field of OB, human behaviour is not like that. **Motivation**, for example, varies in the same person from time to time and from situation to situation (Reflection Box 1.2). (The gauge of the copper wire does not vary according to the way it is feeling!) Neither can we say that research findings from a study of one individual are generally applicable to all individuals. Nonetheless, the more research we carry out into individual behaviour the closer we can get to accurate predictions of how people, in certain circumstances, are likely to react or behave.

1.4 Early work in OB

One of the earliest difficulties encountered by OB pioneers was how to set about researching behaviour at work in a rigorous way. This problem is similar to that faced by psychologists and sociologists, who found it difficult to gain academic credibility in a world where accurate measurement and proof through experimental replication were considered essential.

According to Tyson and Jackson (1992) though "By and large behaviour is not random; on the contrary, it is directed towards an end. Moreover there are differences between people: in similar situations we do not necessarily act in similar ways. But there are fundamental consistencies which allow predictability."

Trying to measure and prove a variety of psychological or sociological phenomena through numerous replications is almost impossible. As a result of this, early researchers soon discovered that it was not possible to move with great confidence from generalized assumptions about how groups of people behave, or tend to behave, to specific and predictable actions for individuals.

Unmeasurable human phenomena such as fatigue, motivation or attitudes, for instance, are so subjective (i.e. they depend on the person you are considering) and even more difficult to assess because they change greatly and unpredictably over time. In the so-called hard sciences, such problems are less troublesome as most phenomena in the physical world possess objective characteristics like weight or size that can be measured accurately.

Tyson and Jackson (1992) report that the science of OB is one based upon disagreement, controversy and alternative viewpoints. According to Robbins (1992) the trick is to be able to decipher under what conditions each argument may be right or wrong.

The World Wars and the period in-between saw massive advances in both the understanding and methods of research into workplace behaviour.

Reflection Box 1.2 What makes people work?

At the beginning of the twentieth century, as the Western world grew ever more industrialized, people-related problems in workplaces assumed greater significance in the eyes of factory owners and managers: specifically, how to get people to work harder, while keeping their salaries at a level that still allows the company to make a profit. It was an American, Frederick W. Taylor, who really got people thinking about people as an actual resource to be used in the workplace.

In 1911, Taylor's book *Principles of Scientific Management*, proposed that managing people was a process that could be carried out using *scientific principles*. In particular, he asserted that any given job could be examined closely so that the most efficient and appropriate way of doing that job could be identified as the **one best way**. Taylor's approach to management was informed by a belief *that human beings work only for money*. Taylor believed that pay was the only real motivator for people in the workplace and that the only way to encourage people to work harder was by offering them a financial incentive.

Taylor was the forefather of **time and motion study** – a procedure whereby the tasks involved in a job are studied to see how much time it takes to do each, and the methods used to perform each task are examined to see whether they are effective. Many companies that adopted Taylor's approach believed that it gave them a real competitive advantage, and the principles were widely adopted throughout US industry as well as in European countries, such as Germany and France.

1   Do you agree with the view that people work only for money?
2   Why do people do work that is not paid for; for example, charity work or volunteer work?
3   Will everybody work more if you pay them more?
4   What do people get out of working apart from the pay?

Research workers in the social sciences tackle these methodological problems by concentrating on measurable effects of behaviour. They ask such questions as 'What sort of behaviour is shown by people who are not satisfied at work?' Dissatisfied people might be late for work or may not come to work at all. Or they may lack concentration and make more errors than are typical. These so-called **indirect measures** can be assessed. This process of translating experiences into measurable sets of behaviours is known as **operationalization**.

Social science researchers also use interviews, questions to generate data that they subsequently analyse, commonly with the help of sophisticated statistical techniques to reveal meaningful and reliable results. They may enhance the validity of their evidence by **triangulation**, taking evidence from a number of points of view to come to a more balanced and reliable judgement.

The research carried out at this time led to the development of some very important ideas that continue to influence management practices in organizations today. During World War I, for example, the UK government established a committee responsible for overseeing the health of workers in the munitions factories. And in 1928 the Industrial Health Research Board (IHRB) was established, a body that researched issues such as sickness and absence, working hours time and motion studies and job design (Marriot, 1970). In America, interest in the work of the German industrial psychologist Hugo Munsterberg (1863–1916) was stimulated by World War I in which psychological testing was used to recruit military personnel, as a means of 'fitting men to the job' (Corsini, 1987).

Another major influence on research in organizational behaviour was the *Hawthorne Studies* that were carried out in the Western Electric Company at Hawthorne in Illinois from 1924 to about 1935. These studies were carried out by a team of academics under the guidance of a Harvard professor, Elton Mayo (Hollway, 1991).

Initially, these experiments, inspired by the concept of *Scientific Management* (a set of theories and beliefs originated in the 1920s by F. W. Taylor which saw great value in the detailed measurement of work in order to streamline and increase worker efficiency), set out to examine the effects of variation in a range of working conditions including various light levels on the productivity of workers. Mayo found, rather perplexingly, that no matter what they did to working conditions, productivity within the group subjected to the variations always increased. This was the case even when illumination was reduced to such an extent that workers could barely see their hands in front of them. This finding led to the term **Hawthorne effect** which refers to the phenomenon whereby human behaviour is affected simply by the act of observation. As a consequence of this the opportunities for conducting accurate **time and motion studies**, where workers are closely observed and timed to see how long a job or element of a job actually takes, will generally give a false reading of the actual situation.

So, following Mayo's conclusions, the organization that takes an interest in its staff, treats them well and takes into account their feelings and needs can expect to get better output than one that does not.

As the Hawthorne experiments progressed, however, the researchers found that, contrary to their expectations, incentives were not the greatest influence on productivity; rather, it appeared that social norms operating within groups of workers were of major importance. The researchers coined the phrase **rate fixing** to refer to the tendency for groups of workers to establish a standard level of productivity with which group members were expected to comply. People working at a rate too far above or below this standard rate were likely to be subjected to informal sanctions such as being excluded from the group's social processes.

Obtaining evidence in the social-science area traditionally utilizes various methods of **interviewing, questionnaires** and **observation** techniques to generate the data to be subsequently analysed. More recent innovations in techniques have included the use of **critical incident diaries, focus group discussions** and **longitudinal studies** into changes in observed behaviour over time. While none of the individual techniques may present a full picture of the area being investigated, the use of combinations of a number of techniques is a way of increasing the level of validity of the evidence obtained.

Work in the OB field regularly draws on established theories from other recognized academic disciplines such as psychology or sociology, but adds a flavour of the organizational context. In this way the theory is used almost as a flashlight to highlight issues and demonstrate contradictions that may be found in whatever organizational situation is being considered. It is this view that we urge you to take when you come across the theories and concepts presented in this and other textbooks. Take from the theories whatever frameworks and examples you can to help illustrate what you are observing, remembering always that evidence which satisfies scientific criteria is better than a shrewd guess.

The student of OB has to be aware of the temptation to believe anecdotal information as though it were fact. Organizational myths about the way people behave may be entertaining, but do not carry any weight unless supported and verified by a valid body of research evidence.

1.5 The individual, the group and the organization

It is customary to analyse OB from three points of view – that of the individual, the group and the organization. This three-stage classification is a good way of learning about the subject of OB. It allows us to consider the impact of organizations on our lives at three increasingly complex levels of analysis, building our understanding as we go. If we take the individual view we look at such things as personality and attitudes, job roles and motivation. If we look at groups we are more concerned with how teams of workers interact and how they are led and developed. When we

TEXT OUTLINE		
THE INDIVIDUAL	THE GROUP	THE ORGANIZATION
		bureaucracy
		change
		complexity theory
		contingency leadership
attitudes		flexibility
commitment	communication	hierarchy
discrimination	group cohesion	knowledge management
diversity	group decision-making	leadership styles
equal opportunity	group norms	male and female leadership
empowerment	group structure	management development
job enrichment	groupthink	metaphorical analysis
job satisfaction	inter-group conflict	organization culture
motivation	multiskilled teams	organization structure
perception	peer pressure	organizational development
performance appraisal	quality circles	organizational effectiveness
performance management	risky shift?	organization environment
personal constructs	self-managed teams	organization life-cycles
personality traits	social needs	organizational systems
psychological contracts	teambuilding	power
role theory	team objectives	pluralism
self-actualization	team-based pay	role model leadership
socialization	team roles	socio-technical systems
values	teamworking	stakeholders
		unitarism
		virtual organizations
THESE TOPICS ARE COVERED IN CHAPTERS 2, 3 AND 8	THESE ARE COVERED IN CHAPTER 4	THESE TOPICS ARE COVERED IN CHAPTERS 5, 6, 7 AND 9

Figure 1.1   A three-category model of the study of OB.

look at organizations we consider issues such as organizational culture, legislative and technological changes and strategies underlying management policies. Figure 1.1 illustrates these three perspectives and shows the nature of the issues relevant to each perspective.

1.6 Contemporary issues in OB

Figure 1.1 provides a map of the different topics that are covered in the book. However, in addition to the topics that are explicitly covered, there are four contemporary themes that recur throughout the book, spanning different topics and chapters. These are diversity, teamworking, organizational culture and flexible working practices.

Diversity is a concept that is concerned with the differences between people and how such differences affect organizational and individual performance. As you will see as you progress through the book, there are many theoretical and practical approaches for designing and managing organizations that are based on the assumption that people in organizations are basically *similar*, rather than *different*. We see this assumption reflected in some approaches to motivation (Chapter 3), in the analysis of organizations (Chapter 7) and even in approaches that are explicitly concerned with increasing diversity (Chapter 8). In these chapters we will be examining the validity of this assumption.

Diversity is also a useful concept for linking the individual, group and organizational levels of analysis in organizational behaviour. For example, in Chapter 2 we focus on a number of ways in which individuals differ and the basis for these differences. In Chapter 4 we see how these differences affect the performance of teams and in Chapters 5 and 7 we see how such differences affect the performance of organizations.

Finally, diversity is a useful concept for highlighting the tensions that exist within the field of organizational behaviour. Organizational behaviour can be criticized on the grounds that some of its assumptions and theories are developed from a managerialist perspective; that is, they are more concerned with the interests of managers than workers (Sofer, 1972). These tensions are explored explicitly in Chapter 8, where we examine the difficulties organizations have in promoting the interests of minority groups. They are also explored in Chapter 7, where we use the concept of power to show how organizations can be thought of as highly contested arenas, in which individuals and groups use their differences to achieve positions of power. As we shall see, such contests do not always further the interests of the organization's official power holders.

The second theme is that of **teamworking**. At the group level of analysis the concept of teamworking is increasingly important to many organizations. Teams are being set up to manage all sorts of organizational problems, with some organizations developing self-managed team-based structures rather than have individuals responsible to a line manager. Introducing teamworking presents a number of challenges to managers and team members. Employees now have to consider the impact of their behaviour on other team members and other teams within the organization. The objective of using teams is to improve overall performance of the organization and not to have high performance teams in some parts of the organization let down by poor performance elsewhere.

As you can see from Figure 1.1, teamworking is covered in detail in Chapter 4. However, in other chapters and topics we can see both the roots and the effects of the increasing emphasis on teamworking. In Chapter 6, for instance, we see how the ever-increasing complexity of the business environment has led organizations to reconsider the way they are structured. In broad terms, many organizations are seeking to reduce bureaucracy and increase their flexibility by introducing flatter structures that facilitate teamworking. Thus teamworking is partly a response to meeting the demands of an evermore competitive business environment. In Chapter 9 the concept of organizational learning shows how organizations are attempting to gain strategic advantage by utilizing knowledge in ways that facilitate organizational performance. Teamworking is seen as playing a key role in knowledge production and dissemination. Finally, in Chapter 5 the shift in emphasis from the study of managers to the study of leaders illustrates how teamworking as a practice demands different sorts of individual attributes to those required in less flexibly organized companies.

The third theme is **organizational culture**, a concept that has received much attention from researchers and writers since the mid-1970s. Organizational culture is concerned with the *human* side of an organization. Specifically, the behaviours, attitudes and values that employees possess. The interest in organizational culture partly corresponds with the shift in the economic base of Western Europe from manufacturing to service industries and the attendant problems of managing employees' behaviour. Simply put, service industries are far more dependent on employees for their success than are manufacturing industries, because the employee *is* the service in many cases. Chapter 7 explores the concept of culture as a topic in its own right, but it is reflected in many topics covered in other chapters. For example, some motivation theories are explicitly concerned with identifying employees' values and attitudes (Chapter 3); organizational commitment is considered to be a highly important concept and is concerned with the extent to which individuals identify with organizational values (Chapters 2 and 4); and organizational development is explicitly concerned with understanding and intervening in these processes (Chapter 9).

The final contemporary theme is that of **flexible working practices**. Where customers or other users of organizational services are demanding 24-hour access and instant responses to their changing needs, the organization that can respond effectively to such demands will reap the rewards. This means that organizations have to be able to adapt to change readily and utilize policies that encourage flexible working, not constrain it. Operating flexibly means moving from a rigid repeatable formula for organizational success to a situation where the organization is prepared to respond quickly and has contingency operation plans to cover all reasonable possibilities.

Creating a flexible organization places demands on both employers and employees. For instance, employers need to be able to retain staff who are 'experts' or 'knowledge workers', but at the same time to have a pool of potential staff who are multi-skilled and who can be employed on a temporary basis to meet production or service demands. These demands mean that organizations need to have some means of selecting appropriate staff. As we shall see in Chapter 2, some selection practices are based on the assumption that individuals and their environments do not change much over time, yet this is a challengeable assumption. How can organizations make 'good' selection decisions if it is not possible to predict human behaviour with any degree of accuracy? The extent to which individuals can be measured and predicted is debated throughout many of the chapters in the book in the form of Reflection Boxes.

From the employee's perspective, flexible working may mean that that job security (the prospect of a permanent steady job) is simply not achievable. Given that many motivation theories were developed at a time when job security was the norm (Chapter 3), what implications does flexible working have for maintaining a motivated workforce? Again, these issues are explored in Reflection Boxes throughout the chapters.

Finally, flexible-working practices can be seen as a response to changing economic and social conditions and, as a set of practices, we need to understand them as located in this broader context. The impact of context on a variety of theoretical and practical approaches to work behaviour is discussed in many of the chapters in the book, and you will be encouraged to think about this as you progress through it.

These four themes were also chosen because they reflect current concerns in organizations. Diversity is assuming more and more importance as the nature of the employment market continues to change. The increase in service-sector jobs has seen increasing numbers of women entering the employment market (*The Economist* (US), 1998), and government policies on social inclusion in both Europe and North America mean that organizations are under increasing pressure to recruit from minority groups. These pressures have led to a focus on diversity issues and drawn attention to the limitations and strengths of approaches aimed at managing or increasing diversity.

Teamworking and flexible working are increasingly dominant working practices in many organizations. The dominance of such practices can be partly understood within the economic context of the 1990s, during which businesses came under increasing competitive pressure because of the workings of the global market and the free-market policies adopted by western governments. This pressure has led organizations to seek to reduce costs, largely through downsizing (or redundancies) and to look at ways of working that can achieve the organization's goals using less manpower than in previous times (Peak, 1997).

Finally, organizational culture has assumed more and more importance as a concept for understanding organizations, partly because the management of diversity, flexible working and teamworking, if they are to work effectively, require the consent and commitment of employees. Organizational culture, with its explicit focus on the more human side of the enterprise (values and attitudes), appears to offer organizations a means of understanding the processes that lead employees to resist change, to develop negative attitudes towards new working initiatives or to lack motivation.

As such, these four themes reflect not only contemporary organizational concerns, but also draw attention to the contextualized nature of science and particularly social science. Put simply, theoretical ideas gain dominance not only because of their rigour but also because they meet the demands of a constantly evolving society. At different times, and in different social and economic contexts, a quite different set of themes might have been selected.

Case Study 1 'Building a flexible organization: British Gypsum' at the back of this book illustrates a real-life example of an organization seeking to introduce more flexibility and the issues they had to deal with. It could be that the demands for increases in flexibility that we are witnessing in many organizations is merely a logical response to the need to be able to cope with environmental change on a scale which has previously not been experienced as the norm.

1.7 Summary

In this chapter we learned that organizations touch all of us in a variety of ways and that some exist for purely commercial reasons and others do not.

We recognized that OB is built on foundations created by a number of relevant disciplines and has now developed into an academic discipline

---

Reflection Box 1.3 Charles Tyrwhitt shirts on the Net

An example of the clear potential benefits of flexibility is reported in the *Financial Times* (13 August 1998). Nick Wheeler, founder of Charles Tyrwhitt (a small mail-order shirt company offering traditional Jermyn Street shirts largely to professional males), recently (1998) entered into a partnership agreement with EDS, the US information-technology services group.

The objective was to extend Wheeler's business to sales on the Internet. EDS estimates that by the year 2002, about 25 per cent of his business will be transacted via the Internet.

Using websites for transacting business is not cheap. The full development of Charles Tyrwhitt's site will cost around £250,000. By working with EDS, Wheeler now has an interactive website selling and marketing the company's products via email to a targetted database at a cost per mailing of 22p compared with the 50p per brochure cost of Charles Tyrwhitt's current marketing vehicle.

Since the site went 'live' in April 1998 the company has received orders amounting to £140,000 and the active customer database is up to 8,000. By being receptive to new marketing and selling techniques, Wheeler has demonstrated a tangible benefit of flexibility and remains optimistic about the prospects of electronic business. He hopes to achieve about 15 per cent (£5m) of his total sales via the website by 2001.

Discussion points

1 What are the drawbacks if any of operating a business wholly on the Internet?
2 What types of customers will be attracted to using the Net?
3 How does an organization need to alter its structure and skills to operate effectively using this distribution channel?

---

with its own methodologies. We also learned that we need to be careful to check the validity of anecdotal evidence.

We read that OB is typically studied from three perspectives. The individual, the group and the organization and that we will be examining each of these in depth throughout the book.

Questions

Self-test questions

1 List all the contacts you make with organizations in your day-to-day life.

2   Why are people the organization's best asset and their biggest potential liability?

3   What are the three traditional levels of complexity used in the study of organizational behaviour?

4   How far do you think that virtual organizations will be able to use technology to replace the functions that traditional organizations perform?

5   How does the use of indirect measures assist in identifying and estimating subjective phenomena?

Discussion questions

1   How can theories be used in OB, when many of the concepts and beliefs are largely unprovable?

2   If some theories of OB are not based on verifiable facts, how can you defend the field from the claim that it is 'just common sense' and not really scientific?

3   What do you think about the contribution of teams to organizational working versus that of an individual?

4   How important do you think the psychological contract is between employees and the organization, how is it changing?

5   Do you see the importance and influence of OB growing in the future, if so why and if not why not?

References and bibliography

Arker, D. and Joachimstaller, E. (1999) The lure of global branding, *Harvard Business Review*, November/December.

Brookes, I. and Bates, P. (1995) The problems of effecting change in the British Civil Service, a cultural perspective, *British Journal of Management*, **5**, 177–190.

Buchanan, D. and Huczynski, A. (1997) *Organisational Behaviour*, London: Prentice Hall.

Corsini, R. J. (1987) *Concise Dictionary of Psychology*, New York: Wiley.

Ellis, S. (1996) A study into strategic change management at Royal Mail, MPhil, University of Luton.

Freedman, S. M. and Phillips, J. S. (1988) The changing nature of research on women at work, *Journal of Management*, **14**(2), 231–251.

George, J. and Jones, G. (1996) *Organisational Behaviour*, Reading, MA: Addison Wesley.

Hale, R. and Whitlam. P. (1998) *Towards the Virtual Organisation*, London: McGraw-Hill.

Herriot, P. and Pemberton, C. (1995) A new deal for middle managers, *People Management*, June, 2–34.

Hollway, W. (1991) *Work Psychology and Organisational Behaviour: Managing the Individual at Work,* London: Sage.

Kissler, G. (1994) The new employment contract, *Human Resource Management*, **33**, 335–352.

Makin, P., Cooper, C. and Cox, C. (1996) *Organisations and the Psychological Contract*, London: BPS Books.

Marriot, R. (1970) The Industrial Research Council, Industrial Psychology Research Group, *Journal of Occupational Psychology*, **44**, 253–260.

Michelson and Morley cited in Zukav, G. (1979) *The Dancing Wu Li Masters, an Overview of the New Physics*, London: Rider.

Pascale, R. (1995) In search of the new 'employment contract', *Human Resources*, **21**, 21–26.

Peak, M. A. (1997) Today's management flavour: Plain vanilla, *Management Review*, **86**(7), 26–30.

Peters, T. (1988) *Thriving on Chaos: A Handbook for Management Revolution*, Palo Alto, CA: Macmillan.

Peters, T. and Waterman, R. (1982) *In Search of Excellence*, New York: Harper and Row.

Robbins, S. (1992) *Essentials of Organisational Behaviour*, London: Prentice Hall (international editions).

Smither, R., Houston, J. and McIntire, S. (1996) *Organisation Development, A Strategy for Changing Environments*, New York: Harper Collins.

Sofer, C. (1972) *Organizations in Theory and Practice*, London: Heinemann.

Storti, C. (1999) *Figuring Foreigners Out – A Practical Guide*, London: Intercultural Press Inc.

Stredwick, J. and Ellis, S. (1998) *Flexible Working Practices, Techniques and Innovations*, London: IPD.

Taylor, F. W. (1911) *Principles of Scientific Management*, New York: Harper and Brothers.

The Economist (US) (1998) A gentle invasion, 18 July, **348**.

Tyson, S. and Jackson, T. (1992) *The Essence of Organisational Behaviour*, London: Prentice Hall.

Zukav, G. (1979) *The Dancing Wu Li masters: An Overview of the New Physics*, London: Rider.

2

Personality and attitudes

Contents

Objectives

After reading this chapter you should be able to:

- differentiate between nomothetic and idiographic approaches to personality
- explain the beliefs about personality that inform each approach
- describe how such approaches influence work-based practice
- define what attitudes are and how they can be changed
- understand the concepts of organizational commitment and job satisfaction

2.1 Introduction

In this chapter we will focus on the individual by examining two aspects of individual behaviour, personality and attitudes. Managers have become increasingly interested in these areas since the 1950s, when studies began to show that these human attributes could be important determinants of work-place behaviour. Chapter 1 discusses some of these historical trends.

In the first section of this chapter we will focus on personality. Personality is being seen as important in an economy increasingly dependent on the service sector. Companies are keen to acquire staff who will be polite and friendly to customers, for instance. In this section, we will look at two different approaches to understanding personality: nomothetic approaches, which assume that everyone possesses the same sorts of personality traits, but in different quantities, and idiographic approaches, which suggest that personality is more or less unique to each person. We will review the implications of each of these approaches for work-based practice.

In the second section, we will examine attitudes, including those related to work performance – specifically, job satisfaction and job commitment. These are increasingly seen as important areas of study because it is believed such attitudes have implications for employee motivation, a topic covered in its own right in Chapter 3.

2.2 Personality

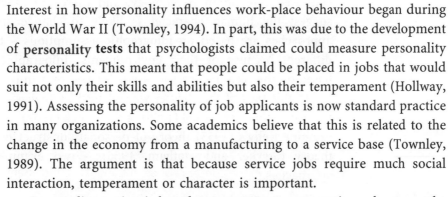

Interest in how personality influences work-place behaviour began during the World War II (Townley, 1994). In part, this was due to the development of **personality tests** that psychologists claimed could measure personality characteristics. This meant that people could be placed in jobs that would suit not only their skills and abilities but also their temperament (Hollway, 1991). Assessing the personality of job applicants is now standard practice in many organizations. Some academics believe that this is related to the change in the economy from a manufacturing to a service base (Townley, 1989). The argument is that because service jobs require much social interaction, temperament or character is important.

Personality testing is based on **nomothetic** assumptions about people: we all possess the same characteristics, but in different quantities, which gives each person their uniqueness (Cattell, 1965). In turn, nomothetic assumptions are based on the idea that personality is trait-like. That is, our characteristics define who we are and are not likely to change (McCrae

Reflection Box 2.1 Can personality tests predict future behaviour?

Personality tests are a popular tool used in selection procedures. Organizations use these tests by 'profiling' a job, to identify a **person specification** (a list of characteristics necessary for successful performance in the job). Each short-listed candidate is then tested and, theoretically, the candidate most like the person specification gets the job. However, this process is based on a number of challengeable assumptions.

First, research shows that organizations actually use such tests to justify their selection decisions rather than actually inform them (Herriot, 1989). Second, these tests actually predict about 10 per cent of the variance in job-related behaviour (Cook, 1998). Put simply, of the 100 per cent of all factors that might affect performance at work, a personality test can account only for about one-tenth of them. Third, jobs change as do people. So, selecting someone for a job on the basis of how both it and the person 'look' at the moment is no guarantee that the apparent degree of fit between the two will remain over time.

1   Should organizations use such tests?
2   What might their value be?

and Costa, 1990). This is an advantageous position for organizations, since it suggests that it is possible to *predict* how people will behave in the future (Reflection Box 2.1). However, the nature of personality is a highly contested domain in psychology, and there are other approaches that suggest the human character is likely to change and develop. These approaches are based on **idiographic** assumptions – that people are all different because of their environments. Idiographic assumptions are based on the idea that personality is learned or acquired (Schwartz, 1989).

In this part of the chapter we will start by reviewing two popular trait theories – those of Cattell (1965) and Eysenck (1967) – before moving onto examine Kelly's (1955) theory of personal construct psychology and role theory (Stryker and Statham, 1986) – two examples of idiographic approaches.

2.3 Trait approaches to understanding personality: Cattell's 16PF test

One of the most widely used trait approaches is Cattell's 16 Personality Factors (16PF). Cattell was an American psychologist. He began his research by combing the dictionary for words that described personality, character and behaviour. He identified about 5,000 words. Cattell then used what he called a **lexical criterion** to reduce this list to a more manageable number. In other words, he made judgements about words that were similar in meaning, such as 'outgoing' and 'sociable'. Having reduced the list, he was left with about 200 descriptors of behaviour which he compiled into questionnaires. He then issued these questionnaires to a large number of people who were asked to make judgements about their own behaviour. An example might be:

I enjoy being with other people

(a) true
(b) not sure
(c) false

Once Cattell had collected a large amount of data in this way, he subjected it to a statistical procedure called **factor analysis**. This mathematical procedure is concerned with identifying data that 'go together'. For instance, people who describe themselves as sociable may also describe themselves as risk takers and as not at all shy. Factor analysis helps to identify these sorts of datasets and to describe the set using an appropriate label. The set described above might be labelled 'extroversion'.

Using factor analysis to analyse his data, Cattell identified 16 factors that he said formed the underlying structure of personality. Table 2.1 gives a description of these 16 factors.

These 16 factors are, according to Cattell and his advocates, a description of the underlying structure of personality. We all possess these traits, but because we all have each trait in different quantities, and because different traits interact with each other differently, the permutations are so vast as to account for the uniqueness of individuals. Since Cattell's work, there have been further attempts to come up with even more elegant models of personality (Digman, 1990), and there is now some agreement that there may be in fact five super-traits that encompass the variation in human personality:

1   extroversion (sociable, assertive);
2   emotionality (anxious, insecure);
3   agreeableness (conforming, helpful to others);
4   conscientiousness (persistent, organized);
5   intellect (curious, open to experience).

Table 2.1 *The 16 factors in Cattell's analysis of personality. The factors as defined by the characteristics of high and low scorers on each trait dimension are listed in order of the amount of variance accounted for by each factor. The labels listed are the currently used verbal approximations for the content of each factor.*

1. Cool	versus	Warm
2. Concrete-thinking	versus	Abstract-thinking
3. Affected by feelings	versus	Emotionally stable
4. Submissive	versus	Dominant
5. Sober	versus	Enthusiastic
6. Expedient	versus	Conscientious
7. Shy	versus	Bold
8. Tough-minded	versus	Tender-minded
9. Trusting	versus	Suspicious
10. Practical	versus	Imaginative
11. Forthright	versus	Shrewd
12. Self-assured	versus	Apprehensive
13. Conservative	versus	Experimenting
14. Group-oriented	versus	Self-sufficient
15. Undisciplined self-conflict	versus	Controlled
16. Relaxed	versus	Tense

2.4 Trait approaches to understanding personality: Eysenck's theory of cortical arousal

Eysenck believed that behaviour is biologically driven; that is, behaviour is simply a response to biological and physiological processes operating in the brain and the rest of the body. Eysenck also believed strongly in the power of heredity to determine what sort of person we will be.

 There is a structure in the brain known as the **ascending reticular activating system (ARAS)**, a part of the brain which, among other things, is responsible for regulating the sleep/waking cycle. Thus, when ARAS activity is very low we tend to feel drowsy, and when it is very high, very alert. Eysenck, like many psychologists before him and like many of us, observed that people could be generally categorized as extroverted or introverted. Extroverted people are, on the whole, very sociable, like stimulation and excitement and enjoy noise, clamour and busy environments. Introverts, on the other hand, prefer to be on their own or with only a very small number of other people. They also avoid stimulation and excitement and tend to prefer peace, tranquillity and solitude. Eysenck proposed that these apparent differences between extroverts and introverts were caused by differential base-level activity in the ARAS. Specifically, Eysenck proposed that extroverts have a very low base-level activity. Because of homeostatic principles (the tendency of the body's systems to achieve balance or equilibrium), the goal of the ARAS is to achieve optimal base-levels of activity. In other words, there is a level of activity that is the *preferred level*, in the same way that the preferred body temperature is 37.4°C. So, the extrovert engages in activities which will stimulate the ARAS, just as someone who feels cold will start to shiver or put on warm clothing. In contrast, the introvert has very high base levels of ARAS activity and hence their goal is to reduce this level by engaging in activities which will be more sedative, just as the person feeling hot might 'strip off' or sweat.

There is evidence to support Eysenck's theory (Carver and Scheier, 1992). Introverts and extroverts do appear to prefer different levels of stimulation. Similarly, research suggests that base levels of activity in the ARAS are different in extroverts and introverts early in the morning. Introverts have higher base levels at these times than extroverts. This, it is argued, accounts for the fact that many introverts tend to be earlier risers than their extrovert counterparts and also explains why they find it easier to concentrate and perform cognitively demanding tasks in the morning. Conversely, extroverts tend to come into their own during the evening, at which time stimulating activities carried out during the day have significantly increased ARAS levels.

Eysenck developed his theory further by proposing that not only was the ARAS an area which was prone to differential base-activity levels but also the emotion centres in the brain, which cluster around a structure called the hypothalamus, are implicated. Basically, Eysenck argued that emotionally unstable people are easily aroused in their brain's emotion centres, whereas emotionally stable people are less easily aroused. Using this as a basis, Eysenck developed a trait theory of personality based on four types (Figure 2.1) and developed a questionnaire that he claimed measured the traits identified in Figure 2.1.

2.5 A critique of trait theories

One of the great difficulties in personality measurement is that we have to assume that people are being honest when they make reports on their own behaviour. The problem is that behaviour is not an objective phenomenon; we tend to try to see ourselves in the best possible light. People who

	Emotionally stable		Emotionally unstable	
Introvert	Passive Careful Thoughtful Peaceful Controlled Reliable Even-tempered Calm	Phlegmatic	Quiet Pessimistic Unsociable Sober Rigid Moody Anxious Reserved	Melancholic
Extrovert	Sociable Outgoing Talkative Responsive Easygoing Lively Carefree Leaderlike	Sanguine	Active Optimistic Impulsive Changeable Excitable Aggressive Restless Touchy	Choleric

Figure 2.1   Eysenck's four 'types' and associated traits [adapted from Eysenck (1975)].

develop personality questionnaires have labelled this tendency 'faking good' (Crowne and Marlowe, 1964), and several test publishers claim to have developed lie scales that reveal when people are attempting to present themselves rather too perfectly.

However, the fundamental issue here is the notion that an accurate picture of an individual's personality is actually obtainable. This is questionable. For one thing, people tend to see themselves differently from situation to situation (Hollway, 1984). Most people completing personality questionnaires agree that it is very difficult to answer some of the questions. For instance, consider the comment: *I would prefer to stay at home with a good book than go to a party.* Most people feel that their answer depends on a number of factors: Whose party is it? What book do you suggest I read? What mood am I in?

Some social psychologists suggest that trait theories provide one perspective on personality but that they are just that – a perspective (Potter and Wetherell, 1987). There are many, many other ways of thinking about human behaviour. They differ chiefly in the extent to which behaviour is seen to be largely the product of heredity (internal factors) or of the environment (external factors). Some psychologists believe that both heredity and the environment have a mutual effect on our behaviour and that the effects of the two are probably not amenable to separate analysis

(Henriques *et al.*, 1984). For example, consider a child who inherits a gene for extroversion. The extent to which that child becomes extroverted depends on his or her parents' behaviour, the culture of the society in which the person is raised and their own life experiences. No one would argue that both genes and environment have had an effect on the person's development, but it is not possible to determine which of the two was mainly responsible.

2.6 Idiographic approaches to personality: Kelly's theory of personal constructs

Kelly (1955) believed that people learn behaviour through observing the behaviour of others. He argued that this process of observation leads us to develop hypotheses about the social world. These hypotheses form what Kelly called our **personal constructs**. These are our own highly individual 'lenses' through which the social world is perceived. For example, I might develop a hypothesis that most people can be judged according to whether they are kind. However, my interpretation of 'kind' will not necessarily be the same as yours. I might see kindness as being related to the giving of love and you might see kindness as being concerned with helping people who are not well off.

We all develop a wide array of such constructs. However, according to Kelly, these are organized hierarchically. In other words, we use some constructs very regularly and others very rarely. Additionally, our constructs can change or disappear depending on our experiences. For example, if I come across many people who I cannot judge using my 'kindness' construct, I might develop a new construct to help me judge people I do meet, such as 'friendly'. Or, I might come into contact with people who are kind in different ways from my original definition. For example, I might find that someone I had originally judged as not particularly kind rallied round me when I was upset.

According to Kelly, another important feature of personal constructs is that they are **bipolar**. In order to be able to make a judgement that a person is 'kind' requires a knowledge of what 'not kind' is. Kelly calls the construct that emerges first as the **emergent construct** and its opposite the **implicit construct**.

Kelly developed a technique for identifying personal constructs, known as repertory grid. Here is an example of how this technique is performed.

Repertory-grid technique

Kelly originally developed this technique for exploring the self-concept, but it is now used in a wide variety of personal (Dalton and Dunnett, 1990) and business settings (Honey, 1979). To produce a repertory grid the individual identifies a list of 'elements' or objects that he or she is likely to have constructs about. In exploring personal constructs about the self-concept, it is usual to identify up to six elements, which might include a person I like, a person I dislike, a person I admire, a person I pity, a person who influences me and myself. Personal constructs are elicited by presenting the individual with triads (threes) of elements and asking them to say whether any element differs from the other two and on what basis. For instance, I might say that the person I like is different from the person I dislike and the person I pity, because he is 'outgoing'. Because of construct bi-polarity, the opposite of outgoing also needs to be established. So I need to specify what the person I dislike and the person I pity have in common that makes them different from the person I like. To continue the example, I might say they are 'insular'. This process continues until the individual has specified every difference he or she can between each triad, and until each element has been presented with every other.

Example of a repertory grid

The result is a grid (Figure 2.2) that can be used to identify relationships between constructs and elements. It is usual in self-concept grids to add 'ideal self' to the list of elements once all constructs have been elicited. The individual then rates each element on each personal construct. In the example above, a five-point scale is being used where five means that the element is very like the emergent construct and one means that it is like the implicit construct; three means it is neither one nor the other.

As you can see in the example, this person sees himself in quite a negative way and his rating of his ideal self shows that this is not a position he values.

2.7 Idiographic approaches to personality: role theory

Role theory also assumes that personality is learned. However, role theory stresses the importance of social roles (Stryker and Statham, 1986). According to this theory we learn to become a girl or a boy through

Elements								
Constructs	A person I like – Dave	A person I dislike – John	A person I admire – Sheila	A person I pity – Chris	A person who influences me – Mum	Me now	Ideal self	
Thoughtful	5	1	5	4	5	3	5	Thoughtless
Stimulating company	5	1	5	1	5	1	5	Boring
Confident and articulate	5	3	3	1	5	1	5	Shy and awkward
Caring and supportive	5	1	3	3	5	4	5	Puts self first
Straight-talking	3	1	5	2	5	2	5	Two-faced
Easy to talk to	5	1	5	2	5	3	5	Lacks interest in others

Figure 2.2   Repertory grid.

observation of other girls and boys (Festinger, 1954). We then take on the behaviours that characterize those roles. This process continues through-out our lives as we learn how to role-play in a variety of social situations – employees, bosses, husbands, wives and parents. According to role theory, therefore, a person is always to some extent acting a part (Goffman, 1959).

Proponents of role theory have been interested in investigating the processes that operate when people take on different roles. Snyder (1974) suggests that some people find it easier to role-play than others, with the consequence that they are better **impression managers**. In other words, some people are able to persuade other people that the role they are playing is the 'genuine' them. Snyder suggests that this ability stems from a psycho-logical characteristic he calls **self-monitoring**. High self-monitors are very aware of their social situation and the impression they are giving. They are able to read social cues accurately and are able to change their behaviour to better conform with people's expectations. In contrast, low self-monitors do not tend to be aware of social situations and the cues presented and tend to enact the role in which they are most comfortable.

Principles of role theory have been successfully used in training programmes (Goldstein and Sorcher, 1974), in which individuals are taught new skills by observing role models. Additionally, interview techniques have been developed to address the problem of impression management; that is, a situation in which a candidate appears very good but, on employment, turns out not to be. Situational interviews, in which people are asked to explain how they would actually deal with real-life job situations, are one example here (Cook, 1998).

2.8 A critique of idiographic approaches

Idiographic approaches are less concerned with the content of personality and more with understanding the processes through which individuals acquire their self-beliefs. Idiographic approaches also suggest that people can and do develop and change their self-beliefs with behavioural consequences.

Idiographic approaches are probably most useful for exploring personal development issues. The repertory-grid technique, for instance, can be used in career counselling and personal counselling (Dalton and Dunnett, 1990) and role theory is useful for thinking about the design of training and induction programmes.

However, it is difficult to 'test' these theories because they are concerned with explanation, not prediction. For instance, role theory does not allow us to make predictions about the roles a person might adopt in the future, nor does personal construct theory allow us to predict how constructs might change. It has been argued that 'testability' is not relevant for such approaches (Bhaskar, 1989), though proponents of trait theories pride themselves on the predictive properties of their theories (see Reflection Box 2.2).

2.9 Attitudes

In this section we are going to look at attitudes, focusing specifically on job satisfaction and organizational commitment. These two attitudes are of great interest to organizations because they are thought to be related to important outcomes, such as productivity, staff turnover and morale. We will begin this section by defining what attitudes are and how we develop

Reflection Box 2.2 Is personality a product of Western thinking?

Some sociologists (Rose, 1996, Du Gay, 1997) have argued that the whole notion of personality is a reflection more of Western culture than of actual human nature. The argument is, very simply, that because Western culture sees the individual as the most important social entity, psychologists have invented concepts like personality and attitudes to explain our behaviour. However, sociologists argue that our behaviour can be explained just as easily by other social entities – class, social values and power. So, the argument goes, the reason why women are often stereotyped as 'passive' or 'gentle' is not because of their personality but because of their subordinate roles in society as wives and mothers: these characteristics are *products* of these roles, not their *basis*.

One of the problems in emphasizing the individual as the main unit in social analysis is that we often forget that work performance is more than a function of the individual's personality and intellect. How good you are at your job depends (among other things) on

- the nature of the work itself;
- the effectiveness of work colleagues;
- the working environment;
- the economic environment.

Can you think of any others?

If we do not take these things into account, we may neglect to understand other aspects of the workplace that are having an effect on performance.

them before moving on to examine the concepts of job satisfaction and organizational commitment.

Defining attitudes

Eagly and Chaiken (1993) suggest that attitudes can be defined in two ways. In some definitions, an attitude is described as combining affective, behavioural and cognitive components that are oriented towards a particular object (Breckler, 1984). For instance, I might have a positive attitude (affective component) towards animal welfare (object), which predisposes me to watch TV programmes that address this issue (behavioural component) and which is underpinned by the belief that animals are as important as humans (cognitive component).

Other social psychologists prefer to define an attitude in affective terms only (Brehm and Kassin, 1996), defining attitudes simply in terms of a positive or negative evaluation of any given object at a certain level of intensity. For instance 'hating' tabloid newspapers or 'loving' soap operas.

The relationship between attitudes and behaviour

People often assume that attitudes are related to behaviour. So, if I express a positive attitude towards animal welfare, you would probably be surprised to see me taking part in a hunt. Researchers have noticed, however, that behaviour is not necessarily predictable from a stated attitude. Context appears to be important (Fishbein, 1980). For instance, the way that we think others might judge us is important in determining whether behaviour can be predicted from a stated attitude. I might be less willing to go on a march against animal cruelty if doing so might lead important people in my life to disapprove of me. Also, the extent to which we believe we are in control of the behaviour is important. For example, I might not be willing to make a speech about animal welfare if I do not believe I have the skills to do so. Finally, people might express an *intention* to behave in a particular way, but then either cannot or do not.

Attitude-discrepant behaviour

A major assumption underpinning much of attitude research is that individuals are motivated by the need for **cognitive consistency**, in which our attitudes and behaviour are in line with each other (Abelson *et al.*, 1968). If we engage in attitude-discrepant behaviour, cognitive consistency theory predicts that we will experience a feeling of cognitive discomfort which we will be motivated to reduce. For instance, if I had been expressing disgust about fox-hunting and then joined a hunt, I should experience some feelings of discomfort and would have the desire to explain what I did in ways that would bring my behaviour and attitudes back in line with each other. Festinger (1957) called this feeling of discomfort **cognitive dissonance** .

Festinger, however, argued that not every attitude-discrepant behaviour would cause cognitive dissonance. What seems to be important is the extent to which people freely commit to attitude-discrepant behaviour and the extent to which they have some knowledge of the consequences of that behaviour.

What has now become the classic experiment on cognitive dissonance was conducted by Festinger and Carlsmith in 1959. Subjects were asked to perform a very dull task which, they were told, was part of an experiment on performance. After performing the task, subjects were asked to tell the next subject that the task was highly enjoyable. Half the subjects were offered one dollar for telling this 'fib' and the other half, twenty dollars. Effectively, therefore, they engaged in attitude-discrepant behaviour. After the experiment was over, all subjects were interviewed and asked to give an honest opinion about how enjoyable the task had been. As predicted, Carlsmith and Festinger found that subjects who had been paid twenty dollars to 'fib' to new subjects said the task was dull and boring, but the subjects who had been paid one dollar said it was mildly enjoyable.

Carlsmith and Festinger argued that this was the result of **insufficient justification**. If you willingly engage in an attitude-discrepant behaviour that you cannot really justify (as in the one-dollar condition), you will find it difficult to accommodate. To reduce the discomfort experienced, therefore, you will change your attitude to bring it in-line with your behaviour. However, if you can justify it (as in the twenty-dollar condition), you will not.

Aronson and Mills (1959) also showed that a person who put a great deal of effort into the attitude-discrepant behaviour was likely to experience high levels of cognitive dissonance which they would reduce by changing their attitude. For instance, research shows that the more effort psychotherapy patients put into their own treatment, the more they believe it has been worthwhile (Axsom, 1989).

Cooper and Fazio (1984) suggest that for dissonance to occur and to produce attitude change, four conditions are necessary:

- the attitude-discrepant behaviour must produce negative consequences (e.g. the person does something boring and claims it was interesting);
- a feeling of personal responsibility for these consequences;
- a belief that the negative consequences of the behaviour were foreseeable;
- physiological arousal occurs as a consequence (actual feelings of discomfort).

Having reviewed what attitudes are and how they can be changed, let us move on to look at organizational commitment and job satisfaction.

2.10 Organizational commitment and job satisfaction

Organizational commitment is generally defined as a positive orientation towards the workplace. Many researchers have attempted to define organizational commitment in ways that might render it amenable to measurement. Allen and Meyer (1990) have defined it as follows:

- **affective commitment** (concerned with how a person feels about their organization);
- **continuance commitment** (the extent to which a person perceives it would be desirable or undesirable to leave the organization);
- **normative commitment** (the person's moral orientation to the organization; that is, the extent to which they feel a sense of responsibility or obligation towards their employing organization).

Researchers into organizational commitment have argued that these three components are quite distinct. So, if someone is affectively committed to their organization, it does not necessarily follow that they will also demonstrate continuance or normative commitment. However, this distinction does not seem to offer much practical help to managers. Research into the three dimensions of organizational commitment shows mixed results. Some researchers claim to have found relationships between levels of affective commitment and work performance, with those expressing more commitment being better at their jobs (Meyer *et al.*, 1993). Other researchers have found no such relationship (Arnold *et al.*, 1998). On the whole, it appears that organizational commitment is good at predicting 'intention to quit' but not much else (ibid.). This is hardly surprising. Someone who dislikes their place of work is unlikely to express the desire to remain there as an employee. In fact, it is doubtful whether these two 'measures' are distinct. Is disliking your place of work really that different from saying, 'I don't want to work here'?

Job satisfaction is defined generally as a *positive orientation* towards one's work or role (Locke, 1976). Like all attitudes, job satisfaction is assumed to have affective, cognitive and behavioural components. So if you are job satisfied, you will generally like your job, you will think positive thoughts about it and yourself in relation to it, and you will behave in ways that enhance your performance.

Interestingly, there is little empirical evidence to support the idea that job satisfaction is related to improved performance. In fact, a study by Smither *et al.* (1989) suggests that the relationship between job satisfaction and performance may be spurious or false. This study showed that people tended to rate the performance of people who were judged to be job satisfied more highly than those who were judged to be dissatisfied. In reality, there were no significant differences in several key performance areas, such as output and efficiency.

Job satisfaction and its relationship to performance is developed further in the next chapter.

2.11 Summary

In this chapter we have looked at two important areas of study at the level of the individual – personality and attitudes.

We have discussed two approaches to personality that are based on quite different sets of assumptions. Nomothetic approaches assume that we all possess the same traits in different (and measurable) quantities; idiographic approaches are concerned with the identification of the processes that produce our self-beliefs.

Each approach has its strengths and weaknesses. Nomothetic approaches are useful for differentiating between people on aggregate, but are probably less useful for an in-depth understanding of any given individual. In contrast, idiographic approaches are more useful for issues of personal development, but are less useful for helping us differentiate between individuals.

Attitudes are of great interest to social psychologists because they can be highly predictive of behaviour. However, as we have seen, this is not always the case. There are several reasons why a person may not behave in ways that are consistent with an expressed attitude. Research does show, however, that engaging in attitude-discrepant behaviour can be experienced as uncomfortable in some circumstances, producing attitude change.

Organizations are also interested in attitudes, especially those thought to influence workplace behaviour. We took a brief look at organizational commitment and job satisfaction. The literature on organizational commitment suggests that people who have a positive attitude towards their jobs are more likely to express the intention of staying in that job. This is an important area for study in a service-based economy in which well-developed interpersonal skills need to be retained by the organization. The research on job satisfaction suggests that its relationship with performance may not be clear-cut, an issue we address more fully in the next chapter.

Questions

Self-test questions

1 Describe three key differences between nomothetic and idiographic approaches to the study of personality.
2 What are the benefits of approaches that assume it is possible to measure personality?
3 How does role theory differ from the theory of personal constructs?
4 What is an attitude?
5 Explain why not all attitude-discrepant behaviours result in cognitive dissonance.
6 Why are organizations keen to understand the processes that lead to job satisfaction and organizational commitment?

Discussion questions

1 To what extent is it possible to both measure personality and predict how it will influence future performance?
2 In what ways can the study of personality help managers become better managers?
3 Discuss the ways that organizations might be able to foster job satisfaction and organizational commitment. What benefits are they likely to obtain from doing so?

References and bibliography

Abelson, R. P., Aronson, E., McGuire, W. J., Newcomb, T. M., Rosenberg, M. J. and Tannenbaum, B. H. (1968) *Theories of Cognitive Consistency: A Source Book*, Chicago: Rand McNally.

Allen, N. J. and Meyer, J. P. (1990) The measurement and antecedents of affective, continuance and normative commitment to the organization, *Journal of Occupational Psychology*, **63**, 1–18.

Arnold, J., Cooper, C. L. and Robertson, I. T. (1998) *Work Psychology: Understanding Human Behaviour in the Workplace* (third edition), London: Pitman.

Aronson, E. and Mills, J. (1959) The effect of severity of initiation on liking for a group, *Journal of Abnormal and Social Psychology*, **41**, 258–290.

Axsom, D. (1989) Cognitive dissonance and behavior change in psychotherapy, *Journal of Experimental and Social Psychology*, **21**, 149–160.

Bhaskar, R. (1989) *The Possibility of Naturalism: A Philosophical Critique of the Contemporary Human Sciences* (second edition), New York: Harvester Wheatsheaf.

Breckler, S. J. (1984) Empirical validation of affect, behavior and cognition as distinct components of attitude, *Journal of Personality and Social Psychology*, **52**, 384–389.

Brehm, S. S. and Kassin, S. M. (1996) *Social Psychology* (second edition), Boston: Houghton Mifflin.

Carver, C. S. and Scheier, M. F. (1992) *Perspectives on Personality* (second edition). Boston: Allyn and Bacon.

Cattell, R. B. (1965) *The Scientific Analysis of Personality*, Baltimore: Penguin.

Cook, M. (1998) *Personnel Selection* (third edition), Chichester: Wiley.

Cooper, J. and Fazio, R. H. (1984) A new look at dissonance theory. In Berkowitz, L. (ed.) *Advances in Experimental Social Psychology*, **17**, 229–267.

Crowne, D. P. and Marlowe, D. (1964) *The Approval Motive: Studies in Evaluative Dependence*, New York: Wiley.

Dalton, P. and Dunnett, G. (1990) *A Psychology for Living: Personal Construct Theory for Professionals and Clients*, London: Dunton.

Digman, J. M. (1990) Personality structure: Emergence of the five-factor model, *Annual Review of Psychology*, **41**, 417–440.

Du Gay, P. (1997) *Production of Culture, Cultures of Production*, London: Sage.

Eagly, A. H. and Chaiken, S. (1993) *The Psychology of Attitudes*, Fort Worth, TX: Harcourt Brace Jovanovich.

Eysenck, H. J. (1967) *The Biological Basis of Personality*, Springfield, IL: Charles C. Thomas.

Festinger, L. (1954) A theory of social comparison processes, *Human Relations*, 7, 117–140.

Festinger, L. (1957) *A Theory of Cognitive Dissonance*, Stanford, CA: Stanford University Press.

Festinger, L. and Carlsmith, J. M. (1959) Cognitive consequences of forced compliance, *Journal of Abnormal and Social Psychology*, **58**, 203–210.

Fishbein, M. (1980) A theory of reasoned action: some applications and implications. In Howe, H. E. and Page, M. M. (eds) *Nebraska Symposium on Motivation*, **27**, 65–116.

Goffman, E. (1959) *The Presentation of Self in Everyday Life*, Garden City: Doubleday.

Goldstein, A. P. and Sorcher, M. (1974) *Changing Supervisor Behaviour*, New York: Pergamon Press.

Henriques, J., Hollway, W., Urwin, C., Venn, C. and Walkerdine, W. (1984) *Changing the Subject: Psychology, Social Regulation and Subjectivity*, London: Routledge.

Herriot, P. (1989) (ed.) *Assessment and Selection in Organisations*, Chichester: Wiley.

Hollway, W. (1984) Fitting work: Psychological assessment in organisations. In Henriques, J., Hollway, W., Urwin, C., Venn, C. and Walkerdine, W. (eds) *Changing the Subject: Psychology, Social Regulation and Subjectivity*, London: Routledge.

Hollway, W. (1991) *Work Psychology and Organisational Behaviour: Managing the Individual at Work*, London: Sage.

Honey, P. (1979) The repertory grid in action, *Industrial and Commercial Training*, **11**, 452–459.

Kelly, G. A. (1955) *The Psychology of Personal Constructs*, New York: Norton.

Locke, E. A. (1976) The nature and causes of job satisfaction. In Dunnette, M. D. (ed.) *Handbook of Industrial and Organizational Psychology*, Chicago: Rand-McNally.

McCrae, R. R. and Costa, P. T. (1990) *Personality in Adulthood*, New York: Guildford.

Meyer, J. P., Allen, N. J. and Smith, C. A. (1993) Commitment to organizations and occupations: Extension and test of a three-component conceptualization, *Journal of Applied Psychology*, **78**, 538–551.

Potter, J. and Wetherell, M. (1987) *Discourse and Social Psychology: Beyond Attitudes and Behaviour*, London: Sage.

Rose, N. (1996) *Inventing Ourselves: Psychology, Power and Personhood*, Cambridge University Press.

Schwartz, B. (1989) *Psychology of Learning and Behaviour* (third edition), New York: Norton.

Smither, J. W., Collins, H. and Buda, R. (1989) When ratee satisfaction influences performance evaluations: a case of illusory correlation, *Journal of Applied Psychology*, **74**(4), 599–605.

Snyder, M. (1974) The self-monitoring of expressive behavior, *Journal of Personality and Social Psychology*, **30**, 526–537.

Stryker, S. and Statham, A. (1986) Symbolic interaction and role theory. In Lindzey, G. and Aronson, E. (eds) *The Handbook of Social Psychology*, New York: Random House.

Townley, B. (1989) Selection and appraisal: reconstituting social relations? In Storey, J. (ed.) *New Perspectives on Human Resource Management*, London: Routledge.

Townley, B. (1994) *Reframing Human Resource Management: Power, Ethics and the Subject at Work*, London: Sage.

3

Motivating people at work

Contents

Objectives

By the end of this chapter you should be able to:

● understand and explain the concept of motivation
● differentiate between content and process theories of motivation
● describe the key ideas and assumptions that inform content and process theories of motivation
● explain the ways that motivation theories are used to design work-based practices aimed at improving work performance
● discuss some of the shortcomings of motivation theories, explain what these are and state why they are important

3.1 Introduction

Understanding what motivates people is particularly important for managers because, without people who are prepared to perform set tasks to a certain level and standard, organizations would not survive. In this chapter we are going to look at various theories that attempt to provide explanations of what motivates people, as well as some common practices that organizations use to try to improve the performance of their workforces.

The chapter is divided into two sections. In the first section we will consider different *types* of motivation theory. It is common to group motivation theories into two main categories: content theories that focus on *what* sorts of factors produce motivation and process theories that attempt to explain *how* motivation and behaviour are related. We will look at each of these groups by describing the key ideas and assumptions that underpin the theories and then discussing the explanatory power of each.

In the second section, the focus will be on understanding how motivation theories can be *applied* to the workplace. To begin with, we will look at incentive schemes and at performance-related pay and appraisal or performance management systems. We will then look at other workplace practices designed to increase motivation such as job design, in which principles taken from motivation theories are used to design jobs and to make decisions about what the content of jobs should be.

3.2 Theories of motivation

Before we consider different theories of motivation, we need to understand what we mean when we use the term itself. Before we go on to discuss the concept at greater depth, stop a moment and consider what you understand by the term. Some people might think of it as a feeling, which is often reflected in our language: "I don't feel very motivated today." Other people think of it as behaviour, which too is reflected in language: "He is incredibly motivated" is a description we might use of a highly productive colleague.

 Psychologists differentiate between drives and motives. A **drive** is an internal force that produces motivated behaviour. For instance, all animals have an instinctive desire for survival and, to this end, have drives to eat and to reproduce. Thus eating and mating are examples of behaviour

Reflection Box 3.1 Motivation – a case of the chicken and the egg?

A common assumption made by most of us is that we need to feel motivated before we can do something. We often put off doing unpleasant or dreary tasks because we tell ourselves we lack motivation. However, experts in positive-thinking techniques suggest that the feeling of motivation is something that can be aroused simply by doing something, even something we did not really want to do in the first place. Susan Jeffers in her book *Feel the Fear and Do It Anyway* suggests that people should force themselves to do tasks about which they feel uncomfortable and over which they are procrastinating because this will foster feelings of motivation. These, she argues, are good for us, because we feel good when we feel motivated to do something. It is a pleasant feeling.

What does this imply about drives?

motivated by the drives of hunger and reproduction respectively. Both of these, however, are motivated by the more fundamental survival instinct. The word 'drive' directs our attention to the fact that motivation is something that pushes us into action.

A **motive** is something we acquire through learning. Thus, at work we might work hard for the motive of promotion because we have learned that this is often the reward for doing so. The idea of reward is central to many motivation theories, as we shall see.

The chief difference between drives and motives is that drives are often conceptualized as unconscious and, therefore, to some extent beyond our control (though see Reflection Box 3.1). Thus, while I can stop myself from eating, I cannot stop myself from being hungry. Conversely, motives are what we acquire as we learn what sorts of things earn us rewards. A baby learns that crying brings its mother, so will use this to draw her attention to itself. However, we acquire motives through drives. The reason the baby cried in the first place was because it was hungry.

As we shall see, motivation theories draw on the concepts of both drives and motives.

Content theories of motivation

Content theories attempt to identify specific things that motivate people. They focus on both **intrinsic motivators** (needs or drives that originate *within* the person, such as desire for prestige or status) and **extrinsic motivators** (things that originate *outside* the person and that can produce desires and needs, such as money). As we shall see, in practice it is difficult to make a neat separation between these two sources of motivation. We are going to look at three content theories of motivation:

- Maslow's hierarchy-of-needs theory;
- Alderfer's existence, relatedness and growth (ERG) theory;
- Herzberg's two-factor theory.

Maslow's hierarchy of needs

Maslow's contention was that human beings seek satisfaction of a number of internal needs or wants (intrinsic motivators). These needs are arranged for most people in an order or hierarchy (Maslow, 1943) (Figure 3.1).

The first-level needs are known as **physiological needs**. They include basic physical requirements such as hunger and warmth. Once these needs are satisfied the requirement moves to a second level, known as **safety needs**. Safety needs include security, the need for predictability and orderliness, and freedom from pain. Both of these preliminary needs could be satisfied by increasing workers' income levels. Maslow's third level of

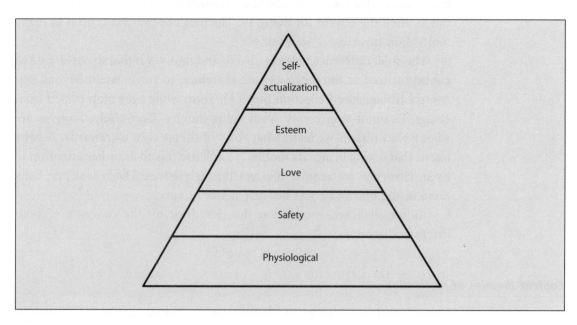

Figure 3.1   Maslow's hierarchy of needs.

motivators is **social needs**, such as affection, a sense of belonging, social activities, friendships and both the giving and receiving of love. Once these needs are satisfied the employee can move on to the next level of **esteem needs** (or **ego needs**), in which self-respect and the esteem of others become important. Status, recognition and appreciation also form part of the needs satisfied at this level.

At the ultimate level of Maslow's hierarchy are **self-actualization needs** At this level, workers are able to reach their full potential. Some will be creative and innovative; others will not. The point is that workers who achieve this level are going to be frustrated by working at a level or pace that is below their best. Figure 3.1 summarizes the theory and the various levels of motivation Maslow identified.

According to Maslow, once a lower need has been satisfied it no longer acts as a strong motivator and satisfying the next level of needs becomes the focus of the individual's attention.

Maslow's theory has attracted much attention and criticism (Salencik and Pffeffer, 1977; Rauschenberger *et al.*, 1980). One criticism is that employees may be able to satisfy their needs outside the workplace, so managers can easily be confused (or just unaware) about genuine levels of motivation at work. In addition, the theory emphasizes satisfaction of needs as the main motivational driver, with the implicit assumption that more satisfaction will filter through to higher productivity. Higher work performance is presumed to be the result of highly satisfied employees, which may or may not hold true.

Theoretically, the idea that we all have these needs organized in this particular way is suspect. People vary in the ways they experience needs. Research has shown that some people are motivated mainly by money, while others are prepared to work in voluntary jobs to experience meaningful work (Mitchell and Mickel, 1999). Furthermore, different life experiences can alter a person's outlook and what he or she perceives to be important. For instance, a person striving for self-actualization through work might get to a point where he or she feels it is a pointless exercise and that there is more to life.

The notion that all needs originate intrinsically is also questionable. Research suggests that needs can develop because of social influences. For instance, the desire for self-actualization is something we might learn because we see the effects it has on others, e.g. happiness (Rose, 1996). Furthermore, research suggests that the development of needs and the way they are related to the social context is probably complex. For instance,

---

Reflection Box 3.2 Is self-actualization a need or a fashion?

This idea of self-actualization can be criticized on the grounds that it is exploitable (Rose, 1996). It is good for business organizations if we are prepared to work excessive hours for no other reason than achieving self-actualization, but is it really good for workers? Media reports about increasing levels of stress in the workforce and the impact of excessive working hours on peoples' family life indicates that what may be sauce for the goose may not be so for the gander.

A second issue concerns the homogeneity (degree of sameness) of any workforce. As we pointed out earlier, motivation is not a stable construct. Levels of motivation vary greatly between and within people. Similarly, what motivates one person may not motivate another. In our society, perhaps, many people are keen to self-actualize, but there are likely to be a substantial number of people who really do see work only as a means to an end and have no desire to engage with it on any other level. Is it ethical for organizations to attempt to force everyone to feel the same way about work? And is it good? Perhaps trying to make people see things in the way that management wants them to alienates people rather than encourages them?

Deci (1971) found that when people were paid for doing a task they already enjoyed they sometimes lost interest in it. So, theories like Maslow's do tend to oversimplify matters.

Overall, there appears to be a consensus between academics and managers that Maslow's hierarchy-of-needs theory is a very useful way of thinking about behaviour but that, in reality, it offers little guidance on how to actually motivate people at work and its theoretical principles are questionable (Arnold *et al.*, 1998). See Reflection Box 3.2 for more debatable aspects of content theories.

Alderfer's ERG theory

Alderfer's (1972) theory is broadly similar to that proposed by Maslow, except that he proposes a three, rather than five-level, hierarchy:

- existence needs (comparable with Maslow's physiological and safety needs);
- relatedness needs (comparable with Maslow's social and esteem needs);
- growth needs (comparable with Maslow's self-actualization needs).

However, Alderfer's theory is distinct from Maslow's in that Alderfer suggests that people may experience the different levels of needs *simultaneously* and may not progress up the hierarchy in the way Maslow suggests. He also acknowledged that the environment might mean that certain needs cannot be met. For example, needs for self-actualization may not be achievable in a work environment that is dull and boring. Alderfer suggested that, if this happened, the individual would substitute other needs as being most important, such as relatedness needs.

Herzberg's two-factor theory

Herzberg's study, carried out in 1959, used 203 accountants and engineers to develop his theory. Subjects were interviewed using the **critical incident method**: they were asked to describe something that had happened at work that they felt particularly good or bad about. The responses obtained were very consistent and led Herzberg to believe that there were two sets of factors involved in motivation at work. One set of factors, which he referred to as **hygiene factors**, prevented dissatisfaction. These were aspects of the job which, while not motivating in themselves, would, if they were not present, lead to severe dissatisfaction and ultimately demotivation. The second set of factors were what Herzberg referred to as the **motivators**. If these factors were present they would lead to superior performance and effort from employees. Figure 3.2 represents the key elements within the two-factor theory and gives examples of both hygiene factors and motivators.

One of the most significant principles that Herzberg introduced was to detach the factors which cause dissatisfaction from those which cause satisfaction and, consequently, motivation. Previously, it was thought that the removal of a dissatisfier (something that was causing the employee problems in the work environment) would automatically lead to an increase in satisfaction levels. Herzberg's work showed that it was not that simple; just because employees were no longer dissatisfied, they would not necessarily become motivated. The opposite of dissatisfaction is not satisfaction but, simply, no dissatisfaction. In order to motivate employees, managers must use motivation factors and not simply remove the dissatisfiers.

Interestingly, neither Herzberg nor Maslow cites money as a significant motivator (beyond a basic level of performance). Yet organizations persist in using financial incentives as their chief motivational tool. Indeed, as

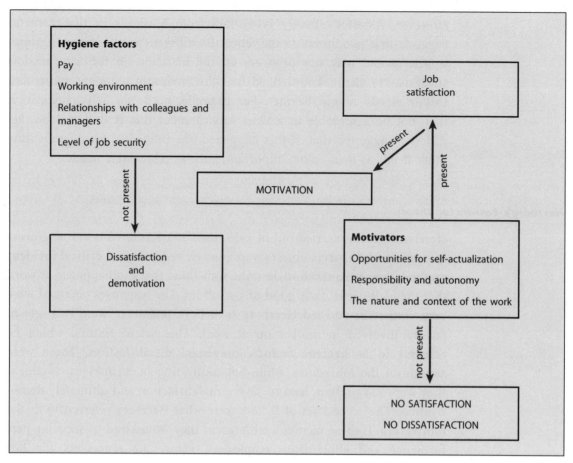

Figure 3.2   Herzberg's two-factor theory.

Case Study 1 'Building a flexible organization: British Gypsum' and **Case Study 3 'Positive aspects of teamworking: total employee involvement at Smith and Nephew'** show, financial incentives can be extremely useful for facilitating acceptance of organizational change. Part of the problem here is that Herzberg's theory masks individual differences: different people have different needs for money (Mitchell and Mickel, 1999). Herzberg's theory has also been criticized on the grounds that replicating his results is easier to achieve if similar research methods are used. For example, what appears to motivate people differs depending on whether they are interviewed or observed. This suggests that the theory is not very robust. Furthermore, research suggests that manual workers are more likely to be motivated by money than are more professional or managerial groups (Goldthorpe *et al.*, 1968). If this is the case, Herzberg's theory may not apply to every work group. And a more recent review of the literature queries the extent to which Herzberg's theory is relevant in the 1990s, because some of Herzberg's hygiene factors, such as pay and job security, are not mentioned as either satisfying or dissatisfying by participants in more recent studies (Ambrose and Kulik, 1999).

Process theories of motivation

Process theories look at relationships that might enhance, or detract from, motivation. Within this category are **expectancy-based models** as described by Vroom (1964) and by Porter and Lawler (1968). The underlying basis of these theories is that people are influenced by what they expect to happen as a result of their actions. Employees must be able to trust that promises on rewards will not be broken or significantly altered, though the level of trust may rely on past experience of the organization's management behaviour. **Equity theory**, as described by Adams (1965), is another process theory, in which the focus is on understanding how people make judgements about their own and other's contributions and rewards. We are going to look at three process theories:

- Vroom's VIE theory;
- Porter and Lawler's expectancy model of motivation;
- Adam's equity theory.

Vroom's VIE theory

This expectancy motivation model is based on three key variables (VIE):

Valence: the *anticipated* satisfaction from the outcome;

Instrumentality: the *extent* to which performance-related outcomes lead to need-related outcomes;

Expectancy: the perceived *probability* that effort will lead to performance-related outcomes.

Vroom defines valence as the anticipated level of satisfaction, which may or may not be matched by the actual result. The valence of certain outcomes may be totally self-contained but, more commonly, results from the 'knock-on' effects of the outcome. For example, some employees may derive increased satisfaction merely by earning more, but others are likely to derive satisfaction from what they can now use the extra income for. In other words, some people may value the *status* that extra money can bring, while others are more concerned with the *pleasure* of acquiring more possessions.

The strength of valence of an outcome depends on the extent to which that outcome is perceived to be related to performance. This is the instrumentality (I) in Vroom's theory, since it is concerned with whether performance is *instrumental* to the achievement of outcomes. According to expectancy theory, the employee has to make a judgement about the probability of the reward coming their way after they achieve the required performance levels. In probability terms, if it is thought to be highly unlikely we would assign it a value of close to 0. If an outcome is more or less certain, but nonetheless not guaranteed, the probability value will be close to 1.

Finally, expectancy is the perceived relationship between effort and performance. If an individual believes that putting more effort into their work (say, in terms of time or concentration) will *improve* their performance, then expectancy (E) will be high. Like instrumentality, values of E can range between 0 and 1.

The combination of valence (the perceived value of the anticipated outcome), the instrumentality (perceived relationship between performance and outcomes) and expectancy (the perceived relationship between effort and performance), determines the employee's motivational force.

Vroom's theory can be summed up as $\sum EIV = $ motivation. An example might make this more clear.

An individual, in considering whether to work harder or more efficiently, may do so on the basis that she [*sic*] expects the following outcomes:

- promotion;
- recognition.

However, in addition to these outcomes, she also expects that she will have to work

- longer hours.

According to Vroom, she will attach a value to these outcomes and estimate the probability that:

- increased effort will lead to an improvement in performance;
- improvement in performance will lead to the outcomes she anticipates.

Let us say that she calculates the value of each of these outcomes on a scale of one to seven. One means that she does not value the outcome at all. Seven means she would value it highly. As we have already said, probability values range between 0 (the outcome is highly improbable) through to 1 (the outcome is certain). We can now calculate the likelihood that this individual will work harder.

Outcome 1 (Promotion)   **Outcome 2 (Recognition)**
Valence = 7   Valence = 5
Instrumentality = 0.5 (a 50 : 50 chance) Instrumentality = 0.2 (low)
VI = 3.5   VI = 1

Outcome 3 (Longer working hours)
Valence = 0
Instrumentality = 1 (certain)
VI = 0

Expectancy = 1 (she is certain that increasing her effort will improve her performance)

$$\sum VI = 3.5 + 1 + 0 = 4.5$$

$$\sum VIE = 4.5(1)$$

$$\sum VIE = 4.5$$

Since the maximum $\sum VIE = 21$ and the minimum $\sum VIE = 0$, there is only a 20 per cent (4.5/21) chance that this individual will work harder. (See Figure 3.3 for a diagrammatic illustration of Vroom's theory.)

This example demonstrates some of the problems with Vroom's theory. Do we actually engage in these sorts of cost–benefit analyses when thinking about working harder? Some researchers have suggested that we tend to make decisions to do things and then justify them after the event, not before (Regan and Kilduff, 1988). Also, as you can see, if you do not value an outcome at all, that particular VI calculation will always be 0, automatically reducing the final VIE sum.

Porter and Lawler's expectancy model of motivation

Porter and Lawler (1968) took the work of Vroom and developed it beyond the idea of motivational force. They looked at employee performance as a whole. Porter and Lawler believe it is important to allow for the fact that

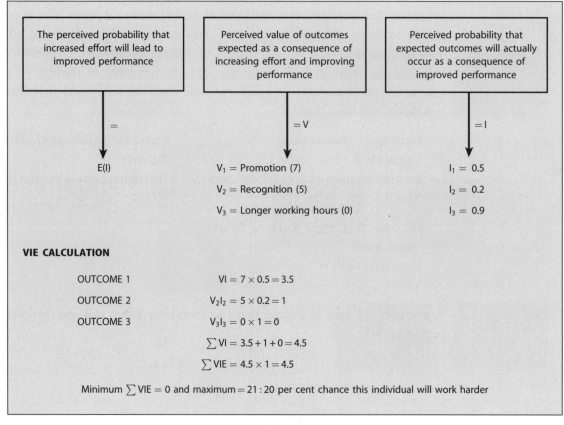

Figure 3.3   Vroom's expectancy theory of motivation.

extra levels of effort do not always lead to improved performance. Any number of extraneous variables will have to be considered, such as the employee's ability, level of training, complexity of the skills needed or technological constraints. This version of expectancy theory sets out motivation, satisfaction and performance as separate variables, in direct contradiction to the idea that satisfaction leads to improved performance (as in Herzberg's theory). Porter and Lawler believe that improved performance leads to greater job satisfaction. Figure 3.4 depicts the Porter and Lawler model of motivation.

Adam's equity theory

Adam's (1965) theory is based largely on the concept of social comparison (Festinger, 1954). Social comparison is a process by means of which individuals compare themselves with other people to arrive at a self-judgement.

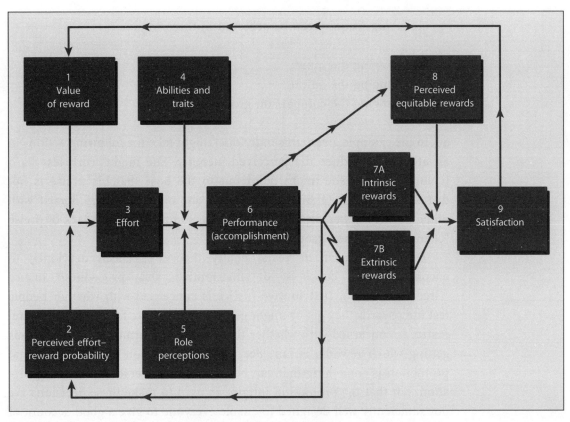

Figure 3.4   Porter and Lawler expectancy model of motivation (Source: Porter, L. W. and Lawler, E. E. (1968) *Managerial Attitudes and Performance*, Copyright © Richard D. Irwin Inc., p. 165).

For instance, in judging how well off we are, we might compare our possessions and lifestyle with those of other people. According to Adams, this is a process we engage in a good deal at work in order to judge the *fairness* of what happens to us. People will be satisfied with their working conditions only if they believe that these are comparable with other people in *similar situations* (Goethals and Darley, 1977).

According to Adams, in assessing the fairness of working conditions we will estimate an input/output ratio. This means we evaluate what we are putting into a job, compared with others, and what we are getting out of the job, compared with others. If we perceive that our inputs exceed our outputs, we will be dissatisfied and motivated to reduce the inequity. So if I think that I am working as hard as my colleagues, but that they are getting treated better than I am (e.g. receiving more praise from the boss), I will experience dissatisfaction and be motivated to reduce the inequity.

Reducing inequity can be achieved in three ways:

- by changing the input;
- by changing the output;
- by changing the comparison group.

So, in the example given, this individual might take the following actions in an attempt to reduce the perceived inequity. She might work less hard (change inputs); she might point out to the boss that his praise is not distributed equally (change outputs); or she might compare herself with other workers in her department who also complain about a lack of praise (change comparison group).

 During the past 20 years, equity theory has been developed to encompass the concepts of distributive and procedural justice (Greenberg, 1987). **Distributive justice** is concerned with whether people feel the rewards they get or might get in the future are fair; and **procedural justice** is concerned with whether the way the organization decides who is getting which rewards is fair. For example, a person might believe that promotion is something that can be achieved by everyone in the organization, but that the promotion interviews used to make these decisions are not sufficiently well designed to enable everyone to give a good account of themselves.

Equity theory and its more recent developments are very useful for understanding why people can become dissatisfied at work and is very helpful for drawing attention to the context within which motivation occurs. Its efficacy as a theory has been tested mainly on the way people make judgements about pay and rewards. Huseman *et al.* (1987) found that people's judgements on the fairness of pay depended on the extent to which they were 'equity sensitive'. In other words, some people are more likely to perceive inequity than others, suggesting that the processes through which such judgements are made are more complex than implied by equity theory. Despite this, research over the past 30 years shows that equity theory's predictions have proved to be very robust.

As you can see, there is no single motivation theory that provides a complete picture of the processes involved. One answer might be to attempt to integrate different aspects of all motivation theories in order to better understand the complexity of motivation. For instance, Harder (1991) examined contradictory predictions from equity and expectancy theory to examine the performance of baseball players. However, the synthesis of the two theories was difficult to achieve. Ambrose and Kulik (1999) suggest that such attempts are not 'inspiring'.

3.3 The application of motivation theories to the workplace

Theories of motivation offer organizations different ways of thinking about how to improve the efficiency and productivity of the workforce. In this section, we will look at some examples of the application of motivation theories to the workplace.

Frederick Taylor and scientific management

One of the earliest attempts to improve workplace efficiency was developed by Frederick Taylor, who we introduced in Chapter 1. In 1911, he carried out a survey of the handling of pig-iron at the Bethlehem Steel Factory. Taylor estimated that a team of 75 men loaded an average of 12.5 tons of iron per man per day. A Dutch labourer called Schmidt was instructed by Taylor to follow detailed instructions on when to sit and rest and how to carry out the various operations to maximum efficiency. The other workers were left to operate the job as they always had. By following the plan worked out by Taylor, Schmidt improved his efficiency by loading 47.5 tons per day. He was able to maintain this level of output for the three years of the study (and in return received a 60 per cent increase in his pay). One by one the other men were selected and trained to handle the pig-iron in the same way, although not all of them were physically capable of achieving the results that Schmidt could. Taylor suggested that all jobs could be analysed and redesigned so as to maximize productivity, a principle he labelled 'scientific management'.

When tasks are not predictable or repetitive, attempting to break them down into a prescribed sequence of physical moves is not straightforward, however. Although some organizations, predominantly in manufacturing or the quasi-industrial fast-food sector, still practise some aspects of scientific management (or 'Taylorism'), many do not. This is because the basic assumption underlying Taylor's work, that motivation can be improved and maintained through financial incentives, has not been supported by study and practice. In general, people appear to rate money as only average compared with other motivators (Kohn, 1993).

What a Taylorist analysis of a job *can* unquestionably achieve is standardization and predictability, often by eliminating the need for employees to think things through for themselves. Indeed, Taylor himself believed that the idea that employees should think up their own working methods would only be detrimental and lead to non-conformity, variations in speeds, materials used and, worst of all, unpredictable outcomes. In addition, the widespread application of Taylorist principles emphasized the differences between workers and managers. The job of the manager was to think out the best methods of working and the job of the employee was to follow instructions accurately.

Although Taylor's ideas are not as popular as they once were, they are still in use. Many organizations successfully use incentive schemes to motivate their staff and performance-related pay is increasingly used as a tool to manage performance.

3.4 Performance management and performance-related pay

Performance-related pay is often used to directly link the performance of individuals (and sometimes groups) to pay. It is often part and parcel of an organization's performance-management system, in which individual performance is appraised or evaluated using sets of job-related criteria. For instance, people might be evaluated against objectives (meeting sales targets, say); or against work behaviours (e.g. attitude to customers). Achievement of a pay award is thus tied to the achievement of these sorts of criteria.

While this is an intuitively good idea, research shows there are problems with it. For instance, some supervisors may not be very good at making judgements about their staff, especially when these judgements are more subjective, such as those made about attitudes. Supervisors may also vary in the experience they have with such systems (Clement, 1987). To overcome such problems, some writers have suggested the use of **360°** **appraisal** (Bernadin and Beatty, 1987; Ott *et al.*, 1990). In a 360° appraisal an individual's performance is appraised by a range of people with whom he or she comes into contact, including customers, colleagues and people below him or her in the organization's hierarchy.

Taylor's approach and modern systems based on it, such as 'piece-rate' schemes (in which employees are paid according to what they produce), are based on the idea that extrinsic motivators are more important than intrinsic motivators. Performance-management systems actually recognize that both extrinsic and intrinsic motivators are important. They also recognize the importance of fairness, both procedural and distributive.

Therefore they use aspects of both content and process theories in their approach to workforce motivation. Other approaches are more explicit in their underlying assumptions, however. Job-enrichment programmes are generally informed by the concept of self-actualization.

3.5 Job enrichment

Job complexity

Turner and Lawrence (1965) pioneered work into the effect that different types of jobs would have on employee satisfaction and absenteeism. Their research led them to predict that many employees would actually prefer jobs that were more complex and challenging. They defined job complexity in terms of six characteristics:

- variety (the different things I do in one day);
- autonomy (how much independence I have over my actions);
- responsibility (how much accountability I have for the success of my work);
- knowledge and skill (the level of ability I bring to the job);
- required social interaction (how much I have to deal with other people to get the work done effectively);
- optional social interaction (how much not directly job-related interaction I need).

According to Turner and Lawrence, the higher a job scores on these characteristics, the more complex it is.

While Turner and Lawrence were able to confirm their predictions on absenteeism, they actually found no direct correlation between job complexity and job satisfaction. On deeper investigation it appeared that the level of job satisfaction depended much more on the workers' individual backgrounds and outside interests than they had first imagined. The ideas that Turner and Lawrence put forward were further developed by Hackman and Oldham (1976) into the Job Characteristics Model (JCM).

The job characteristics model (JCM)

According to the JCM, any job can be described in terms of five core job dimensions:

- skill variety: the degree to which the job requires a variety of different activities;
- task identity: the degree to which the job requires completion of a whole identifiable piece of work;
- task significance: the degree to which the job has impact upon the work of others;
- autonomy: the degree of freedom within the job, independence and individual discretion;
- feedback: the degree to which the job holder receives clear and direct information about the effectiveness of his performance.

Also important in the model is **employee growth need strength**, which is an indication of the extent to which the individual values the job characteristics proposed by the model. The more that an individual values them, the more likely it is that a job low in any of these areas will cause dissatisfaction. Figure 3.5 shows the model and the outcomes predicted by it. The model can be tested using a questionnaire designed by Hackman and Oldham called the **Job Diagnostic Survey** (JDS).

The model was tested by Hackman and Oldham in 1976 using a large sample of employees (more than 600) from seven business organizations, who all completed the JDS. The characteristics of the jobs involved were also assessed by independent observers. The study broadly confirmed the predictions made by the model, with the exception of absenteeism, where a weak and statistically insignificant relationship was observed (Reflection Box 3.3).

Job rotation and job enlargement

One way of breaking up the repetitive nature of over-specialized jobs is by **job rotation**. Employees are given time to learn and perform a variety of functions in one or more sections of the business. Organizations practise job rotation to encourage employees to become multi-skilled, and to give them an opportunity to see more of what the organization is trying to achieve.

Job enlargement also allows employees to 'grow their jobs' horizontally and/or vertically. Again, this can lead to more diversity in the working day and reduce the likelihood of demotivation. As a typical example of a job-enlargement project, let's take an employee who deals with stationery requests. Rather than just receiving and processing these requests, the

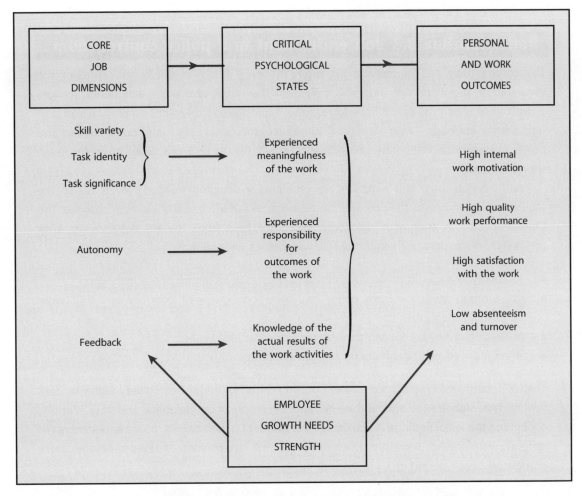

Figure 3.5   Job characteristics model (from Hackman, J. R. and Oldham, G. R. (1976) Motivation through the design of work: Test of a theory, *Organizational Behaviour and Human Performance*, **16**, 250–279).

employee could check and maintain stock records, carry out a full ordering (and invoicing) process, deliver (or arrange to deliver) items to the final users and even brief new staff on the ordering process. In terms of vertical enlargement the employee might also be made responsible for selecting and training new staff and briefing other departments.

Employees are sometimes wary of job enlargement, on the grounds that they may be taking on extra work for no reward. Nonetheless, both job rotation and job enlargement are recognised ways of increasing the level of diversity in otherwise over-specialized jobs and studies have suggested such approaches do bring benefits. For example, Buchanan and Boddy (1983) looked at the effects of job enlargement and found that it

Reflection Box 3.3 Job enrichment in a police control room

The control room or communications room in police forces is the nerve centre of the organization. It is here that incoming calls from the public and other emergency services arrive and to which the police have to respond. Typically, control rooms employ civilian staff on a permanent basis – who are trained to answer emergency calls – and police officers and police managers on temporary secondment, usually for up to 5 years, but often for much shorter periods.

A UK police force was experiencing problems in keeping manning levels up to the required quota in one of their control rooms, because of high levels of sickness absence. The Chief Inspector in charge of the room asked for help from the *HR* department. After preliminary discussions with staff, the following issues were raised:

- too many changes in procedures introduced by new incoming police managers;
- not enough feedback from police managers on how well control-room staff were performing their jobs;
- frustration at never knowing the outcome of emergency calls;
- stress induced by undermanning at peak call times.

The HR department investigated further by using the *JDS*. The job scored very highly on task variety, task significance and autonomy, and very poorly on feedback and task identity, confirming the initial findings. A working group was set up with civilian, police and managerial staff as well as two representatives from the HR department. Various measures were introduced over a period of 1 year including:

- regular feedback sessions between staff and management to discuss procedures and implement negotiated and agreed changes;
- return-to-work interviews following sickness absence.

And 1 year later:

- the sickness rate had improved inasmuch as occasional absence was less, but long-term sickness, the most serious cause of undermanning, remained high;
- staff felt a lot happier about working procedures;
- undermanning remained a problem.

The outcome of this study supports previous research which shows that attempts to improve measurable aspects of organizational performance using these sorts of techniques, increases job satisfaction, but little else (Porras and Berg, 1978).

increased productivity. A study at the Volvo plant in Kalmar, Sweden (Aguren *et al.*, 1976), which also utilized these principles, produced similar results (though this project was later abandoned).

Job enrichment is the precursor of the widespread **empowerment** movement. Empowerment aims to give employees greater autonomy and freedom to respond in much the same way as the move towards job enrichment. While job enrichment attempted to point out the opportunities for employees who wished to become more involved and proactive at work, an empowered workforce is much more akin to a demand that employees must be prepared, and sufficiently skilled, to do much more than merely fulfil the requirements of their basic job description.

Job-enrichment programmes draw on the concept of self-actualization, assuming that people will find more interest and satisfaction in a job that challenges them. Examples of these applications can be found in many organizations and, as we have said, there is research to support their propositions. However, motivation is a complex phenomenon and there is no one approach that could be said to be 'correct'.

3.6 Summary

In this chapter we reviewed content and process theories of motivation. Content theories are concerned with explicating extrinsic and intrinsic factors (such as pay or the need to self-actualize) that produce motivated behaviour. While these theories provide useful frameworks for thinking about motivation, they are universalist in their assumptions: they assume people are all the same. It is clear from studies that have examined content theories that, in fact, people differ markedly in the extent to which intrinsic or extrinsic motivators are perceived as important. Furthermore, the context of work has an effect on what motivates people. Working in a boring job can heighten reliance on relatedness needs; working in a challenging autonomous job might lower them.

Process theories are concerned with developing models that show the relationship between needs, motives and behaviour. Expectancy-based theories solve many of the problems noted about content theories because they are explicit in recognizing the extent of individual differences. However, while they are useful for looking at case-by-case situations, they are rather less useful for looking at what happens within a group, largely because these theories are based on the assumption that it is the *perception*

Reflection Box 3.4 How might changing work contexts affect motivation?

With more and more people working short-term temporary contracts, it might be expected that motivation would be at an all-time low, since, according to need theories, safety and security needs are being compromised by such conditions. However, the economy today is buoyant (in the service sector) and there is no evidence that such conditions are having an adverse effect on organizational performance.

Some authors (Handy, 1994) have tried to make predictions about the possible effects of these changes on employee attitudes, suggesting, for instance, that successive career changes might make it more likely that a person will show more commitment to their own CV than to any specific organization, with obvious consequences for the behavioural expression of loyalty.

Some people believe that temporary contracts are very healthy for organizations because they actually ensure that people remain motivated out of the desire to have their contracts renewed. Furthermore, short-term contracts mean that employers can jettison staff who turn out to be ineffective.

On the other hand, a spokesperson from the Henley Management Centre believes that organizations might be in danger of losing skilled staff if they cannot offer people more job security. Skilled people are highly employable and can change jobs with relative ease. The spokesperson thinks that an increase in the turnover of skilled staff might lead organizations to reconsider the utility of numerical flexibility (the shedding and acquiring of staff according to need). Developing initiatives for the retention of skilled staff may become more of a priority.

The fact that motivation theories seem unable to predict how people will behave in response to changing social conditions suggests that it is a concept that is probably related to these conditions as well as to an individual's psychological make-up. Do the theories we have covered take adequate account of the social context of work?

of one's own desires and environment that are keys in determining behaviour.

Equity theory goes some way to addressing these problems by examining motivation in terms of perceived inequities at the group level. Equity theory predicts that an imbalance between one group's outputs/ inputs and another's will motivate attempts to reduce that inequity. Research is very supportive of this broad idea. However, equity theory has less to say about the content of motivation. Why do some people desire money and others status? Why is one person motivated by voluntary work in unpleasant squalid surroundings and another repelled at the thought of such tasks?

Many of the motivation theories we have looked at in this chapter were developed at a time when work context was very different from what it is today. Only 20 years ago, it was common to train for a career and remain in it until retirement. Most people remained loyal to one company for much of their working lives. They were employed on permanent salaried contracts, and enjoyed a company pension plan and other benefits. Today, the norms for many working people are short-term temporary contracts, many career changes and almost permanent job insecurity. Reflection Box 3.4 looks at the implications of such changes.

Questions

Self-test questions

1. What is the difference between content theories and process theories of motivation?
2. Differentiate between intrinsic and extrinsic motivators, providing two examples of each.
3. List the key principles of scientific management.
4. What is 360° appraisal and why might this system be preferable to traditional boss/subordinate appraisal?
5. Describe the Job Characteristics Model and its main predictions.
6. Describe three changes in the work context that have occurred in the past 30 years.

Discussion questions

1. On what grounds can theories of motivation be criticized?
2. When attempting to increase productivity, what can organizations do about the fact that different people are motivated by different things?
3. Since there is little evidence to suggest that enriching jobs does more than increase job satisfaction, is this a viable way to spend money?
4. How might organizations set about retaining staff who have expert skills and knowledge?
5. Which theories covered in this chapter best explain the processes discussed in **Case Study 4 'More positive aspects of teamworking: NatWest rings the changes at a call centre'**?

References and bibliography

Adams, J. S. (1965) Inequity in social exchange. In Berkowitz, L. (ed.) *Advances in Experimental Social Psychology*, New York: Academic Press.

Aguren, S., Hansson, R. and Karisson, K. G. (1976) *The Volvo Kalmar Plant: The Impact of New Design on Work Organization*, Stockholm: The Rationalisation Council.

Alderfer, C. P. (1972) *Existence, Relatedness and Growth*, New York: Free Press.

Ambrose, M. L. and Kulik, C. T. (1999) Old friends, new faces: Motivation research in the 1990s, *Journal of Management*, **25**(3), 231–290.

Arnold, J., Cooper, C. L. and Robertson, I. T. (1998) *Work Psychology: Understanding Human Behaviour in the Workplace*, London: Pitman.

Bernadin, H. J. and Beatty, R. W. (1987) Can subordinate appraisals enhance managerial productivity? *Sloan Management Review*, **28**(4), 63–73.

Buchanan, D. A. and Boddy, D. (1983) Advanced technology and the quality of working life: The effects of computerised controls on biscuit-making operators, *Journal of Occupational Psychology*, **56**, 109–119.

Clement, R. W. (1987) Performance appraisal: Nonverbal influences on the rating process, *Review of Public Personnel Administration*, **7**(2), 14–27.

Deci, E. L. (1971) Effects of externally mediated rewards on intrinsic motivation, *Journal of Personality and Social Psychology*, **18**, 105–115.

Festinger, L. (1954) *A Theory of Social Comparison Processes*, Stanford, CA: Stanford University Press.

Goethals, G. R. and Darley, J. (1977) Social comparison theory: An attributional approach. In Suls, J. M and Miller, R. L. (eds) *Social Comparison Processes: Theoretical and Empirical Perspectives*, Washington, DC: Hemisphere.

Goldthorpe, J. E., Lockwood, D., Bechofer, F. and Platt, J. (1968) *The Affluent Worker: Industrial Attitudes and Behaviour*, Cambridge: Cambridge University Press.

Greenberg, J. (1987) A taxonomy of organizational justice theories, *Academy of Management Review*, **12**, 9–22.

Hackman, J. R. and Oldham, G. R. (1976) Motivation through the design of work: Test of a theory, *Organizational Behaviour and Human Performance*, **16**, 250–279.

Handy, C. B. (1994) *The Empty Raincoat: Making Sense of the Future*, London: Hutchinson.

Harder, J. W. (1991) Equity theory versus expectancy theory. The case of major league baseball free agents. *Journal of Applied Psychology*, **76**, pp. 458–464.

Herzberg, F., Mousener, B. and Snyderman, B. B. (1959) *The Motivation to Work* (second edition), London: Chapman & Hall.

Huseman, R. C., Hatfield, J. D. and Miles, E. W. (1987) A new perspective on equity theory: The equity sensitivity construct, *Academy of Management Review*, **12**, 222–234.

Jeffers, S. (1991) *Feel the Fear and Do It Anyway*, London: Penguin.

Kohn, A. (1993) *Punished by Rewards*, New York: Houghton Mifflin.

Maslow, A. H. (1943) A theory of human motivation, *Psychological Review*, **50**, 370–396.

Mitchell, T. R and Mickel, A. E. (1999) The meaning of money: An individual-difference perspective, *Academy of Management Review*, **24**(3), 568–581.

Ott, M. J., Esker, S., Caserza, C. and Anderson, S. (1990) Peer interviews: Sharing the hiring process, *Nursing Management*, **21**(11), 32–33.

Porras, J. I. and Berg, P. O. (1978) The impact of organizational development, *Academy of Management Review*, April.

Porter, L. W. and Lawler, E. E. (1968) *Managerial Attitudes and Performance*, London: Irwin.

Rauschenberger, J., Schmitt, N. and Hunter, J. E. (1980) A test of the need hierarchy concept by a Markov model of change in need strength, *Administrative Science Quarterly*, **25**, 654–670.

Regan, D. T. and Kilduff, M. (1988) Optimism about elections: Dissonance reduction at the ballot box, *Political Psychology*, **9**, 101–107.

Rose, N. (1996) *Inventing Ourselves: Psychology, Power and Personhood*, Cambridge University Press.

Salencik, G. R. and Pfeffer, J. (1977) An examination of need satisfaction models of job attitudes, *Administrative Science Quarterly*, **22**, 427–456.

Turner, A. N. and Lawrence, P. R. (1965) *Industrial Jobs and the Worker*, Cambridge, MA: Harvard University Press.

Vroom, V. H. (1964) *Work and Motivation*, New York: John Wiley.

4

Groups and teams

Contents

Objectives

At the end of this chapter you should be able to:

- understand why people need to join groups
- be aware of the reasons why organizations have introduced teamworking
- evaluate the main differences between groups and teams
- be aware of the roles required in teams
- recognize the negative aspects of teamworking
- explain the significant features of group cohesiveness
- understand the principles of developing effective teams and teamworking
- be aware of the features of team-based decision making
- be aware of the features and benefits obtainable from self-managed teams
- understand and recognize situations where conflict might arise in groups and teams

4.1 Introduction

In the next two chapters you will see the terms group and team, or group working and teamworking used interchangeably. This is not because we see no distinction between the two terms, but simply a recognition that in many situations we effectively ignore any distinction.

Even where the concept of teamworking is far removed from that of a mere group, in practice the two are often treated as if they were the same. Is a queue of people standing waiting for a bus a team or a group? They all share a common goal, but the queue could not strictly speaking be considered a team. They may not even know the name of the person standing next to them and they are not in any way working together as a unit.

The blurring of this distinction in organizational terms is not wholly surprising. Managers will often talk of teams and groups in the same breath, and employees may see themselves as group members or team members depending on what they are concerned with at the time. Organizational terminology also adds to the confusion: when we talk of work groups and work teams, we do not always imply any distinction.

4.2 Why do people join groups?

Many people join groups, clubs or societies for reasons that are nothing to do with work. You yourself may have joined a society at the college or university of which you are a member. Other people join dramatic societies, sports clubs or groups to socialize.

There is strong evidence that men and women seek to join others as a natural part of life and that they enjoy the socializing effect of being with other human beings (Berscheid, 1985, cited in Myers, 1994). Table 4.1 gives some of the reasons why most people like to be members of groups or teams.

Do any of the reasons put forward in Table 4.1 apply to you? How would you feel if you were not able to become a member of a group or team either inside work or outside?

According to Heller (1997) working in groups is an excellent way of building the effective interpersonal relationships that organizations need. Relationships at work are generally strengthened by three kinds of behaviours (Allcorn, 1989):

Table 4.1 *Reasons for joining groups or teams.*

Security	Employees will feel stronger and more confident when they can act together. Collective bargaining with employers can also re-balance the uneven power relationship between employer and employee.
Task achievement	Some tasks in organizations are not possible unless tackled by groups or teams. Collective ability and skills should be greater than individual ones especially where synergy can be used to improve efficiency or quality of output.
Social need	Inclusion in a group can give individuals status and self-belief. Social relationships also help to improve communications and stimulate interest, leading to increased job satisfaction.
Power	Negotiation pressure can be applied more effectively if the group is large and is supported by active members.

Adapted from Mullins (1996).

- imitation;
- reciprocity;
- reinforcement.

Imitation occurs when verbal or non-verbal signals are sent and received which emphasize areas of agreement and joint understanding. Imitation leads to attitudinal changes and feeds into the culture of the organization.

Reciprocity occurs when group colleagues work together towards some joint goal. One group member may assist another in return for help in a different area. Cooperation between group members is often achieved on the basis of reciprocity.

Reinforcement of interpersonal relationships occurs when employees obtain rewards for acceptable or approved behaviour. This may or may not involve financial rewards. Praise from a manager or even another group or team member is an example of the way that reinforcement can lead to the encouragement of good group behaviour.

As organizations are increasingly emphasizing the role of teamworking and in some cases trying to encourage self-managed work teams, we need to be clear about what a team actually is and how it differs from a group (Reflection Box 4.1). According to Montebello (1995), "Increasing numbers of companies are abandoning the outmoded tradition of dividing work processes into compartmentalized functions and simplified tasks." A compelling account of the reason for the change is provided by

Reflection Box 4.1 Am I a group member or a team member?

The answer to the question is: it depends what you mean by group or team. Most people will argue that there is a distinct difference between a group and a team. In organizational terms, a *group* could be any set of people who happen to have something in common. (For an accurate definition of a group see Chapter 1.)

All the employees who work on a particular shift, or who work at a specified grade, will commonly be referred to as a group. In this instance the term group is really no more than an administrative convenience. A *team* implies something much more than just a circumstantial connection. A team often requires some entry criteria to distinguish who is and who is not a member.

An established team will also have sets of rules about behaviours that are acceptable and not acceptable. If membership is both automatic and non-negotiable as in 'all the members of shift A' then the classification, and subsequent behaviour of the members, is more likely to be a group than a team.

Consider the following questions:

1   Are all the people in the room with you now a group or are they a team?
2   Make a list of the groups you belong to and all the teams you are in, what is the main difference between the two lists?

the same author, "Companies are discovering that teamwork helps them to gain speed, shed unnecessary work, and consistently deliver eye popping gains in productivity, quality and job satisfaction."

Executives questioned for a survey by Hoerr (1989) were found to be very positive about the prospects for teamwork in organizations. The top expected benefit being increased quality, followed by improved productivity, increased morale and a decreasing in the layers of required management.

The word team does conjure up different images for different people. Some people think instantly of sports teams, others might think about surgical-operating teams. Nonetheless, all teams have a number of features in common. Katzenbach and Smith (1993) declare that "A team is a small number of people with complementary skills who are committed to a common purpose, performance goals, and approach for which they hold themselves accountable."

Figure 4.1   A bus queue.

Being a member of a team means displaying loyalty to the goals and efforts of the team. Sometimes this might mean sacrificing personal achievement in favour of that of the team. Team membership also means, in some circumstances, sharing in the setting of the goals and even working out how best to achieve them.

Being a member of a group implies little in terms of loyalty, although group members, like our bus queue, might well have shared interests. Does Figure 4.1 show a team or a group?

4.3 What do organizations need – more groups or more teams?

The answer is that they need both, for different reasons. Groups can give the organization some administrative convenience. For example, negotiation of pay and workers' conditions is often done in terms of groups of workers. Allocation of all sorts of organizational resources such as

Table 4.2 *Distinction between groups and teams.*

Attribute	Group	Team
Nature	Arbitrary, uncoordinated and lacking cohesion	Motivated, tightly knit and managed
Timeframe	Ongoing	Specific timescale
Function	General or multiple	Specific ad-hoc task
Goals	General, multiple or vague	Specific, single and defined
Responsibilities	General or common	Internal allocation of roles and responsibilities
Accountability	Vague and diffuse	Mutual with performance goals
Communication	Weak	High degree of interdependence and interaction
Bonds	Common interests	Shared commitment and objectives
Motivation	Weak	Strong
Membership	Diffuse, diverse, cross-functional and relatively open	Selected and homogeneous or complementary
Size	Could be large or small	Comparatively small
Integration of new members	Ad hoc	Organized
Leadership	Weak	Clear

Adapted from Coulson-Thomas (1997).

accommodation, car parking and catering can all be broken down into various categories of employee groups for convenience.

However, more significant organizational issues usually need teams. Issues such as quality improvement, empowerment, organizational development and change all rely on the contributions that are made available through teamworking.

Organizations are quick to publicize examples of team successes and Figure 4.2 gives a flavour of the typical benefits claimed.

Time and effort spent on developing and promoting both the value of teams and effective teamworking can clearly be repaid in productivity terms, which is why many organizations see effective teamworking as the way of the future. If the organization is seeking to provide round-the-clock services, teamworking will be more likely to offer consistency of quality than individual working. Teams provide social and structural support for their members, and can expand innovation and creativity as ideas are discussed and modified within the team. Teams also offer organizations some continuity while individual employees are absent or

Company	Team mission	Results
AT&T Credit Corporation	Cross-functional teams formed to improve efficiency and customer service	Improved productivity (800 versus 400 applications per day) and customer service (decision time on loan approval reduced by 50 per cent)
Federal Express	Clerical teams organized to improve efficiency and customer service	Reduced costs $2.1 million in first year and reduced the number of lost packages and billing errors by 13 per cent
GE Appliances	Production teams organized to reduce manufacturing cycle time by 90 per cent and increase product availability	During first 8 months, reduced cycle time by more than 50 per cent and increased product availability by 6 per cent. Decreased inventory costs by more than 20 per cent
Kodak	Production teams organized to generate ideas about improving the efficiency of operations	Improved productivity (works of three shifts now completed in one)
ORYX Energy	Interdepartmental teams assembled to eliminate unnecessary work	Reduced costs $70 million in a single year
Rubbermaid	Cross-functional teams organized to conduct market research on new products	Increased revenue – sales of new product 50 per cent above projection

Adapted from Montebello (1995).

Figure 4.2   Teamworking successes.

leave the organization, because a **multi-skilled team** can generally cover for absent colleagues.

Less common, but nonetheless disturbing, are examples of organizations where teamworking has broken down and performance, both individual and organizational, deteriorates, which is why it is crucial that organizations and managers devote time and energy to team maintenance and development.

Organizations seeking to build up a strong group culture might inadvertently encourage behaviour which is not only unacceptable but is in some cases downright dangerous.

4.4 The significance of work-group cohesion

Group cohesion as defined by Lott and Lott (1965) is "that property which is inferred from the number and strength of mutual positive attitudes among members of the group".

Reflection Box 4.2 Negative aspects of teamworking: peer-group pressure at Salomon Brothers

In the 1980s Michael Lewis wrote of the steps taken by Wall Street bankers, Salomon Brothers, to indoctrinate their new trainees into the 'culture' of the organization. The company was trying to train young traders to be capable of competing with the best and winning. Lewis said of the training programme:

'Life as a Salomon trainee was like being beaten up every day by the neighbourhood bully. Eventually you grew mean and surly. . . . The firm never took you aside and rubbed you on the back to let you know that everything was going to be fine. Just the opposite: the firm built a system around the belief that trainees should wriggle and squirm.'

(Lewis, M. (1989) *Liar's Poker*)

1   What do you think of this type of team pressure being exerted as a training scheme?
2   Why do you think that Salomon Brothers used this technique?
3   How else does the culture of an organization affect the way that teams operate?

According to Mullins (1996) **cohesive groups** will not necessarily result in higher productivity or higher quality. Indeed, high levels of group cohesion might lead to increased effort being placed on the social interaction between group members at the expense of organizational priorities. Such a view is echoed by the work of Seashore (1954) who investigated the effects of group cohesion in an industrial setting and found that, unless organization managers guarded against it, the increased cohesion of work groups would lead to increases in satisfaction of group needs *not* organizational needs.

Argyle (1989) presents a different picture, arguing that a high degree of cohesion leads to greater interaction between members and mutual help leading to social satisfaction. In organizational terms this may be translated into less absenteeism and lower labour turnover. These two factors will lead to higher productivity in themselves.

Even Mullins (1996) concludes that "Strong and cohesive work groups can therefore have beneficial effects on the organization." We believe that cohesive groups are the ones that will generally outperform all others. They will stay together through thick and thin, and be able to offer extra backing to colleagues when required.

Groups become cohesive when the members are motivated to stay in the group. Members of cohesive groups are characteristically committed

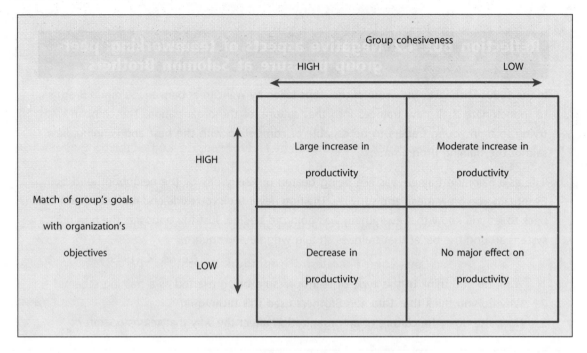

Figure 4.3   Group cohesion and group performance [adapted from Coulson-Thomas (1993)].

and supportive of each other and will be able to resist external threats. Cohesive groups are also capable of ensuring that members conform closely to group norms and performance levels.

Buchanan and Huczynski (1997) believe that the following factors are the main determinates of group cohesiveness:

- attractiveness of the group;
- opportunity to interact with all other members;
- sharing of common goals;
- difficulty of entry to the group;
- status congruence (consensus between group members over hierarchy);
- equity of reward for members;
- success of the group;
- stable membership;
- external threat to group;
- small size.

The tendency of cohesive groups to spend time on social (non-work) activities can act against the proposition that groups or teams are more productive than individuals. To avoid too much social activity, group goals must be closely related to those of the organization. Figure 4.3 illustrates the possible relationships between group cohesiveness and organizational productivity.

Some problems associated with groups

Although a cohesive group can be extremely effective, Janis (1982) showed that too much cohesion can be bad for you. He studied the behaviour of the American Government during the Cuban Missile Crisis that nearly caused a nuclear exchange between the USSR and America. One of his conclusions was that the degree of cohesiveness within the group dealing with the crisis was so high that they focused on the morale and dynamics of the group to the exclusion of almost all else.

Janis coined the term **Groupthink** to describe this phenomenon. The main features of groupthink are outlined in Table 4.3.

Reflection Box 4.3 gives a dramatic example of the possible consequences of groupthink and leads us to ask these questions:

1 What made the team working in this example fail to recognize the significance of the information they had?
2 What safeguards can be used to ensure that overconfidence in teams does not lead to errors of judgement?

Table 4.3 *The groupthink phenomenon – one of a number of group dangers.*

Invulnerability	A belief that the group is unbeatable.
Rationalization	The group is able to deflect and dismiss any criticisms of its behaviour or any evidence that it is not behaving well. Team members bolster each other's explanations: "They're only saying that because. . . ."
Morality	The group believes that their actions are morally correct.
Values	Individuals within or outside the group who express opposition to the group's values are denounced.
Pressure	Group members are put under immense pressure to conform to the group's norms and actions. Such pressure is used to stifle debate.
Self-censorship	Members suppress or deny any negative opinions they have about the group.
Unanimity	The group engineers total agreement and interprets ambiguous signals, such as silence, as a sign of agreement.
Mindguards	Individuals informally appointed to reinterpret any negative information that flows into the group about its behaviour as positive or irrelevant.

Adapted from Janis (1982).

Reflection Box 4.3 Negative aspects of cohesive teamworking: Challenger Space Shuttle Disaster

In 1986 within minutes of the launch from Cape Canaveral, Florida, the Space Shuttle Challenger exploded in full view of the cameras relaying the pictures of what was expected to be another successful launch to millions across the world.

All seven members of the crew were instantly killed, including a civilian schoolteacher, Christa MacAuliffe. A post-event analysis of the cause of the explosion traced the fault to a defective 'O' ring rubber seal that failed to do its job. The 'O' ring was rendered faulty by the freezing temperatures experienced overnight on the launch pad. More significantly the Presidential Commission cited poor decision making as one of the causes of the disaster.

Further investigations have claimed that information was available to prevent the disaster, but the group in charge of the launch did not take account of the advice or information offered to them.

Some of those involved in the analysis of the disaster believe that the negative aspects of teamworking were a contributory factor to the final decision to launch despite contrary advice from Morton Thiokol, the builders of the rocket boosters. NASA management personnel argued with the engineers from Thiokol that the 'O' rings would be adequate, as they had proven to be for the numerous previous launches and tests. Morton Thiokol's superiors, under pressure to approve the launch, were able to devalue Thiokol's opinions by casting doubt on the reasons for any dissent. A past record of success can often lead groups to ignore evidence that is contradictory to what has gone on before.

Overconfidence led the group to disbelieve doubters and not to fully evaluate the risks involved. In the Challenger Shuttle case, while the physical cause of the problem was indeed the 'O' ring, it could be argued that the flawed decision-making process of the group contributed to the disaster (reported in Esser and Lindoerfer, 1989).

Apart from groupthink, very cohesive groups can also create a number of other problems, including the invasion of work-group norms into inappropriate behavioural arenas and an overdependency by individual members on group support.

4.5 Developing effective groups and teams

If organizations want to make teamworking the focus of their operations they have to put some thought and effort into managing and developing teamworking skills and team-based solutions, where individualism

Figure 4.4   Typical outdoor training activities for managers.

previously ruled. Team-development interventions such as 'Outward Bound' weekends or team events outside of the workplace are used extensively by organizations such as HSBC, Barclays Bank and British Telecom, as a way of forging stronger relationships and subsuming individual ambitions for the welfare of the team (Figure 4.4). This type of training is very experiential (i.e. people learn from what they experience), and allows team members to share problems and issues in order to develop better ways of working back in the normal workplace.

Working in organizational teams in a factory or an office is not like joining the local netball side. Like any sporting team one can confidently assume that the goal of the team is simply to win as much as possible and have a good time doing it. So members are unlikely to disagree with the team goals. If I do not like the team, or it is badly organised, I can leave and join another. We can see that employees in organizational teams do not generally have the same freedom to quit. They may also have less opportunity for input to the team's goals and might not even agree with or understand them.

One of the first conditions for effective teamworking is to ensure that team members are properly communicated with and fully aware of their responsibilities. Montebello (1995) argues that team-development schemes that emphasize relationship building at the expense of task achievement is the wrong way to go. He believes that effective teams stem from addressing *task* and *relationship* issues simultaneously.

Experiments on individual conformity in groups were performed by the American social psychologist Asch (1951). He asked subjects to observe slides showing a simply drawn line. The same subjects were then shown a second slide, containing a number of lines of differing lengths. The task was to judge which of the lines in this second group was nearest in length to that originally shown. This task was undertaken by groups of five or six people, but only one of the group was an experimental subject: the others were accomplices of Asch. He found that the experimental subject tended to agree with the accomplices even when they had been told to make judgements that were clearly wrong.

Since then, numerous studies in social psychology have demonstrated that group norms exert a powerful effect on the behaviour of individuals. Work groups, which are generally much more formal than free-forming groups outside employment, can develop rigid codes of conduct which create conformity among group members which can frustrate the goals and objectives of the organization. The Hawthorne experiments, discussed in Section 1.4, confirmed this by revealing the practice of 'rate-fixing' in work groups: a phenomenon in which groups develop norms concerning productivity and causes individuals to work at roughly equal rates.

According to Feldman (1985), conformity to group norms stems from the degree of obedience shown to the legitimate authority of formally defined superiors; that is, the extent to which subordinates conformed to their manager's opinions and requests. In this research three types of response were found to be typical:

- Acceptance based on conscious suppression of personal interests – the subordinate, in order to win approval from the manager, is prepared to act in ways which he/she acknowledges are contrary to his/her own beliefs.
- Acceptance based on unconscious distortion – the subordinate 'denies' his/her behaviour is in conflict with his/her own beliefs.
- Secret rejection – in which subordinates appeared to conform to managers when in their company but secretly followed their own agendas.

Feldman's study suggests that, at least in organizations, the appearance of conformity does not necessarily mean that people accept group norms. They may be motivated to conform for a variety of reasons. Some people may have high needs for inclusion, which means that they are highly dependent on group support to bolster a sense of personal well-being. For these people, conforming to a norm, even one that they don't really accept, is considered to be worthwhile because of the benefits of being a member of the group.

The following list illustrates the main characteristics of group norms:

- Norms can come from the task of the group.
- Norms develop about the non-formal objectives or goals of the group.
- Norms can be used to distinguish between members and non-members of the group.
- Norms specify the internal regulations of the group.
- Norms of attitude, opinion and belief develop in the group.
- Norms of acceptable and unacceptable behaviour towards other groups are established.
- Norms offer a degree of predictability and allow managers to prejudge how a group might react.

Getting the norms of the group right will enable the organization to set and develop the standards of performance that they want from the group. One model of effective teamworking developed at the US-based JC Penney Catalogue Center is called the METHODS model. Methods is an acronym made up of the first letters of the seven principle features: measure; encourage improvement; teach; hear; optimize; dream; succeed.

Measure   Evaluation of team performance ascending to clear predetermined standards. There are seven areas of measurement applicable to teamworking:

- problem solving;
- results and accomplishments over the time-span;
- impact: the significance or otherwise of what was achieved;
- relationships internal to the team;
- task: the timely completion of paperwork and assignments;
- communication external to the team;
- degree of project difficulty, depending on strength and resources of the team.

Encourage improvement

By the use of key goals the team must be encouraged to look all the while for ways of improving. Three types of goals should be considered:

- essential goals required for the team to continue;
- problem-solving goals to propose a more appropriate or desirable condition;
- innovation goals to make something good even better.

Teach   A personalized curriculum and training programme for all team members must be created. All change comes from learning, so a team that educates itself and others as well will change and improve.

Hear   Listen to the feedback that the group gets. Use the information gained to reduce conflict, improve satisfaction of client groups and question current processes.

Optimize   Innovation and role modelling can help to optimize the effectiveness of the team or group. The culture of the team must be one in which experimentation is allowed and encouraged. People who are excited and encouraged by their work are more likely to innovate and share ideas than those who are cynical.

Dream   Spend a little part of every day dreaming. Not in idle time-wasting but in imagining better and more productive ways to work and work together. Every great achievement starts with a dream: somebody wanted to do the impossible. So do not underestimate the power of dreaming. Poor performing teams do not dream.

Succeed   The final principle. The chances of achieving this will be greatly enhanced by teams who are able to work with and through the METHOD principles.

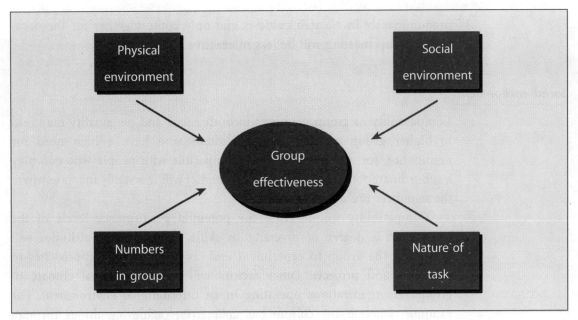

Figure 4.5   Factors leading to group effectiveness.

One factor detrimental to the effectiveness of groups is the make-up of the group itself. According to Coulson-Thomas (1997), "In many organizations, little thought appears to be given to the selection of team members in order to bring together complementary skills, or to the allocation of roles within the team relating to the work of the team itself."

With the increasing availability of research-based techniques (e.g. the work by Belbin and Margerison/McCann covered in Section 4.7) managers now have much more support to call on when they are putting together new teams or want to improve the performance of existing ones.

No one can guarantee if a group will be a success, but a number of factors can be shown to contribute to improving the chances of group success. Figure 4.5 shows one classification adapted from the work of Harvey and Brown (1996).

Physical environment

A group's physical environment affects interaction within the group. Even items as apparently trivial as the layout of the workroom will affect who interacts with whom. Circular tables are likely to encourage more participation, with interchangeable leadership, while teams that work predominantly in isolated cubicles and only come together for the occasional group meeting will be less interactive.

Social environment

Compatibility of group members in both needs and personality may lead to higher group productivity. Individuals who have a high need for dominance, for example, are more compatible with people who can play a subordinate role. The level of group conflict will inevitably increase where the members are not compatible.

Compatibility will increase the potential performance levels of the group, but a degree of diversity in skills, opinions and attitudes will also allow the group to experiment and create innovative approaches to problems and projects. Other factors will affect the social climate of groups in organizations operating in an international environment. For example, whether the culture has collectivist (achieving things through people working together) or individualistic (achieving through independent working) values can be important.

Numbers in group

Typically, productivity is lower in large groups than in small ones. Group size has several effects, including the degree of participation possible and the strength of bonds between members. Large groups have more resources to call upon, but these will be balanced by the difficulties of getting agreement between large numbers of people on a course of action.

Nature of task

Two characteristics of group tasks have a major impact on how effective that group will be. If the task requires a high degree of cooperation (e.g. a hospital surgical team), small groups will generally be more effective than large ones. It is easier to manage the cooperation and coordination of smaller numbers. The second factor concerns the degree of complexity of the task.

Complex tasks often benefit from a more decentralized style of management and control, so that action, decisions and options can be exercised at a lower level within the group. Only if tasks are simple and relatively repetitive (e.g. tasks carried out by an employee working in a fast-food restaurant), with restricted and predictable outcomes, can groups deal with a centralized more directed style of management.

Another category – resources which the group has at its disposal – could also be added to the model, as this would have a further impact on norms about workloads, what is regarded as high quality and how improvements in effectiveness could be achieved.

4.6 Stages of group development

For a group to work effectively, there must be time to allow the group to become an effective unit. Tuckman (1965) presented a universal theory of group development to illustrate the way that groups change over time (Figure 4.6).

In the first stage, which Tuckman calls **forming**, the group comes together and begins to form its own working relationships. The second stage, called **storming** by Tuckman, occurs when the various elements of the group work together to settle any disagreements and set priorities. The third stage is when the group is beginning to jell. During this stage, referred to as **norming**, the ground rules of behaviour and standards are set. Leadership and **followership** patterns will also be established.

By the fourth stage, the **performing** stage, the effectiveness of the group can really be judged. Provided that all the spadework has been done in the earlier stages, the group will be better able to achieve objectives and work cooperatively. When the group is to disband and disengage, the model also suggests that a final stage, **adjourning**, has to be endured. The organizational consequences of the adjourning phase are often represented by falls in both productivity and efficiency as the former team members readjust. A final period of 'mourning' could be added to the model to describe this downturn, which will need to be taken into account as new teams are put together.

One criticism of the Tuckman model is that it does not suggest any recommended time-scale for the movement of the group through the various stages. Some groups, with experienced members who have worked together before, might achieve the performance stage within a week, while others might take seemingly forever to get to effective performance.

An alternative approach, based on psychoanalytic theory, is proposed by Srivasta *et al.* (1977) and is based on the premiss that individuals do not arrive in a group with blank minds – they come

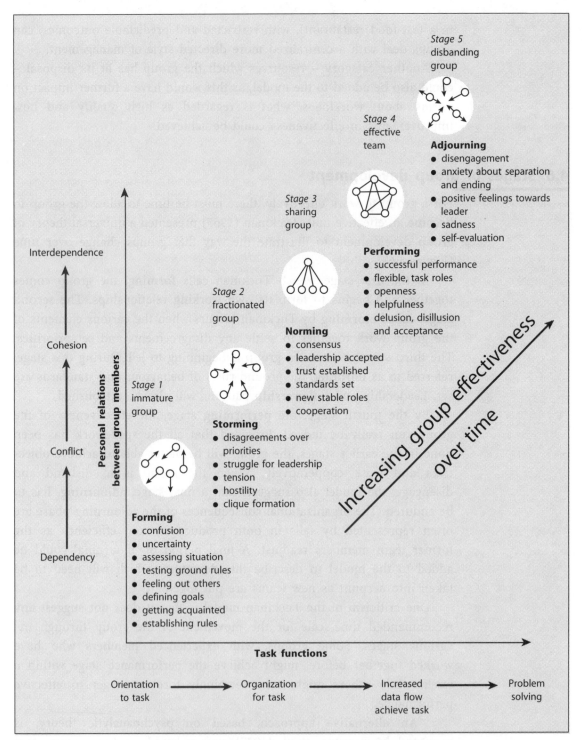

Stage 5
disbanding
group

Stage 4
effective
team

Adjourning
- disengagement
- anxiety about separation and ending
- positive feelings towards leader
- sadness
- self-evaluation

Stage 3
sharing
group

Performing
- successful performance
- flexible, task roles
- openness
- helpfulness
- delusion, disillusion and acceptance

Stage 2
fractionated
group

Norming
- consensus
- leadership accepted
- trust established
- standards set
- new stable roles
- cooperation

Interdependence

Cohesion

Stage 1
immature
group

Storming
- disagreements over priorities
- struggle for leadership
- tension
- hostility
- clique formation

Conflict

Increasing group effectiveness over time

Personal relations between group members

Dependency

Forming
- confusion
- uncertainty
- assessing situation
- testing ground rules
- feeling out others
- defining goals
- getting acquainted
- establishing rules

Task functions

Orientation to task → Organization for task → Increased data flow achieve task → Problem solving

Figure 4.6   The Tuckman stages of group development [based on Tuckman (1965); Tuckman and Jenson (1977); and Jones (1973)].

with an already-formed idea of their own identity. This identity has been developed in a variety of social arenas from home to work and parts of it will be very central to the person's sense of self and will probably not be that amenable to change.

When we join groups some parts of our identity will be challenged by other members. Similarly, we as new members are likely to question the way the group does things (its norms) and the sorts of things it believes in (its values). This process of mutual challenge and adjustment is called the **inclusion process.** Individuals who cannot adjust to a group may leave it. A group whose members cannot adjust to a new individual may break down. On the other hand, the group that stays together and works through the various issues that new members create is likely to develop successfully.

A group that does successfully pass through these stages will eventually reach a point at which the needs of group members are being met. In a similar way to Tuckman, Srivista suggests stages of group development as follows:

Stage 1 Anxiety versus safety

In the initial stage of group development individuals are highly concerned with their own individual identities. They want to be accepted by each other, but they all to differing degrees want to retain important aspects of self. At this stage, therefore, group members are unwilling to let out too much detail about themselves for fear of being rejected.

The leader is very important at this stage. It is the leader that the group looks to in terms of developing a feeling of acceptance or rejection. The leader will often be blamed at this stage for any disquiet or dissatisfaction within the group. The group may not spend enough time thinking about how to structure its activities at this stage and may be rather prone to rushing into action without enough thought.

Stage 2 Similarity versus dissimilarity

In the second stage people become more externally focused and less egocentric. They start to think about other group members and feel less anxious about themselves. Pairings form between members who perceive they share things in common.

The relationship with the group's leader may start to change at this time and most members will become less dependent on the leader's opinions and approval. However, expectations of the leader may still remain high and blame for dissatisfaction, levelled at the leader or the outside environment, is likely to remain.

The activities of the group continue to lack focus and, as feedback from the world outside the group begins to arrive, tentative norms are formed: "Shall we try this? Why don't you take on this role?"

Stage 3 Support versus panic

During this stage the focus for individuals becomes wider than the initial pairings and people become concerned about how to assert their identities within the broader group. It is at this stage that people test out their identities more widely and risk being rejected or 'put down' by other group members. It is here that potentially damaging conflicts can occur. The task becomes the main focus of the group and clarifying procedures and roles is an increasing preoccupation.

Towards the end of this stage a consensus about the identity of the group as a whole begins to emerge and the leader's role changes from one of offering internal support and approval to one of representing the group's interests and identity appropriately to the outside world.

Stage 4 Concern versus isolation

As the group's focus becomes more and more task and goal oriented, there is much negotiation about processes pertinent to the group rather than individuals. The emergent norms are discussed, challenged and modified. Values and attitudes are debated and tested against the group's goals and purpose.

The pairings that characterized the group in its early stages tend to relax to allow more flexibility within the group. Some people may begin to feel isolated.

Relationships become more important than self and people are more prepared to compromise on valued aspects of their own identity in order to retain the integrity of the group.

Stage 5 Independence versus withdrawal

At this point individuals' identities become integrated once more. Changes and modifications are established as part of the new identity but individuals no longer feel threatened. Individuals perceive themselves as highly different from each other, but in a positive way. At this stage some members may feel they cannot commit to the demands of the group in terms of emotion or participation and withdraw.

The group is now oriented towards reality and its actions tend to be well coordinated and geared towards goal achievement. The leader becomes more of a facilitator and is fully integrated into the group's activities.

Stages 1–5 have been adapted from Srivasta, S., Obert, S. L. and Neilson, E. H. (1977) Organisational analysis through group processes. In Cooper, C. L. (ed.) *Organisational Development in the UK and USA*, London: Macmillan.

4.7 An introduction to team roles

Within any group or team there will be a number of roles to be performed. Take the analogy of a football team. If all the players are gifted skilful artists, capable of astounding the crowds with their creativity and flair, the team won't necessarily flourish. Equally, if all the players are athletic fit workers, capable of winning the ball but have little imagination, the team will be equally flawed. Only a combination of the various skills and gifts required to make the complete team will be effective.

In a similar way the operation of a work team needs a balance of all the skills required to achieve results. Away from the sports arena, a similar phenomenon of effective teamworking can be seen in the operation of a choir or orchestra. The overall sound produced will be far superior if the many 'voices' involved are in perfect harmony. If one player or singer wishes to show off, the whole rendition will suffer.

A number of models of the essential roles played by members of effective teams have been developed. One of the most commonly used is that based upon the research of Belbin (1981). Belbin identified *eight key roles* as being significant ingredients in the success or otherwise of the team. These eight areas provided essential contributions to the team effort and if any area was missing or inadequate the overall team would suffer. According to Belbin the eight key roles are:

- implementer;
- coordinator;
- shaper;
- plant;
- resource investigator;
- monitor evaluator;
- teamworker;
- completer–finisher.

Table 4.4 *The Belbin team roles.*

Roles and description	Team contribution	Allowable weaknesses
Plant	Creative, imaginative, unorthodox. Solves difficult problems	Ignores details. Too preoccupied to communicate effectively
Resource investigator	Extrovert, enthusiastic, communicative. Explores opportunities. Develops contacts	Over-optimistic. Loses interest once initial enthusiasm has passed
Coordinator	Mature, confident, a good chairperson. Clarifies goals, promotes decision making, delegates well	Can be seen as manipulative. Delegates personal work
Shaper	Challenging, dynamic, thrives on pressure. Has the drive and courage to overcome obstacles	Can provoke others. Hurts people's feelings
Monitor–evaluator	Sober, strategic and discerning. Sees all options. Judges accurately	Lacks drive and ability to inspire others. Overly critical
Teamworker	Cooperative, mild, perceptive and diplomatic. Listens, builds, averts friction, calms the waters	Indecisive in crunch situations. Can be easily influenced
Implementer	Disciplined, reliable, conservative and efficient. Turns ideas into practical actions	Somewhat inflexible. Slow to respond to new possibilities
Completer	Painstaking, conscientious, anxious. Searches out errors and omissions. Delivers on time	Inclined to worry unduly. Reluctant to delegate. Can be a nit-picker
Specialist	Single-minded, self-starting, dedicated. Provides knowledge and skills in rare supply	Contributes on only a narrow front. Dwells on technicalities. Overlooks the 'big picture'

Strength of contribution in any one of the roles is commonly associated with particular weaknesses. These are called allowable weaknesses. Executives are seldom strong in all nine team roles (from Belbin, M. R. (1996) *The Coming Shape of Organization*, London: Butterworth Heinemann, p. 122).

A more detailed explanation of each of these roles is contained in Table 4.4.

Belbin came to these conclusions after monitoring the performance of a number of teams and groups on a variety of management training exercises. The most consistently successful teams were those which displayed a good balance of the team roles.

Belbin followed up his work by adding a ninth category – the specialist. This role was added because of a realization of the need for professional expertise in much project work and its recurring importance as an issue in career development.

An alternative view of the roles that occur within teams is provided by the work of Margerison and McCann (Team Management Systems). This combines sociological (roles) and psychological (preferences) approaches to teamwork, to show that people have particular **work** **preferences** that relate to the roles they play in a team. A knowledge of these roles and their relationships to individual work preferences is essential if the team is to become a high-performing one.

The eight team roles identified by Margerison and McCann form the model known as the Team Management Wheel. Each double-barrelled role name reflects both the type of work preferred by individuals with this role (*what* people enjoy doing) and their preferred approach (*how* they enjoy doing it).

The eight Margerison–McCann Team Management Systems team roles are as follows:

- reporter–adviser;
- creator–innovator.
- explorer–promoter;
- assessor–developer;

- thruster–organizer;
- concluder–producer;
- controller–inspector;
- upholder–maintainer;

A more detailed description of the major characteristics of each of these roles can be found in Table 4.5.

Table 4.5 *The Margerison-McCann Team Management Systems Team Roles.*

Team role	Major characteristics	General behaviour
Reporter–adviser	Supporter, helper, tolerant; a collector of information; dislikes being rushed; knowledgeable	Usually not aggressive; not time conscious; enjoys finding out; issues interpreted personally; tends to 'put off' decisions
Creator–innovator	Imaginative; future-oriented; enjoys complexity; likes research work	Often irregular work patterns; may miss deadlines; continually searching for new ways
Explorer–promoter	Persuader, 'seller'; likes varied, exciting, stimulating work: easily bored; influential and outgoing	High energy level; knows lots of people; good at getting resources; a visionary; a good communicator
Assessor–developer	Analytical and objective; developer of ideas; enjoys prototype or project work; experimenter	Moves from task to task; action-oriented; dislikes routine; gregarious but independent
Thruster–organizer	Organizes and implements; quick to decide; results-oriented; sets up systems	Makes things happen; action via deadlines; will exert pressure; impatient; may overlook people's feelings
Concluder–producer	Practical; production-oriented; likes schedules and plans; takes pride in reproducing goods and services; values effectiveness/efficiency	Time conscious; follows through to end; dislikes change; prefers routine; makes schedules work
Controller–inspector	Strong on control; detail-oriented; low need for people contact; an inspector of standards and procedures	Critical of inaccuracies; enforcer of regulations; meticulous; quiet and reflective; concentrates in depth on a few issues at a time
Upholder–maintainer	Conservative, loyal, nostalgic; supportive; personal values important; strong sense of right and wrong; work motivation based on purpose	Welds the team together; prefers advisory role; can negotiate well; usually has strong feelings

Source: *Team Management Systems Handbook*, Prado Systems, 1999. Reproduced by kind permission of TMS Development International Ltd, 128 Holgate Road, York, YO24 4FL.

By adopting various strategies, a team should try to cover as much of the model as possible, as a balance of roles is a critical factor in successful teamwork.

Experience tells us that, despite the implications of the studies we've just looked at, the majority of teams in organizations are not put together with much sophistication. Team membership is quite often arbitrary or based more on organizational functions and convenience than real team-working principles.

Remember that data which is based on self-reporting of what people like to do, or how they like to work, does not automatically imply that the respondent will be good at working that way or the best person to work in that role.

Thus, while team-role approaches are useful for taking a snapshot of a team at any particular time, and giving an organization some means of mapping where any problems or benefits are occurring, we have to be wary of their use and applicability beyond this.

4.8 Group decision making

Much attention has been given to the way that groups make decisions. In particular, the focus of research by Hall (1971) has been on understanding those situations in which groups make better decisions than individuals. As a result of his studies, Hall developed a set of guidelines for group decisions (Table 4.6).

People in group situations will often gain the confidence to make decisions that are far more radical than any of the individuals in the group would make on their own. Even if an individual does not support the decision, it would be more difficult to go against the

Table 4.6 *Halls group-decision guidelines.*

- Avoid arguing for your own position, state your point lucidly and logically, then listen to others' reactions and views.
- Do not assume that someone must win and someone must lose, if a stalemate occurs look for the next best alternative.
- Do not change your mind simply to avoid conflict.
- Avoid conflict-reduction techniques such as voting or tossing a coin.
- Differences of opinion are natural and to be expected; seek them out and involve everyone in the process of making the decision.

weight of a large group opinion. For example, if an individual has to make a decision about a risky venture – say investing a large amount of money in a volatile commodity – he or she would feel more comfortable if a group of people had already made the decision to invest. This sort of behaviour is known as **risky shift**.

However, because group decision making can be so advantageous for problem solving in particular, many companies deliberately utilize these processes in **quality circles**. The quality circle, an idea originally developed in Japan, is a group of employees who as part of their working life come together temporarily to solve particular organizational problems or talk over issues.

4.9 Self-managed/autonomous work teams

Research undertaken at the Tavistock Institute in London in the 1950s and 1960s identified some of the direct benefits of self-managed (autonomous) teams. Encouraged by these studies a number of organizations experimented with structures which allowed more use of autonomous work teams. The most widely known example became known as the Scandinavian Experience, in which self-managed teams at Volvo and Saab car plants were found to have improved both job satisfaction and organizational performance.

Case Study 5 'Hot Groups' at the end of this book looks into a specific type of team which is often self-managing, the so-called 'Hot Group'. Hot Groups are high-performing sources of innovation and creativity that some organizations deliberately set up to create an environment where things can and must be done differently.

Such diverse organizations as Dutton Engineering in Northampton and First Direct financial-service call centres are looking again at autonomous teamworking to improve competitive capability and flexibility of response. Moss-Kanter (1983) put the argument that organizations facing turbulent business environments might benefit from abandoning rigid segmented staff structures and move to more integrated team-based approaches.

Peters (1989) popularized very effectively the view that excellent organizations based much of their success on self-managed work teams that provided the basic blocks on which to build competitive advantage. Chaston (1998) claims further that there is growing evidence that a number of major corporations have been using self-managed teams for many years but have avoided publicizing their use on the grounds that the concept conferred significant commercial advantages!

An early reported example of a self-managed workteam was detailed by Peters (1989) at Johnsonville Foods Wisconsin sausage factory in the USA. Johnsonville Foods became a celebrated case because relatively unqualified, but highly trained, team members made all kinds of management decisions and took responsibility for such things as hiring, reward decisions, quality improvement and a range of other issues that workers, whether in teams or not, are not normally expected to take.

Examples of how teamworking is being integrated into the fabric of organizations include evidence from Digital Equipment, the US based computer company, where long-term teams might typically spend the first 2 days of its operation building team dynamics to get the project up and running. The Inland Revenue in the UK has recently introduced 'team listening' sessions in which the entire office staff sit down on a monthly basis for discussion and feedback on performance indicators and group problems.

The same term is used by Do It All, the do-it-yourself retail chain, to describe the activity carried out by their store managers, who are expected to arrange social activities on a monthly basis for all members of the team. For teams to communicate effectively internally they need uninterrupted time away from their usual activities. Finding this time represents a real cost in 'service downtime' that must be borne by the organization.

Evaluating the contribution of a team member to the organization presents something of a dilemma. Two key aspects of performance have to be addressed. First, how effective was the individual contribution to the team effort (in other words, were they a good 'team player'?) and, second, how effective was the overall team in terms of the agreed objectives? When these two questions are answered the final assessment will fall into one of the categories in Figure 4.7.

As can be seen in Figure 4.7 one of the dangers occurs in the bottom left corner where individuals take a free ride on the skills and ability of other team members, thereby hiding their own poor performance. In the top right sector individual excellence, where it is not tailored to the needs of the team, only serves to defeat the purpose of teamworking. One way of encouraging more effective teamworking would be to incorporate it into organizational reward systems. Team-based pay has yet to become a predominant basis for reward in organizations, even in the ones that

Reflection Box 4.5 The rise of the virtual team

The virtual-work team is an organizational phenomenon that is appearing as a direct result of the increased communication possibilities afforded by recent technological developments. Virtual teams are a flexible resource that can bring intellectual or technical skills together temporarily to solve organizational problems in the same way that conventional teams can but, in the virtual team, the work is accomplished electronically.

Without the need to meet, the location of the team members is largely irrelevant. Although the majority of virtual teams meet up from time to time, even this can be overcome by the use of videoconferencing or teleconferencing.

Virtual teams are more likely to be self-managed because of their very nature. Virtual teams can free the organization from constraints of time, geography or staff availability. If a 24-hour service is required, the virtual team can be a true organizational asset. But simply connecting everyone via e-mail or Internet technology does not create a team. The virtual team, like any other, needs to be focused on and harnessed to the organizational goals before it can become effective.

Chris Brennan, who has worked on virtual-team development at both the Lotus Institute and IBM and is now an independent consultant in virtual-team development, believes that a facilitated face-to-face team-development session is vital in the first formative stages if the team is to operate effectively at a distance thereafter: "Our work suggests that the complication in a virtual team is to do with discipline and alignment. If you have 10 people located in 10 different places and they are not at all sure that they know what they are doing, chaos breaks out. It is critical that they establish a relationship and trust each other."

Peter Cochrane, Head of Research at British Telecommunications Labs in the Research and Development arm of BT, believes that younger employees adapt more readily to the concept of virtual teamworking: "The people we employ are usually around 25–27 years old. They are used to teamworking from their education and they don't come with this stupid management culture that says 'information is power'."

For Cochrane, the key to effective virtual teamworking is really no different from that of conventional teams. He does offer some words of warning, though, to those organizations that are thinking of moving into virtual teamworking: "A lot of things that happen in physical space have to be changed. The notion of control goes out of the window, along with management in its strictest sense. Anyone who tries to control the information becomes the single biggest risk to the project."

1   What do you think are the negative and positive aspects of virtual teams?
2   How does that fact that a virtual team does not physically meet affect the socialization aspects of team-working?
3   How possible is it that the virtual team will eventually replace traditional teams in organizations?

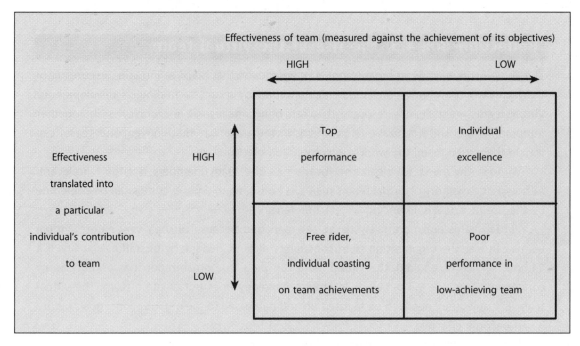

Figure 4.7   Evaluating the team and individual team-member effectiveness [adapted from Coulson-Thomas (1993)].

emphasize the role that teams play. The advantages of introducing team-based rewards include:

- reinforcing teamworking and cooperative behaviour;
- encouraging groups to improve;
- promoting the sharing of information and skills;
- clarifying team objectives and mapping paths to meeting them;
- underscoring the teamwork ethic and emphasizing it as a core organizational value.

An example of an organization which has introduced team-based pay to its service teams is the Inland Revenue. In 1996, having already introduced individual performance-based pay, they set up a trial system which tied an individual's further pay rise to whether or not the team met or exceeded its objectives (Reflection Box 4.6). In the first year of operation the vast majority of teams met their objectives.

A survey by Coulson-Thomas (1993) covering 100 organizations employing over 1 million employees, uncovered much evidence of the difficulties of teamworking. This is summarized in Table 4.7.

Reflection Box 4.6 Team-based pay for all?

If the advantages of teamworking are so great to both individual and the organization why don't organizations put their money behind team-based pay schemes? What advantages and drawbacks can you think of in doing this? How would you feel if your pay was dependent upon the efforts and results of everyone else in your team? Do you think that team-based pay would encourage cooperation or conflict?

Suppose you, as a student, were given an average mark for all the people in your group, regardless of what you personally achieved and how you individually performed in your exams and assignments. Would this make you cooperate with your classmates and even help them study in order to boost your average? Or would you be demotivated because whatever you did you would not get a result that was a direct reflection of your efforts?

The same survey also contains further evidence about what organizations are actually using teams for (see Table 4.8).

At its best the self-managed-team concept can engender loyalty, commitment, enthusiasm and a culture of unprecedented efficiency and cooperation. At its worst self-managed teamworking can be fraught with frustration, stifled by bureaucracy and ruptured by disputes and rivalry. In some organizations the best efforts at teamworking can degenerate into time-consuming committees which offer nothing more than a delay in organizational processes.

Table 4.7 *The difficulties of self-managed teamworking.*

- Internally focused groups might be able to deliver structural change or flatter organizations, but they can easily lead an organization to lose sight of its customers and their requirements.
- Teamworking needs support in terms of skills development for both team leaders and team members. Information technology to support teamwork and empowered teams is yet to be used widely.
- Group objectives are often expressed, if at all, in non-quantifiable terms so that measurement and the subsequent reward of group outputs is more difficult than it should be.
- Cross-functional teams are less common and multi-level teams rarer still, leading to the potential reinforcement of departmental or sectional barriers.
- Many organizations lack good 'team-working role models' because past policies have played down the contribution of teamwork.

Table 4.8 *The most common uses of teamworking in organizations.*

- The most important uses of groups and teams are to deliver customer satisfaction and achieve total quality. (An added benefit is the removal of departmental barriers and the encouragement of cross-functional cooperation.)
- Changing corporate culture by involving employees in increasing the speed of response to customers were also common objectives of group working.
- High-achieving teams were found to be those which operate in a cross-functional way, cutting through functional boundaries that inhibit the delivery of value to customers.
- The future areas where teamworking was expected to increase most were in the field of customer relations, building closer relationships with customers and suppliers.

It should be no surprise to Western students of organizational behaviour that the potential for disaster is so prevalent. The education and training culture of the West is far more concerned with the performance of individuals than the notion of the team (Townley, 1989). Often, the typical characteristics and attitudes that we have been encouraged to display as individuals can serve only to undermine effective teamworking.

4.10 Inter-group and intra-group conflict

Conflict in work groups is inevitable from time to time, especially if groups or teams come under pressure to perform. Some level of conflict is normally considered to be a healthy way of ensuring creativity and innovation and preventing the group becoming stale.

When conflict is so great that it becomes destructive and harmful, action must be taken to reduce its effects and ultimately remove the source of the conflict. Inter-group conflict describes a situation in which groups are in dispute with other groups in the same organization. An example might be where a production department disagrees with the design department over changes to a specification that, while improving the finished product, would make the production more complicated or time consuming. Intra-group conflict occurs when members of the same group fall out. Here an example might be where two employees in the same team have different views on how best to complete the same job.

Sherif (1966), an American social psychologist, was one of the first to study inter-group conflict. Sherif and his colleagues took a large group of young boys to a summer camp. When the boys arrived at the camp they were split into two groups. The groups were then allocated tasks in direct competition with each other.

Under competitive conditions the boys began to exaggerate the strengths and qualities of their own group and the weaknesses and limitations of the other group. Sherif called this the **in-group, out-group phenomenon**. Later experiments showed that the in-group, out-group phenomenon could be eradicated only if the two groups were set tasks that required a higher degree of collaboration.

In the UK, Tajfel and his colleagues (1978; 1982) designed another series of experiments to look at inter-group relations. They put people into two groups using arbitrary criteria (such as which modern painter they liked), so the selections were completely random. Individuals were then given the opportunity to make judgements about members of their own group and members of the group to which they did not belong. Members of both groups were equally unknown to the individual subjects.

Tajfel found that subjects made unfavourable judgements about the group to which they did not belong and favourable judgements about the group to which they did belong.

These experiments shed light on the reasons for inter-group conflict in organizations as well as the potential for group loyalty. In large organizations it is quite common to find inter-group conflict between members of different groups or departments (e.g. between managers and workers). In organizations such conflict usually takes the form of negative stereotypes (e.g. 'all managers are out for themselves').

Inter-group conflict can reduce communication between groups and lead to various degrees of non-cooperation, from downright refusal to carry out certain requests to more subtle forms of disruption, such as taking more time than necessary to complete a job. At times, inter-group conflict can lead to very serious consequences, such as the strike threats experienced by Ford UK in 1999, which were grounded in accusations of racism between certain groups at the Dagenham plant.

Intra-group conflict is often cited as a major source of stress for individuals at work (Quick and Quick, 1984). Reflection Box 4.7 describes a typical case.

The following list offers examples of behaviour likely to lead to destructive group conflict:

- Restricting information so that one group member implies that he or she has information which will answer a group problem but will not communicate it to the rest.

Reflection Box 4.7 Intra-group conflict or bullying?

A group of individuals working together in an administrative department in a public-sector organization developed a serious case of intra-group conflict. Three members of the group had worked together for several years. They had good relationships with each other and had established their own ways of performing the tasks of their department. The fourth member had recently joined the department, having been promoted from elsewhere in the organization. They all worked in an open-plan office, supervised by a manager who had her own office, but who interacted reasonably regularly with the team. The manager was also quite new to the department.

Within weeks of joining the group, the newest member began to feel that the longer-serving group members did not like her. She felt they 'picked on her' for the slightest misdemeanours, and she also felt they demanded too much conformity from her. For instance, she felt that not only did the group demand that tasks were completed in certain ways but that she was also expected to share their beliefs, opinions and views on a whole range of matters from who they did and did not like in the workplace to what they considered to be fashionable clothing.

At first, if the new group member did not comply with the others she was given a frosty look. However, over time the situation grew much more tense, to a point at which they actually stopped talking to her altogether. She also believed they were talking about her behind her back and would sometimes come into the office to find them giggling in a way she found quite disturbing. Eventually, she spoke to a member of staff from a different department about the problems she was experiencing. She said she didn't want to speak to her own line manager, the office supervisor, as she felt this might make matters worse. The members of staff concerned apparently told her that this department had a reputation for being bitchy and that she ought to seek a transfer as soon as possible.

Unfortunately, her colleagues found out that she had spoken to this particular member of staff and the situation in the office apparently became intolerable. They not only refused to talk to her but actually made it extremely difficult for her to perform her job properly. For instance, they would omit to tell her important information or refuse to help her to do tasks she was unfamiliar with.

Unable to cope with the atmosphere in the office, the new member of the department eventually took sickness absence before resigning her position.

1   How did the conflict situation arise and how could it have been avoided?
2   How should the newest member of the group have behaved when she joined?
3   How could the group have made it easier for the new member?

- Deliberate distortion of the facts to present or preserve a position.
- Factionalism (subgroups form to undermine the overall group position).
- Insults or disrespectful comments which are aimed at subverting the group.
- Withdrawal by one or more of the group by sulking or by simply ignoring the group's problems.
- Members speak in order to be heard rather than to make effective contributions.
- Delaying tactics, such as changing the subject or deliberately confusing the issue with excess data.

The following examples list behaviour likely to cause constructive group conflict:

- Exploration of and discussion of alternative solutions to a problem.
- Brainstorming and innovation or creativity sessions.
- Sharing of information and experiences.

The previous two listing have been adapted from Tajfel, H. (1978).

Cognitive explanations

In attempting to understand conflict between groups, the focus has largely been on **cognitive explanations**; that is, the idea that conflict can be explained by understanding the ways we process information about each other.

It is widely accepted by psychologists (e.g. Cohen, 1993) that we store information in our brains in **schemas**. Schemas are not actual structures but are explanations of the way information is dealt with. Schemas enable us to *categorize* information, to automatically process information and to retrieve or recall information.

As we develop as children and learn how to differentiate between different objects on the basis of properties they possess, we store that information in ways that enables us to categorize new objects as and when we encounter them. For instance, a child will initially develop a schema for animals, which is different from his or her schema for furniture. This enables a child to recognize that a table is different from a sheep – even though both might have four legs! As we encounter more and more examples of different objects (chairs, coffee tables, cats and dogs) our schemas become increasingly complex to account for the wide variety of objects that might belong in any single category.

Schemas also help us to recall and retrieve information. If you were asked to learn a list of 30 words, you would find it a lot easier to remember them if you were able to categorize them in some way. For instance, words beginning with the letter B or organic things or properties of fruit or whatever. Categorizing things in this way is known as **schematic processing**.

Stereotypes are schemas that contain information about certain groups of people. Brislin (1993) claims that we use stereotypes to make judgements about members of certain social categories, even if we don't know the individual concerned.

The notion that we may develop negative attitudes to groups to which we do not belong because we distort our perceptions of them implies that there is a 'correct' way to perceive people (Henriques, 1998). For example, managers may not be very popular with people at the bottom of the hierarchy. Stereotyping explains this by suggesting that people at the bottom of the hierarchy may misperceive their managers.

In fact, we can see the idea at work in various modern-day management practices. Consultation exercises, management by walking around, team briefings, empowerment programmes and 360° appraisals are all examples of trying to reduce the differences between teams and create an opportunity to feel part of one bigger group.

Table 4.9 offers, by way of a recap on some of the issues we have covered in this chapter, some of the more common advantages and disadvantages of teamworking.

4.11 Summary

In this chapter we have looked at the significance of teams and groups for the field of OB. In considering the psychological motivation behind group membership for many people we have outlined the social needs served by affiliation and group membership.

We pointed out the differences between groups and teams that, as a student of OB, you need to be clear about because many people confuse the two.

We saw that the variety of roles that people play in work teams can be different from when they behave as individuals and that by combining

Table 4.9 *Do's and don'ts of teamworking in organizations.*

DO	DON'T
Support and develop team attitudes	Simply announce that the team exists
Allow teams autonomy of action	Constrict the team unduly
Give the team clear objectives	Expect immediate top performance
Appreciate the stages of team development	Expect all to be good team players
Attempt to balance the skills of the team	Appoint team leaders arbitrarily
Allow teams to make their own decisions	Dictate all aspects of team behaviour
Allow new entrants to join the team	Exclude new members
Ensure that team loyalty is developed	Allow team loyalty to hide inadequate performance of individuals

the various qualities of its members a team can often produce results that are far in excess of what each of the individuals alone can achieve.

The significance of work-group cohesiveness was considered as a factor that allows a team to grow strong and develop its identity. A few words of caution were also supplied to consider when one is thinking about teamworking and organizational groups. If the group becomes the focus for setting and achieving goals rather than the organization, there could easily be some **misalignment**; that is, the group could go off pursuing aims and objectives that they were happy with but the organization did not see as important.

In this chapter we have seen how some of the best aspects of teamworking need to be managed and they cannot be taken for granted. In the field of sports a well managed and balanced team will have a very good chance of beating a team made up of superior individuals. The same is true in organizations.

Not all organizations can recruit the cream of employees. Sometimes they have to use teamworking-based solutions to make up for the fact that many employees have skill or experience shortages in certain areas, while they might equally excel in others.

In the final section of the chapter we looked at some of the myths and realities of teamworking. We believe that the main learning point should be to recognize that effective teamworking needs a change in the traditional management style for many organizations. A tightly controlled and rule-bound team will not be able to use creativity and innovation in what it does, thereby losing one of the main advantages it holds over an administrative group of individuals.

The overall lesson from this chapter is that groups and teams offer excellent opportunities for individuals and organizations to meet and exceed their goals, but they must be managed effectively to ensure that the negative aspects of group and team-working do not outweigh these benefits.

Questions

Self-test questions

1   Explain the meaning of the following terms as they relate to group working:
    *   group cohesiveness;
    *   formal and informal groups;
    *   team roles.
2   According to Belbin, what are the main roles that need to be present to create effective work groups?
3   What could cause the misalignment of group or team goals with organizational ones?
4   What are the main negative aspects of teamworking?
5   What are the four stages of the Tuckman model of group development?
6   What are the pros and cons of self-managed work teams?
7   What are the main factors likely to raise or lower the effectiveness of work groups?

Discussion questions

1   How do you think the norms of group behaviour develop over time and how can they be altered?
2   According to Harvey and Brown a few key factors will influence the effectiveness of a group. Can you think of other issues and factors that might also play a part?
3   According to the concept known as risky shift, what is the danger that group decisions can create?
4   Team-based rewards promise some advantages but they also carry drawbacks. How would you feel about being rewarded for team-based results rather than individual performance?
5   What do you see as the key features of a group and how does it differ from a team?

6 What do you feel you would enjoy most about working as a team member and what would be less enjoyable?

7 Why would an informal group tend to be less effective at achieving complex tasks or objectives?

8 For what psychological or sociological reasons do you think people join groups?

9 What do you see as the factors that lead to increased cohesiveness in a work team?

4.13 References and bibliography

Allcorn, S. (1989) Understanding groups at work, *Personnel*, **66**(8), 28–36.

Argyle, M. (1989) *The Social Psychology of Work* (second edition), London: Penguin.

Asch, S. E. (1951) Effects of group pressure upon the modification and distortion of judgements. In Guetzgkow, H. (ed.) *Groups, Leadership and Men*, New York: Carnegie Press, pp. 177–190.

Belbin, M. (1981) *Management Teams, Why They Succeed or Fail*, London: Heinemann.

Brislin, E. (1993) *Understanding Culture's Influence on Behaviour*, Orlando, FL: Harcourt Brace Jovanovich.

Buchanan, D. and Huczynski, A. (1997) *Organisational Behaviour, An Introductory Text*, Prentice Hall.

Chaston, I. (1998) Self-managed teams: Assessing the benefits for small service-sector firms, *British Journal of Management*, **9**, 1–12.

Cohen, G. (1993) Everyday memory and memory systems: The experimental approach. In Cohen, G., Kiss, G. and le Voi, M. (eds) *Memory: Current Issues* (second edition), Buckingham: Open University Press.

Coulson-Thomas, C. (1993) Harnessing the Potential of Groups, a survey undertaken for Lotus Development, London: Adaptation Ltd.

Coulson-Thomas, C. (1997) *The Future of the Organisation*, London: Kogan Page.

Esser, J. K. and Lindoerfer, J. S. (1989) Groupthink and the space shuttle Challenger accident, *Journal of Behavioural Decision Making*, **2**, 167–177.

Feldman, S. P. (1985) Culture and conformity: An essay on individual adaptation in centralized bureaucracy, *Human Relations*, **38**(4), 341–357.

Hall, J. (1971) Decisions, decisions, decisions, *Psychology Today*, November.

Harvey, D. and Brown, D. (1996) *An Experiential Approach to Organisational Development*, New Jersey: Prentice Hall.

Heller, R. (1997) *In Search of European Success*, London: Harper Collins Business.

Henriques, J. (1998) Social psychology and the politics of racism. In Henriques, J., Hollway, W., Urwin, C., Venn, C. and Walkerdine, V. (eds) *Changing the Subject: Psychology, Social Regulation and Subjectivity*, London: Routledge.

Hoerr, J. (1989) The payoff from teamwork, *Business Week*, July 10, 56–62.

Janis, I. L. (1982) *Victims of Group Think: A Psychological Study of Foreign Policy Decisions and Fiascos* (second edition), Boston, MA: Houghton Mifflin.

Katzenbach, J. R. and Smith, D. K. (1993) *The Wisdom of Teams: Creating the High Performance Organization*, Boston: Harvard Business School Press.

Lewis, M. (1989) *Liar's Poker, Two Cities True Greed*, London: Hodder and Stoughton.

Lott, A. J. and Lott, B. E. (1965) Group cohesiveness as inter personal attraction: A review of relationships with antecedent and consequent variables, *Psychology Bulletin*, **64**, 259–309.

Margerison, C. J. and McCann, D. J. (1996) *Team Management: Practical New Approaches*, Management Books 2000.

Margerison, C. J. and McCann, D. J. (1999) *Team Management Systems Accreditation Handbook*, Prado Systems Ltd, 2nd edition.

Montebello, A. R. (1995) *Work Teams that Work*, Petaling Jaya, Malaysia: Quest.

Moss-Kanter, R. (1983) Change masters and the intricate architecture of corporate culture change, *Management Review*, **72**, 18–28.

Mullins, L. (1996) *Management and Organisational Behaviour*, London: Pitman.

Myers, D. (1994) *Exploring Social Psychology*, New York: McGraw-Hill.

Peters, T. (1989) *Thriving on Chaos*, Pan Books.

Quick, J. C. and Quick, J. D. (1984) *Organizational Stress and Preventive Management*, New York: McGraw-Hill.

Seashore, S. E. (1954) *Group Cohesiveness in the Industrial Work Group*, Ann Arbor, MI: Survey Research Centre, University of Michigan.

Sherif, M. (1966) *Group Conflict and Cooperation: Their Social Psychology*, New York: Harper & Row.

Srivista, S., Obert, S. L. and Neilson, E. H. (1977) Organisational analysis through group processes. In Cooper, C. L. (ed.) *Organisational Development in the UK and USA*, London: Macmillan.

Tafjel, H. (1978) Intergroup behavior: Group perspectives. In Tajfel, H. and Fraser, C. (eds) *Introducing Social Psychology*, Harmondsworth: Penguin.

Tafjel, H. (1982) *Social Identity and Intergroup Relations*, London: Cambridge University Press.

Townley, B. (1989), Selection and appraisal: Reconstituting social relations. In Storey, J. (ed.) *New Perspectives on Human Tesource Management*, London: Routledge.

Tuckman. B. W. (1965) Development sequence in small groups, *Psychological Bulletin*, **63**, 384–399.

J. C. Penney Methods Model is described in *Team Performance Management*, **2**(3) (1966).

5

Organizational leaders and managers

Contents

Objectives

By the end of this chapter you should be able to:

- understand what leadership is and how it differs from management
- evaluate the sources of leadership power
- be aware of the theories that attempt to explain differences in leadership style
- describe how contingencies require different leadership styles
- make an informed judgement about the future of leadership

5.1 Introduction

People have been debating the nature of leadership for as long as records have been kept, certainly as far back as the ancient Greek philosopher Homer. People continue to be enthralled by the topic. Recently, some business leaders have even replaced the great leaders of military or politics as influential role models.

If you asked someone to name a great leader, the names of Jack Welch, Percy Barnevik, Ricard Semler, Anita Roddick, Richard Branson, Bill Gates or Sir John Harvey Jones would be just as likely to be mentioned as those of Tony Blair, General 'Stormin' Norman Schwartzkopf or Bill Clinton.

Leadership has to provide a focal point for an organization and give employees the confidence to follow and believe in the strategy and goals set.

Aristotle (384–322 BC) expressed the view that to be a good leader one has first to learn the skills of 'followership', believing that he who has never learned to obey cannot be a good commander. More than ever in today's business climate managers have to operate as leaders *and* followers as organizations look increasingly to expertise in preference to age as a determinant of authority.

Another crucial distinction in the role of the modern leader is pointed out by Sir Adrian Cadbury, former head of Cadbury Schweppes, who said "Good leaders grow the people below them, bad leaders stunt them; good leaders serve their followers, bad leaders enslave them" (1999).

According to Mosley, Pietri and Megginson (1996) "leadership is a process of influencing individual and group activities toward goal setting and goal achievement. ... In the final analysis the successful leader is the one who succeeds in getting others to follow."

Bryman (1996), offers the following slightly different definition of leadership, "Leadership is the creation of a vision about a desired future state which seeks to enmesh all members of an organisation in its net."

There are many alternative definitions you will find in other books, but they all agree that leadership is a crucial activity in organizations and one that often determines the success or failure of major organizational initiatives.

5.2 Management versus leadership

Much concern centres on the role of organizational leadership in the future, now that more flexible styles of working and new structures of

Table 5.1 *Management versus leadership.*

Managerial skills and behaviour	Leadership skills and behaviour
Planning	Inspiring
Controlling	Motivating
Communication	Envisioning
Evaluating	Behaviour modelling
Monitoring	Involving
Teamworking	Promoting learning
Directing	Team building

organization are replacing the old-fashioned bureaucratic hierarchical patterns of management. There is a growing distinction between management and leadership (Table 5.1). While the traditional management view (detailed later in Chapter 9) emphasizes planning and control, modern leadership is more concerned with exercising influence and inspiring people rather than enforcing required behaviour. Mosley, Pietri and Megginson (1996) believe that leadership is an important part of management but that it is not the same thing. For Kotter (1990) the crucial difference can be found in the view that the manager's task is to concentrate on control to provide order and stability, whereas leaders must concentrate on aligning, inspiring and giving people the confidence to welcome change.

Case Study 3 'Positive aspects of teamworking: total employee involvement at Smith and Nephew' at the end of the book gives an excellent example of an organizational situation when the aspects of leadership and management have been confused leading to less than optimal results.

Table 5.1 lists the major differences between management and leadership.

Peters and Austin (1985) provided an extensive list of the characteristics and behaviours that typified leadership in contrast with management:

- visible and available – 'one of the troops';
- in touch with individuals;
- able and willing to listen;
- tough, fair and persistent;
- trusting of people and with respect for them;
- looking for controls to remove;

- preferring discussion to written reports;
- able to see mistakes as opportunities to learn and develop.

Whereas the manager or non-leader (as they describe it) is typically:

- invisible, giving orders to staff;
- uncomfortable with people;
- good talker;
- hard to reach;
- trusts only words and numbers on paper;
- unfair and arrogant;
- looking for new controls and procedures;
- sees mistakes as punishable offences and opportunities for scape-goating.

5.3 Sources of leadership power

Power is the potential ability to influence the behaviour of others. Leaders hold power either by virtue of the resources they control or by exercising personal sources of power and influence. These sources might be legitimized by the leader being elected or appointed. Alternatively the leader might have power by virtue of some skill or ability that only they have. Typical sources of leadership power are categorized in Table 5.2.

Table 5.2 *Typical sources of leadership power and influence.*

Legitimate power	Power coming from a formal position in the organization and from the authority attached to it.
Reward power	Power stemming from the leader's ability to bestow rewards, financial or otherwise.
Coercive power	Power to punish or recommend punishment.
Expert power	Power resulting from the leader's knowledge or skill regarding the tasks performed by followers.
Referent power	Power coming from the leader's personality characteristics that command identification and respect.
Elected power	Power derived from votes of interested parties, such as trade-union representatives.
Resource power	Power to allow use of exclusive resources, such as land or capital.

5.4 Leadership styles

Leadership style is a very personal and infinitely variable thing, although a number of classifications have been developed to help us understand the way different leaders behave. Often theoretical descriptions of leadership style are not as useful as the anecdotal or observational evidence that many who have worked with great or highly successful leaders are happy to disclose. Descriptions of typical leaders' personalities can often give a clue to the type of leadership style that they would normally employ.

Table 5.3 illustrates the views of Bobo (1997) on leadership, indicating some of the commonly occurring styles. As can be seen, there is a wide variety of styles and leadership behaviours that can be observed. Most leaders will utilize a range of styles in accordance with their reading of the situation. Note that all the classifications emphasize the role of the leader in changing or improving things not simply controlling them.

Early efforts to describe the ideal leader looked at **leadership traits** Traits theory, as witnessed in the work of Stewart (1963), attempted to describe all the features that a good leader displays. One difficulty with this theory is that the list grows ever longer the more successful leaders you consider. Eventually, it becomes so cumbersome that you begin to ask yourself if any one person can ever possess all the qualities they need to become a great leader. Could it be the case that effective leadership can still be arrived at even though the person designated to be the leader does not necessarily have all the qualities listed?

There are also a number of contradictions if we start to compare leaders from different fields of endeavour. For example, the qualities

Table 5.3 *Leadership styles.*

Style	Typical behaviour	Drawbacks	Advantages
Activist leadership	Pursuit of specific (own) causes; poor eye for detail sees big picture	Not in tune with organization	Good in crisis; gets things done
Laid-back leadership	Takes little seriously	Little enthusiasm generated	Can fulfil a holding role
Ambivalent leadership	Decisions often revoked; lacking in training or skill	Cost to organization as policies have to be reworked	May be more effective after training
Analytical leadership	Seeks too much information before decision making	Paralysis by analysis; too slow to be effective	Won't be easily swayed
Autocratic leadership	Rules with a rod of iron; 'my way or the highway'	Bullying and unwilling to use others' ideas	Direct and clear instructions to staff

Reflection Box 5.1 Leadership style in action: is Hewlett Packard's MBWA the best way to lead?

One organization which attempted to combine the qualities of both management and leadership is Hewlett Packard. They used a style of management which became known as 'Managing by Wandering Around' (MBWA). The MBWA principle centres on the belief that the most effective form of management comes from developing a network of influence, both formal and informal. These channels of communication include talking with key subordinates, customers and suppliers, monitoring what competitor organizations are up to and keeping an ear open to contacts from outside the organization.

The manager has to literally walk about to establish and maintain the channels of communication. The technique first came to light through the activities of company founder, Bill Hewlett, who was well known for leaving his office and 'wandering around' the plant, greeting people and questioning what they were doing.

Other companies have moved to copy the 'HP Way'. The founder of McDonald's, Ray Croc, regularly visited store units and did his own personal inspection of 'Q S C and V' (Quality, Service, Cleanliness and Value), the themes he preached regularly. In order to 'walk the walk', Ray would pull up in the car park of a McDonald's and perhaps pick up any litter he found outside before lecturing the in-store staff on the importance of keeping the environment clean and tidy.

1   Do you think that MBWA is a good way of showing leadership?
2   What other messages does MBWA send to staff?
3   What are the negative aspects of MBWA?

needed for a professional sports' team leader or coach or manager are very different from those that would be needed for a leader from the Church or the leader of an orchestra. Table 5.4 shows some typical leadership traits.

As can be seen, the columns often contain traits which could arguably fit into other columns. For example, is drive a physical or personality category? There may also be traits that are not included in the table and ones that researchers simply have not yet identified.

Pettinger (1996) describes the way that leadership styles vary from **dictatorial** (in which employees have no input to the decision-making process and are just told what to do) to **democratic** (decisions are taken only after full consideration of employees' views). In-between are **consultative** (the leader consults those affected by the decision and may possibly

Table 5.4 *Leadership traits.*

Physical	Personality	Social	Intelligence and ability	Work related
Active	Determined	Credibility	Judgement	Achievement
Energetic	Originality	Popularity	Knowledge	Drive
Relaxed	Creativity	Charm	Communication skills	Responsibility
	Self-confidence	Sincerity		Task oriented
		Diplomacy		

modify his or her position before making it) and **participative** (the leader encourages employees to propose their own solutions and work out the implications of what is, in effect, their decision).

The key point to recognize here is that none of the styles is universally applicable. The effective leader is one who is able to operate across the range of styles as is appropriate.

Tannenbaum and Schmidt (1973) provide a model for leadership behaviour which described the style of leadership as a **continuum**, reflecting varying amounts of employee involvement and leadership control (Figure 5.1).

The autocratic versus democratic style of leadership suggests that it is the behaviour of the leader rather than his or her personality that determines effectiveness. This throws some weight behind the idea *that leaders can be coached or trained, as opposed to the view that leaders are born not made*. Effective behaviour patterns are something that we can all learn if we know what they are and are given the opportunity to practise and develop them.

Research into effective leadership is focusing more and more on the behaviour of leaders than on their personalities and the most widely acknowledged of these studies was undertaken at the Ohio State University in the USA in the 1940s [see Schriescheim and Bird (1979)]. These studies identified two major leadership behaviours:

Consideration: extent to which the leader is mindful of subordinates, respects their ideas and feelings, and establishes mutual trust. Considerate leaders are approachable, provide open communications, develop teamwork and are oriented towards their subordinates welfare.

Initiating structure: extent to which the leader is task oriented and directs subordinates towards goal attainment. Leaders who

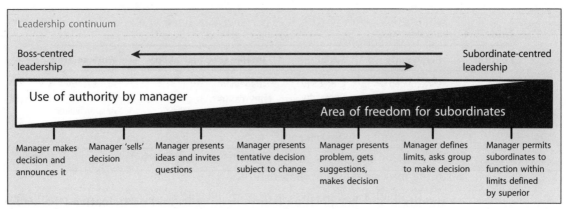

Figure 5.1   The leadership continuum [from Tannenbaum, R. and Schmidt, W. (1973) How to choose a leadership pattern, *Harvard Business Review* May–June. Copyright © 1973 by the President and Fellows of Harvard College.]

favour this style typically give instructions, spend time planning, emphasize deadlines and provide explicit schedules of work activities.

An important thing to remember is that both of these factors are interdependent. A leader can exhibit high or low tendencies in either or both of the behaviours. Figure 5.2 illustrates the types of leadership behaviours that were found by the Ohio State researchers.

In quadrant A the leader shows low levels of both consideration and initiating structure behaviour. This would indicate less-than-effective leadership and may signify that the leader is lacking the necessary skills or motivation. A leader who occupies this quadrant is one that is not adding significant value to the organization. The most common situation

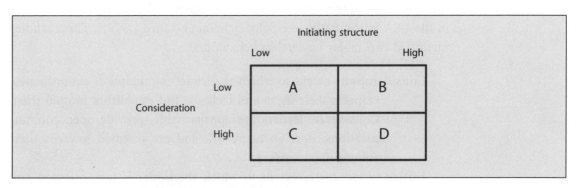

Figure 5.2   Leadership styles identied by the Ohio State studies.

when this occurs is with inexperienced leaders who need further development and support.

Quadrant B indicates a leader who is highly structured and works mostly through a directive approach. This type of leader will be closest to the traditional view of the task-oriented industrial or operational manager. Where the organization is in a stable environment and needs quick results this style will be more applicable. This position is more likely to be successful in the short term, as less attention is paid to developing and sustaining relationships.

In quadrant C, leaders give more weight to considerate behaviour and are less concerned with the direction of subordinates. Such leaders are more likely to employ participative styles or communicate more openly. For complex and changing tasks where cooperation and teamworking are essential this type of leadership will be appropriate.

Leaders who fall into quadrant D are able to combine behaviours that illustrate a high concern for both key factors. The Ohio State research suggested that the leader who is described by the features of quadrant D is the most likely to achieve better performance and greater satisfaction than any of the other styles. This quadrant also represents a more sustainable position for the leader over the long term.

 Blake and Mouton and later Blake and McCanse developed the Ohio research further and constructed a similar two-dimensional leadership theory which has become known as the **leadership grid**. The three-dimensional model and its major subsequent management styles are shown in Figure 5.3. Each axis on the grid has a nine-point scale: 1 means 'low concern' and 9 means 'high concern'.

Team management (point 9,9) is believed to be the optimum combination and is recommended to managers because it embodies the view that members of the organization should be working together to achieve objectives.

Country-club management (point 1,9) is used by the authors to describe a management style in which primary consideration is given to the *people* aspects but not to output or results.

Authority-obedience management (point 9,1) is the consequence when efficiency or cost control becomes the main focus of the manager's objectives.

Impoverished management (point 1,1) indicates that managers are operating ineffectively, lack a philosophy of what good

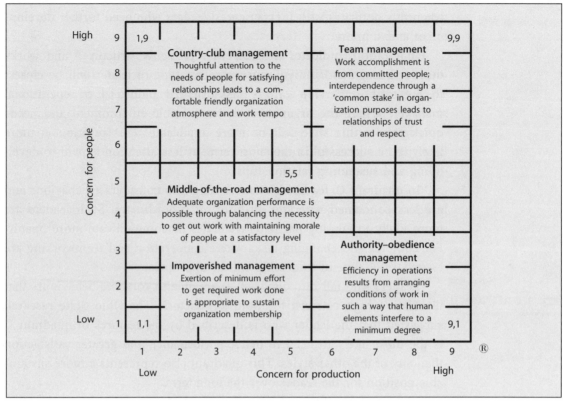

Figure 5.3
Blake and McCanse leadership grid [from Blake, R. R. and McCanse, A. A. (1991) *Leadership Dilemmas –* ® *Grid Solutions*, Gulf Publishing Company. Houston, Texas 800-231-6275. Used with permission. All rights reserved.]

leadership and management is about and, as a consequence, exert little effort on either type of behaviour.

Middle-of-the-road management (point 5,5) occurs where moderate concern is shown for both factors and the result is generally to achieve an adequate level of output while maintaining everyone's satisfaction and morale levels.

Is there one ideal style of leadership?

We could argue that the practice of actively involving employees in goal setting, through the use of participative-management techniques so that both task and people considerations are to the fore, represents the ideal style of leadership as we currently understand it.

Work by Misumi in House (1987) evaluated 34 studies over a 35-year period commencing in 1949 and concluded that of all the various styles identified, the best was the one that focused on both production *and* interpersonal relationships. This view is strongly supported by the evidence of Blake and McCanse's 'team leadership style'.

On the contrary side of the debate, several studies argue that there is no ideal style and that different situations dictate the use of different styles. The view that leadership style is highly situational and the most effective style will be contingent upon such things as the people, the task, the organization and other environmental variables provides support for the view that one best style cannot be identified.

The consequences of this view for the development and teaching of leadership imply that effective leadership will best be achieved by helping leaders and managers recognize the situations when each style would be appropriate.

5.5 Contingency theory of leadership

Several theories have emerged to explain how leadership styles should change when situations themselves change. Fiedler's (1967) contingency theory of leadership combines an organizational situation with the desired style of management. He used a **least preferred co-worker (LPC)** questionnaire to determine the predominant style of the leader. Those who rated their least preferred co-worker negatively were said to be task oriented, while those who rate their least preferred co-worker positively are said to be more relationship oriented, because they saw positive values even in someone that they did not like to work with.

Fiedler then compared this predominant style to the actual situation or **contingency** faced by the manager. Situations were classified as follows:

- Leader–member relationships: the group atmosphere and members' acceptance of the leader. When members have trust, respect and confidence in the leader, relations are considered good.
- Task structures: how the tasks carried out are specified. Routine repetitive assembly-type operations are highly structured, whereas creative and ill-defined tasks are usually unstructured and are more difficult for the manager to control.
- Position power: the extent to which the leader holds authority over the members. Position power can be enhanced if the leader has access to sources of power (reward, punishment, evaluation and direction). If not, he or she has little control over the member's activities.

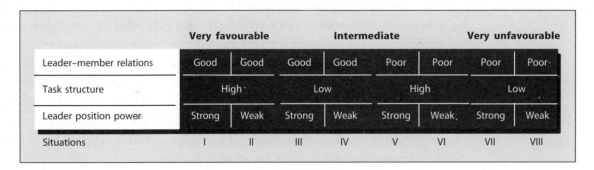

	Very favourable		Intermediate				Very unfavourable	
Leader–member relations	Good	Good	Good	Good	Poor	Poor	Poor	Poor
Task structure	High		Low		High		Low	
Leader position power	Strong	Weak	Strong	Weak	Strong	Weak	Strong	Weak
Situations	I	II	III	IV	V	VI	VII	VIII

Figure 5.4   Fiedler's classification of leadership situation favourableness [from Fiedler, F. E. (1972) The effects of leadership training and experience: A contingency model interpretation, *Administrative Science Quarterly* **17**, 455. Reprinted by permission of *Administrative Science Quarterly*.]

Combining these three situations yields a list of eight possibilities which are illustrated in Figure 5.4.

Situation I is the most favourable and situation VIII is the least favourable. In situation I the leader has all the cards, position power is strong, leader–member relationships are good and task structure high. In the worst situation, situation VIII, leader–member relations are poor, task structure is low and the leader's position power is weak.

Fiedler next considered the effect of situational favourableness on the style of the leaders themselves. His findings are shown in Figure 5.5.

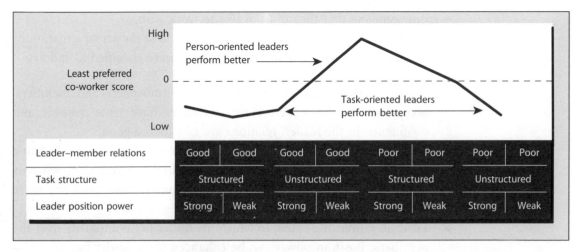

Figure 5.5   How leader style fits the situation [from Fiedler, F. E. (1972) The effects of leadership training and experience: A contingency model interpretation, *Administrative Science Quarterly* **17**, 455. Reprinted by permission of *Administrative Science Quarterly*.]

Task-oriented leaders were found to be more effective when the situation faced was either highly favourable or highly unfavourable (at the two extremes of the continuum). Whenever situations fell between extremes the managers with a more people or relationship-oriented style were found to be more effective.

Fiedler believed that the difference was due to the fact that when the situation was either extremely favourable or unfavourable members of the work group would benefit from a more structured approach which a **task-focused manager** can provide. In extremely favourable situations the group members needed only to take charge and provide direction for them to perform well. In extremely unfavourable situations the leader needs to provide highly structured well-defined directions, strong signals and authority. The **person-oriented leader** will be preferred in conditions of intermediate favourableness because performance is negotiated rather than directed.

For leaders to make best use of the Fiedler theory they must be aware of both the way they prefer to work and the situation they are facing. They must know their own preferred leadership style (and how to change it if the need arises) and whether they can expect to face favourable or unfavourable leadership situations. When this level of understanding is achieved the theory suggests that application of the correct style to the correct contingency will pay dividends.

5.6 Role-model leadership

Grand strategies and visions can all seem pretty meaningless if the leaders and managers who have to impart them do not model themselves on the values implied. Some companies, such as Disney and Rank Xerox, define role-model behaviour for their managers and actually assess them against this ideal.

Some companies believe encouraging a variety of images to reflect what it takes to be a 'trailblazer' or **role-model leader** in their company. An example of such a list is offered in Table 5.5.

The list in Table 5.5 is long, but it serves to highlight the point that leaders as **role models** will be judged on what they do and not what they say. Reflection Box 5.2 illustrates something of the ways that two of the best known and successful modern business leaders in the Western world claim to work.

Table 5.5 *The role-model 'trailblazer' at the Belgian insurance group Fortis*

Trailblazers have to:

- make tough and easy choices to reach a goal;
- decide the best course and go for it;
- inspire with enthusiasm for the chosen approach;
- contribute through their own effort and initiative;
- apply energy now, but looking to the future;
- make the road their own even when others have been there before them; that is, differentiate their leadership;
- look for and overcome obstacles and be determined to forge ahead;
- know they need the support of a strong team;
- put together know-how and experience;
- use the strength of diversity to move together in a shared direction;
- be persevering and tenacious, climbing higher with each little step;
- record and celebrate success along the way and look ahead to fresh challenges.

Adapted from Coulson-Thomas (1997).

5.7 Male or female leadership

We describe the glass-ceiling concept in detail in Chapter 8. It can be best described as an invisible barrier (either deliberately created or inadvertently imposed) which prevents women rising beyond a certain level within an organization. You need to decide if the term is simply a popular myth or if there is evidence to prove its existence?

As an example of some of the evidence available Mani (1997) noted that approximately half of American federal civil servants are female but only 13 per cent of executives are female.

Sometimes the barrier becomes more visible when organizational policies are shown to be discriminatory. Legislation which outlawed deliberate sex discrimination and the recognition of the unfairness of discriminatory practices have reduced the effects of the glass ceiling, but most surveys which compare male and female salaries and job opportunities still point to significant disparities.

To argue that the presence of more women managers will change organizations means we must be able to show that clear differences in business style, attitude or behaviour exist between the sexes. Many of the issues relating to women working in organizations is presented in Chapter 8. Writers such as Popp and Muhs (1982) and Steinberg and Shapiro (1982) suggest that organizational changes, characterized by greater teamworking, less hierarchical structures and minimal control, favour the approaches taken and skills shown by many women managers.

Reflection Box 5.2 Cases in leadership

1. Percy Barnevik ABB

Percy Barnevik left his role as Chief Executive of Asea Brown Boveri, a group of more than 1,000 businesses, in 1997, having joined the organization in 1980. Educated at Stanford University, Barnevik established an international reputation for outstanding leadership skills and ability. He is widely regarded by his peers and those within and outside ABB as the embodiment of exemplary modern leadership. Barnevik's style was personal and direct. He was an excellent communicator and made English the common organizational language to ease cross-border communications. Barnevik spent a minimal amount of time at his head office and travelled around the world talking directly to employees in the many businesses within the group.

One of the legacies of Barnevik's leadership was the smooth handover to his successor, Goran Lindahl. Barnevik worked hard to ensure that the succession would be smooth because he recognized that the company's shares might suffer when he left. The wholesale restructuring of ABB under Barnevik's tenure left the organization with a multicultural management structure. Seven nationalities are represented on the ABB Board and a cadre of capable managers provide the strong 'corporate glue' of Barnevik inspired common values. Barnevik dismissed fears that the new structure would fail once he departed. He emphasized that over the 10 years since the company's last main restructuring the company no longer relied so heavily on the 'one great leader' idea. Adapted from 'The secret of his success' (Arkin, 1997).

2. Jack Welch of General Electric Company

Many people believe that Jack Welch is the best and most successful leader in Corporate America. Welch's style is direct and clearly focused on the business imperatives of a group that spans the globe and which has been able to capture many of the benefits of size while minimizing any drawbacks.

Many managers struggle to cope with the demands of motivating and communicating with a far smaller team than Welch's. Some chief executive officers (CEOs) strive to squeeze adequate performances from companies a fraction of the size of GE, so how does Welch sit so confidently on top of a business empire of around $320 billion in assets, $92 billion in sales and more than 250,000 employees in 100 countries? A large part is believed to be down to sheer force of personality, an unbridled passion for winning and an obsessive attention to detail.

He is also said to be almost brutal in the candour of his communication at meetings but, above all, he believes in the ability of his people to deliver.

Welch is a high profile CEO and puts effort into getting to know company employees and has made a significant competitive advantage out of the informality he insists on within such a giant business. Welch believes in simple business principles and is often heard to compare the

Reflection Box 5.2 (cont.)

operations at GE with a grocery store where satisfying customers and providing goods and services that they want is all that really matters.

Welch inherited a formal and traditional hierarchical structure of nine levels of management, which resulted in the slowing of internal communication to a snail's pace. Now all his employees call him Jack and communication channels are far faster. He also inherited a calendar speckled with corporate presentations that were more about show than effect, which have now been transformed into Welch's very own levers for leadership.

Communication tops the list of activities that Welch undertakes throughout the year. Each January the company's top 500 executives meet in Boca Raton to discuss and set the coming year's agenda. The main event of the gathering is Welch's wrap-up session delivered on stage and under spotlights in front of two video recorders. During this session Welch becomes a cross between preacher and guru, highlighting the priorities for the coming 12 months and, more importantly, what will not be acceptable from the gathered executives.

Welch's belief in the use of effective communication comes from a recognition that no business leader can simply *will* something to happen, nor can he or she expect to tell a few senior executives and wait for the change to occur. Welch doggedly repeats the message over and over again. He also uses other symbols and signals to reinforce the message wherever possible. Handwritten notes exemplify his informal style and have tremendous impact on workers who expect to receive all corporate communication in memo form. Welch plans and sets precise performance targets for all those who report to him directly.

Another of Welch's leadership principles is differentiation. He believes that giving people across-the-board increases or penalties is the exact opposite of what organizations should be doing – that is, as people obviously contribute to organizational success in vastly different manners they should be rewarded and managed likewise.

So what does the great leader himself look for in those he appoints to become leaders? In every potential leader Welch is looking for what he calls 'E to the fourth power', which is the term used to describe people who have enormous personal energy, the ability to motivate and energize others, 'edge' (the GE word for being increasingly competitive) and the skill to execute these attributes. Adapted from 'Jack – A close-up look at how America's number one manager runs GE' (Byrne, 1998).

Questions

1   How do the two role models reflect the theories of leaders and leadership?
2   How do the two examples use actions that display what they want employees to do?
3   How do they model the behaviour they wish to see others in the organizations copy?

Stereotypical images of male managers (more task focused and aggressive) and women managers (caring and concerned for relationships above task) are precisely that – stereotypes. Nonetheless, views of the distinctions between male and female managers are strongly held. In 1995 Mant wrote, "We are beginning to see a substantial increase in the numbers of women entering the professions particularly in medicine and family law. These are fields where women's natural gifts ought to confer advantages to them over many males."

Wajcman (1996) studied the behaviour and attitudes of senior men and women managers in large multinational companies. Her research indicated that, in terms of management style, similarities between men and women far outweigh the differences. Wajcman argues that there is in fact no such thing as a 'female' management style and that women who have achieved senior management positions are in many respects indistinguishable from the men in equivalent positions.

In reality, a good manager needs to be able to use the full spectrum of 'hard' and 'soft' skills as described by the leadership grid we introduced earlier in this chapter.

An investigation by Margerison and McCann (1995), which aimed to identify and quantify similarities and differences in male or female managerial styles, pointed more towards the *similarities* of female and male managers. Their analysis covered a survey of 8,200 men and 5,000 women across a range of industries and countries. Asking people what they felt was the most important aspect of their work generated eight major categories. Table 5.6 illustrates how these varied between male and female respondents.

Table 5.6 *Different preferences between male and female managers.*

Major work preferences	Male	Female
Advising	3	5
Innovating	11	9
Promoting	10	10
Developing	18	15
Organizing	25	24
Producing	24	25
Inspecting	8	9
Maintaining	2	3

Reflection Box 5.3 Male versus female leadership

1   Using your experience and the evidence you have just read (and after reading Chapter 8) do you think there are any signicant differences in style or ability between male and female leaders?

2   What different skills and attributes would you expect male and female leaders to display?

The figures in Table 5.6 represent the per cent of respondents to the survey who rated each of the categories as an important part of their work. For both sexes organizing and producing scored highest and maintaining and advising scored lowest.

This evidence suggests that, overall, men and women have very similar approaches to managerial work. Margerison and McCann believe that women, if anything, reinforce the male preference towards development and implementation rather than counterbalancing the teamwork effort in any way.

It is likely that the vast differences in style observable between managers of the same sex are far greater than any characteristics that can be attributed to male or female management styles.

Despite the research there remains a belief that male and female leadership styles differ and that some organizations will be able to benefit from capturing the appropriate skill differences (Reflection Box 5.3). While leadership and management continue to be seen as a predominantly male activity, associated with control and command (at least in Western corporate culture), it is understandable that female employees who seek to operate in a male-dominated business environment will continue to be under scrutiny.

5.8 The future of leadership

As long as we have organizations there will be a need for leaders. Leaders have to do more than simply manage the organization. They have to provide a vision and inspiration to all those they communicate with.

What, then, are the likely priorities for organizational leaders beyond the year 2000? According to Senge (1990) our view of leadership itself must change radically if we are to improve the effectiveness of organizations in the future, "Our traditional views of leaders as special people who set the direction, make the key decisions, and energise the troops are deeply rooted in an individualistic and non-systemic world view. Especially in the West, leaders are heroes, great men (and occasionally, women) who rise to the fore in times of crises. At its heart, the traditional view of leadership is based on assumptions of people's powerlessness, their lack of personal vision and inability to master the forces of change, deficits which can be remedied only by a few great leaders."

For Senge, the new vision of leadership is very closely tied to the concept of the **learning organization,** about which we will learn more in Chapter 9. Leader behaviour in the future must centre much more on stewardship of the organization. New-style leaders must be able to build the organization in such a way that people are able to continually expand their capabilities, to improve their skills and their ability to improve the organization.

This view of organizations, which lets people grow and develop, contrasts sharply with those early Taylorist principles of organizational design, which embraced principles of speed, repetition, cost efficiency and above all conformity.

According to a leadership consultant and former Chief Executive of Hay/McBer the era of knowledge management calls for a new style of leader. The new era calls for an increased emphasis on three key leadership skills for the new **knowledge-based organization:**

- **Orchestrating:** seeking to influence and direct the organization from afar.
- **Acting as a focal point for organizational learning:** developing systems and procedures that will allow the fostering and capture of organizational knowledge.
- **Facilitating 'different types of thinking'** about business problems, or product and service innovations.

5.9 Summary

In this chapter you were introduced to the concept of leadership and some of the theories that surround it. You will have seen how distinctions can be made between leadership and management, and why some leaders are able to command tremendous power over organizations and individuals.

You also saw how different leadership styles are used and the ways in which good leaders apply the most effective style in the right situation or contingency.

You also read about two shining examples of organizational leadership and were able to see how they embody much of the theory and rhetoric of leadership in their everyday work.

We summarized the debate over male and female leadership styles and left you to reflect on the differences.

The final section on the future of leadership and organizations should leave you in no doubt about the contention that both are going to have to change significantly over time.

Questions

Self-test questions

1 What is leadership and how does it differ from management?
2 Where does leadership power come from and how can it be lost?
3 What are the different leadership styles that can be used?
4 What skills and abilities will the leader of the future need?

Discussion questions

1 Is a good leader necessarily a good manager and vice versa?
2 What do you think is the best leadership style?
3 Name some great leaders you have heard of and what you think makes them so good?

References and bibliography

Arkin, A. (1997) The secret of his success, *People Management*, 23 October, 27–30.

Bobo, J. (1997) A look at leadership and one great leader in particular, *National Underwriter*, **101**(27), 7 July, 33.

Blake, R. and McCanse, J. (1986) *The New Managerial Grid*, Houston: Gulf.

Bryman, A. (1996) *Leadership and Organisations*, London: Routledge and Keegan Paul.

Byrne, J. A. (1998) Jack – A close-up look at how America's number one manager runs GE, *International Business Week*, 8 June, 40–51.

Cadbury, A. (1999) Comments noted in *The Times* 'Leadership into the 21st Century', 9 February, in association with The Industrial Society.

Coulson-Thomas, C. (1997) *The future of the Organisation*, London: Kogan Page.

Daft, R. (1994) *Management*, Dryden Press.

Fiedler, F. (1967) *A Theory of Leadership Effectiveness*, New York: McGraw-Hill.

House, R. (1987) A path goal theory of leader effectiveness, *Administrative Science Quarterly*, **16**, 321–338.

Kotter, J. (1990) What leaders really do, *Harvard Business Review*, May–June 1990, 113–130.

Mani, B. (1997) Gender in the federal senior executive service: Where is the Glass Ceiling?, *Public Personnel Manager*, Winter, 545–558.

Mant, A. (1995) Changing work roles. In Tyson, S. (ed.) *Strategic Prospects for HRM*, London: IPD Publishing.

Margerison, C. and McCann, D. (1995) Are men and women different at work?, *MCB University Press*, **44**(5).

Mosley, D., Pietri, P. and Megginson, L. (1996) *Management Leadership in Action*, New York: Harper Collins.

Peters, T. and Austin, N. (1985), *A Passion for Excellence*, London: Fontana.

Pettinger, R. (1996) *Organisational Behaviour*, London: Macmillan Business.

Popp, G. and Muhs, W. (1982) Fear of success and women employees, *Human Relations*, **35**(7), 511–519.

Schriesheim, C. A. and Bird, B. J. (1979) Contributions of the Ohio State studies to the field of leadership, *Journal of Management*, **5**, 135–145.

Senge, P. (1990) *The Fifth Discipline*, London: Century Business.

Steinberg, R. and Shapiro, S. (1982) Sex differences in personality, traits of female and male Masters of Business Administration students, *Journal of Applied Psychology*, **67**(3), 306–310.

Stewart, R. (1963) *Managers and Their Jobs*, London: Macmillan.

Tannenbaum, R. and Schmidt, W. (1973) How to choose a leadership pattern, *Harvard Business Review*, May–June.

Wajcman, J. (1996) Desperately seeking differences in management style gendered, *British Journal of Industrial Relations*, **34**(3), 333–349.

6

Organizational analysis: structure and systems

Contents

Objectives

By the end of this chapter you should be able to:

- perform a rudimentary organizational analysis using the structure and system metaphors and explain the advantages and disadvantages of each approach

- explain how the organization's environment influences its internal functions

- use organizational analysis to show why an organization might have difficulties adapting to changing environmental conditions

- appreciate how organizational analysis can help the understanding of patterned behavioural responses among employees

6.1 Introduction

Organizations are as unique as the individuals that make them up. No two organizations are the same. Even if you have done the same job in two different organizations, each will have their own unique style or ways of doing things. A large-scale organization may well show significant differences from department to department or site to site, but nonetheless there will usually be some key things that all who come into contact with it can recognize and relate to. One purpose of organizational analysis is to understand why this is the case.

If we want to analyse organizations, where do we start? What is an organization anyway, other than a collection of the individuals and groups that make it up? The reality is that the whole is greater than the sum of its parts. Think of Marks and Spencer, a company that has been with us for more than 100 years. There is probably no one working there now who worked there 60 years ago, yet Marks and Spencer continues to have its own unique 'Marks and Spencerness'.

How, then, should we think about whole organizations? Stop for a moment and ask yourself how organizations work. What images do they conjure up? Some people think of the human body: it works as a unit, yet its organs – the heart, lungs, circulatory and nervous systems – each have their own specific functions. What kind of entity do you think best describes how organizations work?

Thinking about organizations in terms of objects is a very useful way of analysing them and is known as **metaphorical analysis**. Using metaphors to analyse organizations encourages us to notice things about them that we might not otherwise have done. For instance, the human-body metaphor described above might lead us to examine how different departments are *connected* together so that we can understand the interdependent nature of them. Alternatively, it might lead us to examine how the **inputs** to a hospital (unwell people) are turned into **outputs** (well people).

Of course, metaphors can also lead us *not* to notice certain things as well. So looking at organizations as if they were human bodies blinkers us to some extent to the processes involved in, for example, organizational conflict. What happens when departments are purposefully working to undermine each other, a situation that is not readily analysed using the human-body metaphor.

In this chapter, we will be focusing on two metaphors that are popularly used in organizational analysis – structure and systems.

The **structure** metaphor encourages us to think about organizations in terms of physical structures, such as machines and organisms. We shall look at how organizations appear to have shifted in the course of the twentieth century from machine-like structures to more organic (lifelike) structures and we will attempt to understand why this has happened. We will also examine the emergence of the flexible firm and focus on some of the structural properties of this type of organization.

The **systems** metaphor makes us think about organizations in similar ways to those we used to describe the human-body metaphor, largely as interdependent systems that transform inputs into outputs. We shall see that this is a highly *rational* metaphor that tends to ignore the more unpredictable and unforeseen processes that go on in organizations.

We will conclude the chapter by taking a brief look at **complexity theory**, a form of organizational analysis that combines both structural and systemic features of organizations, while accounting for both the dynamism and instability of the organization and its environment.

As we shall see, each metaphor has its strengths and limitations and you will be encouraged to identify these yourself. We will also attempt to show you how analyses of the organization are related to individual and group categories.

6.2 Organizations as structures

A familiar feature of organizations is the **organizational chart**, which shows how all the people who work there fit into the overall structure. See Figure 6.1 for a typical example.

One major feature of organizational structure is **hierarchy** – the various levels that exist in the company. Structure can also be defined in terms of people's roles: that is, the jobs that people do. This information is also included in a typical organizational chart, as shown in Figure 6.1. Structure can also be defined in terms of objectives – what is the organization trying to achieve? Thus, structure can be defined in terms of:

- hierarchy;
- roles;
- purpose.

Why is structure important?

Up until the twentieth century business owners did not pay the attention to structure that is typified by businesses today. Organizational life was far

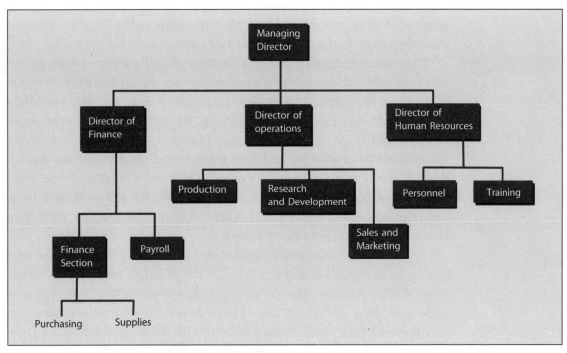

Figure 6.1   Organizational chart for company X.

simpler, there were fewer competitors, relatively stable markets and generally smaller and more simply designed companies. In general, people did not commute great distances to their place of work and limited access to education meant that shop-floor workers had far fewer and less lofty career aspirations than people today. All in all, by today's standards, life at work appeared, relatively speaking, straightforward for the owners of factories and for the managers who ran them.

One of the major effects of the Industrial Revolution was to change the national economy from one based largely on agriculture to one based on manufacturing. As a result, the nature of working life changed fundamentally. People travelled to work rather than working from home or going to the farm down the lane. The sheer size of new factories meant that large numbers of people were employed; and they needed discipline to ensure that they did what they were paid to do.

As factories and organizations became ever larger more and more roles were created to enable them to run effectively. People were needed to supervise and manage others; people who could understand facts and figures were needed to calculate profits and losses; specialist skills were required to operate and repair machinery; and specialist departments were needed to export goods and import raw materials.

Organizations became less easy to manage. Growing specialism meant that people found themselves placed into groups or departments. Furthermore, those departments had to work together to make sure that the whole organization was efficient. Additionally, as factories grew ever more complex and more and more people came to be employed within them the problem of control became ever more central. Factory owners had to think about how to make sure that people came to work on time, were working the hours they were paid to and doing the job as efficiently as possible. Who could ensure that other employees were doing what they were supposed to? Enter the *manager*.

So, as organizations grow bigger they automatically develop some sort of structure. In the late nineteenth and early-twentieth centuries the structures of most organizations was very similar indeed. At this time a German sociologist, Max Weber (1881–1961), undertook his study of organizations and the structural features they shared. His work has been one of the biggest influences in the study of organizations.

Bureaucracy: the ideal type

Weber (1984) was concerned with developing the principles of a blueprint or ideal type of organization. A key principle was **hierarchy**. Every organization should consist of levels of people, operating by the principle of **hierarchical relationships**. These are relationships that operate by **legal authority**. In simple terms, hierarchical relationships are based on the belief that certain patterns of rules and rights are 'legal'. For instance, we tend not to question our manager's rights to tell us what to do and how to do things. Weber pointed out that this type of authority was quite different to that which had operated in previous times. Earlier, the reason people had power over others was because of **tradition.** For example, in stable and unchanging times the Church exercised traditional authority over its flock. Weber's blueprint organization, based on the principles of hierarchy and legal authority, was the **bureaucracy**, defined as having the following features:

• hierarchical ordering of positions; that is, levels of power and authority;

- authority: managers needed legal authority or the power to enforce sanctions and rewards;
- regulation of activities: all jobs should be described in terms of the tasks and activities of which they are composed. The way different jobs relate to each other should be clearly stated;
- impersonal rules: any job will have certain rules and regulations that have to be followed. These rules and regulations are part of the job, not of the person doing the job;
- appointments based on qualifications: jobs should be filled by people who have the appropriate skills and abilities.

In developing this blueprint Weber was not suggesting that all organiz-ations should contain exactly those features he had identified, simply that it could be used as a device for looking at real-life phenomena so that they could be better understood. So, for Weber bureaucracy was the ideal form of organization. We should remember, however, that Weber's ideas were a product of the times in which he lived. Bureaucracy was indeed in the early part of this century an ideal that many organizations tried to achieve. Today, the term 'bureaucratic' can have pejorative connotations, implying an organization is inefficient or ineffective. While it is true that bureaucracies do have some disadvantages, as we shall see, they can also be highly advantageous in some contexts.

The classical school

Following Weber's work a number of scholars became interested in organ-izational forms and methods of management. The classical school of organ-izational scholars started writing about principles of organization. Some of the most prominent writers in this field were Henri Fayol, a Frenchman and three Americans, Mooney and Reilly (General Motors executives) and Mary Parker Follett (an academic).

The classical school were prescriptive in what they had to say about management and they really believed that there was only 'one best way' to organize. Developing Weber's ideas on bureaucracy these writers thought about organizations as if they were **machines**. Hence the term 'machine bureaucracy'. An efficient organization should, like an efficient machine, have working parts that were fully functioning, that worked interdepen-dently and that did its job as efficiently as possible with little waste. Of course, one of the features of any machine is that it does what it does irrespective of the **environment** it is in. In other words, it is a **closed system.** In reality, however, few organizations are closed systems because they are influenced by (and in their turn they influence) the environment in which they operate. For instance, an organization will be affected by market conditions, by economic conditions, by competition and by numerous other factors. Can you think of other ways in which organizations are affected by the environments they are in?

After 1945 people began questioning the idea that bureaucracy was the best type of organizational form. There appear to be a number of reasons for this. First, a number of academics began to write about the **dysfunctions** of bureaucracy; that is, the problems which bureaucratic organizations create. For example, Merton (1968) identified the concept of 'retreatism'. People unable to find a solution to a problem will pass it 'up the line' to a higher hierarchical layer, responding to problems by saying, "I'm sorry, it's not my job." See Reflection Box 6.1 for further examples of problems associated with bureaucracy. Second, there was a spurt in economic activity, particularly in the newly emerging plastics and electronics industries, after 1945 (the end of World War II), which led to a need to think about new ways of organizing because, as we shall see, bureaucratic structures tend not to be responsive to rapid changes occurring in the organization's environment.

Contingency theories

With these developments in both the economic and academic arenas it became clear that there was not 'one best way' to organize. And in 1962 an economic historian, Alfred Chandler, published his work on **contingency.** Chandler developed his ideas by looking at companies in the United States that had had to grapple with huge industrial changes over a single generation. Chandler concluded that new economic demands, including more and more diverse markets and increased competition, had led the bulk of these organizations to move to a multi-divisional decentralized form of organization. Senior managers no longer kept a tight rein on each separate department; instead, organizations were split into divisions according to product or market. For example, food factories were no longer organized by function, such as marketing and sales, but into divisions such as biscuits and canned food. Also, each division was managed by someone who was given considerable freedom to decide how best to run that particular part of the company.

Reflection Box 6.1 Some problems with bureaucracies

As firms get bigger a certain amount of bureaucracy is inevitable. Systems are needed to keep track of such things as customer orders, complaints and personnel records, among many others. Apart from the difficulties with bureaucracy that have been identified by such writers as Merton (1968) and March and Simon (1984) there are also potential problems with the ways that decisions are made in bureaucracies.

Simon (1984) differentiates between programmed and non-programmed decision making in organizations. Programmed decision making makes use of already existing solutions. For example, if a customer complains a set procedure will be initiated involving taking details about the complaint and issuing a standard letter from the customer-services manager. Non-programmed decisions occur when there are no existing solutions to problems and employees are required to think on their feet.

Bureaucratic organizations tend to favour programmed decision making. While this is a useful way of standardizing the company's responses to problems it can also lead to a lack of attention to individual cases. Imagine you had put a complaint into a company about a dishwasher that kept breaking down and all you received in response to your complaint were a series of reassuring letters from the customer-service manager, but no attempt to resolve the problem once and for all.

What other problems might there be with programmed decision making and what might organizations do to resolve them?

Chandler's specific argument was that organizations were changing their structure because of different strategies adopted by senior executives. And the reason senior executives were adopting different strategies (to achieve long-term goals) was because of the challenges imposed by the external environment – the economic conditions and the markets. So, for Chandler strategy is *contingent* on the external environment and structure is *contingent* on strategy.

The relationship of an organization with its environment

Increasing numbers of scholars were examining how an organization's structure is influenced by its environment. The machine metaphor, with its notion of an organization closed off from its environment, was clearly limited. Scholars began to recognize the need for concepts that saw organizations as more open to their environments.

Burns (1984) looked at various organizations in Scotland. They discovered that if an organization's environment was unstable and uncertain a more flexible structure became necessary. What they meant was that if an organization faces stiff competition and if its market is subject to rapid changes a bureaucratic structure will not be able to respond quickly enough. They based this conclusion on the behaviour of the then newer electronics industries, in which product developments were occurring at such a rate that organizations were constantly having to find new and better ways of marketing their products. They had to develop new markets and had to make rapid decisions about what to do to survive.

Burns and Stalker suggested that companies operating in such conditions required what they called an **organic** structure, typified by loosely defined roles, flexible and informal communication networks and a high degree of commitment to the enterprise by employees (the people responsible for dealing with decisions and with handling information). This is quite different from a bureaucracy, in which roles are strictly defined, communication networks very formal and in which decisions are made at some appropriate point in the hierarchy. Conversely, they said that bureaucracies were suitable for some environmental conditions, specifically when the environment is stable and certain.

Another key study in this area was carried out by two American researchers, Lawrence and Lorsch (1984), who looked at the relationship between different internal arrangements of an organization and its environment. They developed the concept of **integration and differentiation** to describe how companies needed to develop different units to deal with a highly segmented environment. That is, they needed departments that could research market trends (research and development departments); departments that could respond to customer demands (production); and departments that could deal with the recruitment of appropriate labour (personnel). The greater the number of different departments required to deal with the organizational environment the greater the degree of **differentiation** within the organization.

At the same time there was a need to have links between these various units so that the company could retain consistency in management and efficiency (**integration**). For example, a company might need to develop various units to deal with its business, such as marketing, research and development, and administration. These departments have little in common either technically or in terms of values. Achieving coordination is difficult but necessary if the organization is to survive. Marketing needs to know what Research and Development are doing, for example.

What is needed, Lawrence and Lorsch argued, is some method of *communication*. They observed that successful organizations had developed things like special roles (such as project-management teams) to bridge the gaps between the various units. Lawrence and Lorsch found that the more diverse the environment of an organization in terms of markets, competition and so on the more differentiated the internal structure needed to be; and the greater the extent of differentiation the greater the need for integration methods.

Flexible firms

Since the late 1970s another structural type of organization has been identified. This is the **matrix structure**, an example of which is shown in Figure 6.2. The matrix organization is designed for high levels of functional flexibility. Rather than assigning employees to set roles and departments they are assigned, as need dictates, to project teams. These teams, in turn,

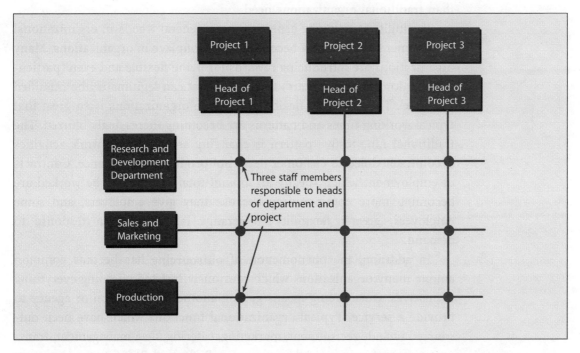

Figure 6.2   A matrix structure.

are headed or managed by the person with the most appropriate skills and expertise. As the matrix diagram shows this means that employees in these types of organization may have several managers at any one time. Although matrix organizations may look like an excellent means of organizing in a highly turbulent environment they do create their own problems, such as clashes of loyalty and uncertainty about job responsibilities. This issue is explored further in the next chapter.

The growing call for increased flexibility and the effects of such changes on the way that people operate mean that new approaches to managing organizations are required. As with many aspects of organization theory the degree of organizational flexibility achievable varies widely between organizations. In most cases established and more bureaucratic organizations are much more resistant to **flexibilization**. They have traditions and widely understood procedures which make them far less receptive to changing their *modus operandi*. Newer organizations, with less of a history to hold them back, tend to offer more potential for new approaches to working. At the extreme of flexibility the concept of the **virtual organization** (explored in Chapter 4) is allowing many businesses to set up and develop highly transitory network-based groups to carry out business with far fewer restrictions on time, place or physical resources than traditional organizations need.

Flexibility is only one aspect of more general trends in organizational development that are now becoming commonplace in organizations. Many organizations are introducing rewards for being flexible and even (particularly for knowledge workers) for doing what can legitimately be classified as 'work'. The degree of flexibility in some organizations is so great that typical working times and patterns are becoming increasingly blurred. The traditional nine-to-five pattern is changing as employees' work activities become scheduled to customer need, not producer convenience. Contracts of employment which specify an *annual* total of hours to be worked are becoming more commonplace because they give employers, and some employees, greater flexibility to arrange labour time in response to demand.

In addition, the phenomenon of **outsourcing** has become common among many organizations which previously insisted on doing everything themselves. Outsourcing means getting another organization or agency to provide a service. Typical organizational functions which have been outsourced include recruitment, marketing, catering, fleet management, transportation and even payroll services. See Reflection Box 6.2.

Reflection Box 6.2 The benefits of flexibility

The motives behind this increase in organizational flexibility are worth considering. A major engine behind the changes is the need for greater efficiency and, as you will see in **Case Study 1 'Building a flexible organization: British Gypsum'**, the move towards flexibility can indeed produce significant savings in terms of reduced labour costs. When organizations have come under economic pressure the potential rewards from a more efficient flexible approach are tempting. Another force behind the move towards greater flexibility is the need for speed. When market pressures and customer tastes are changing rapidly, and largely unpredictably, the ability to provide an agile and effective customer response is a highly prized asset. Organizations which are nimble enough to change production lines or revamp products and services to capture technological advances will be able to steal a march on their competitors. Predicting the future of organizational structures and strategies has itself become a growth industry and many have put forward views on what might happen. Whitlam and Hale (1998) argue strongly that the shape of the future is going to be virtual; that is, the success or otherwise of organizational structures will in the future depend on capturing the techno-logical possibilities to employ networks in place of bureaucracies. One technological development that will be available to assist overstretched management resources that typify many organizations is the rise of the 'knowbots', electronic assistants capable of presenting managers with greater resources of knowledge and data at their fingertips. Those who can build and master these electronic assistants and expert systems will find the speed and accuracy of their management significantly enhanced.

It is worth remembering, however, that predictions about social changes are not always accurate. In the 1960s, for example, it was widely predicted that by 1999 we would all have a robot in our homes.

What sorts of factors can you identify that in the future may well have an impact on the nature of organizations? What sorts of effect might such factors have?

The pros and cons of the structure metaphor

The structure metaphor is a very useful way of analysing an organization. One of its particular strengths is in highlighting the importance of the context within which organizations operate. This is especially the case for contingency approaches which examine the organizational environ-ment in some depth and which can help organizations think more carefully about the appropriateness of their structure.

The structure metaphor does have a number of drawbacks as well. Chief among these is the fact that it downplays the behavioural elements of organizational life. Many organizations recognize the need to be structured more flexibly in a turbulent environment but find that changing structure does not necessarily change the behaviour of employees. An organization with a long history of bureaucracy will not find it easy to encourage its employees to take responsibility and make decisions because of 'retreatism', for example. Furthermore, people create their own informal structures which may be more significant than the formal ones. For example, people may form coalitions specifically to oppose some or other policy decision.

In addition, the structure metaphor tends to leave unaddressed questions of power. Many problems in organizations (as we will see in Chapter 7) are caused by power imbalances which in turn are related to their structural properties; specifically, the fact that power is located at the apex of an organization. Because the structure metaphor takes hierarchy for granted, processes such as conflict and resistance tend to be treated as if they were problems caused by people. In fact, it is more plausible to suggests that conflict and resistance are inevitable outcomes of hierarchy. See Reflection Box 6.3.

6.3 Organizations as systems

The structure metaphor helps us examine how people in organizations are controlled according to the positions they hold, the rules governing their jobs and the roles they perform. Contingency theories take this a step farther by examining how rules, roles and hierarchy are related to events in the external environments, particularly the extent to which the environment is stable or turbulent. The systems metaphor takes contingency theories a step farther. The systems metaphor regards organizations as **open systems**; that is, they have an interdependent relationship with their environment. Thus, just as human beings depend on the environment for survival and in turn affect their environment simply by existing, so organizations depend on the environment for their inputs and likewise affect it with their outputs.

Before we go any farther make a list of all the inputs to an organization of your choice and then think of all of its outputs.

If we think about organizations using the systems metaphor we can also think about organizational survival or extinction in terms of **natural**

Reflection Box 6.3 Is hierarchy inevitable?

Kathy Ferguson (1984) has suggested that bureaucratic organization leads to certain patterned responses of behaviour from employees. Presthus (1962) identifies these as:

- upward mobility;
- indifference;
- ambivalence.

Upward mobility is the desire to progress one's career within the company. Indifference is the desire for security within the job but no real desire to advance one's career and ambivalence is exhibited by people who are disillusioned with the organization and who are unable to conform to the organization's expectations. Ferguson points out that these three responses are produced by the system of bureaucracy itself and not necessarily by the characteristics of people displaying these patterns of behaviour. In other words, being upwardly mobile today does not mean that you will be tomorrow because your career success is largely in the hands of the organization's power holders.

Day in and day out in organizations we can see these patterned responses. When people feel dissatisfied with their jobs because they have failed to get promoted or because they don't agree with a particular policy initiative they usually blame other people in the organization rather than questioning the system that produces these types of problems.

Is hierarchy inevitable? Could you envisage an organization in which nobody was actually in charge?

---

selection. The idea of natural selection, based on Charles Darwin's theory of evolution, suggests that some organizations are likely to survive and flourish simply because they are better adapted to their environment. Evolutionary theory suggests that the reason why certain species become extinct is because they are not suited to the environment in which they are located. In heavily industrialized areas of England light-coloured specimens of a particular species of white moth (*Tethea duplaris*) became extinct because it was easily spotted and eaten by predators in an environment dominated by soot and grime (dark-coloured specimens survive).

So, the systems metaphor causes us to ask questions about the organization's relationship to its environment to help us understand its behaviour. Using this metaphor we might say that bureaucratic organizations work best and are more likely to survive when they are located in

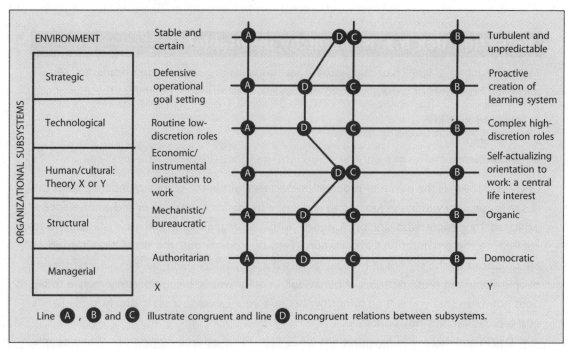

Figure 6.3   A scheme for analysing organizational subsystems [adapted from Burrell and Morgan (1979)].

stable environments, where there is little economic or technological change and low levels of competition. Can you think of any organizations that might be better off structured bureaucratically?

Conversely, if the environment is highly turbulent, an organic structure is probably better because it is receptive to changes and allows the organization to respond quickly.

The systems metaphor is also concerned with understanding how the constituent parts of an organization relate to each other. We have a central nervous system, a digestive system, an endocrine system and so forth. Each of these subsystems has important specialist functions, but each is closely interdependent with all the others. Thus, the central nervous system is dependent on the digestive and circulatory systems to provide it with the nutrients it needs to function and the digestive system is dependent on the central nervous system to provide it with the appropriate signals to perform its requisite tasks – prompting us to eat, for instance.

Organizational subsystems

We can analyse organizations using the systems metaphor by thinking of them as being made up of subsystems. Burrell and Morgan (1979) developed a useful scheme for this purpose (Figure 6.3).

Table 6.1 *Subsystems.*

Environment: stable or turbulent

Is the organization operating in a highly competitive environment? Do changes occur frequently that have a big impact on the way the organization operates? Is it difficult to keep track of the actions of competitors and the behaviour of markets? If the answer to these questions is yes, then the organization is operating in a highly turbulent environment.

Strategic subsystem: proactive or defensive

Does the organization have a clear strategy about where it is going and how it is going to get there? Does it have procedures and methods for monitoring the environment and tracking and anticipating changes? Does the organization learn from its mistakes? Or does the organization wait for changes to occur in the environment before deciding what to do about them? Are mistakes seen as a sign of weakness? Do people try to avoid making errors? Is the concern with ensuring mistakes do not happen again rather than analysing why they occurred in the first place?

Technological subsystem: complex or routine

Technology in this sense refers to the methods used to achieve the organization's chief task. This can obviously involve information technology but also embraces human skills and knowledge. To what extent are the organization's systems for performing its core tasks flexible? Can the system deal with unexpected occurrences? Are people given discretion to make decisions about non-routine events? The greater the flexibility in this subsystem the more complex the subsystem can be said to be.

Human-cultural subsystem: theory X or theory Y

McGregor (1960) claimed that managers tend to judge employees using one of two basic sets of assumptions about human nature. One set, theory X, constructs people as lazy and unambitious, requiring a 'carrot and stick' to motivate them. In contrast, the other set, theory Y, constructs people as having both the desire and potential for self-fulfilment through work. Simply giving people responsibility and autonomy will motivate them. Thus, this subsystem is concerned with identifying whether the organization holds mainly theory X or theory Y beliefs about the people who work there. Are people in the organization largely concerned with work as a means to an end, or are they more concerned with work as an end in itself? Are people generally self-motivated and willing to put in extra effort or do they need incentives to motivate them? Does the organization encourage people to be committed by valuing a job well done? Or is it concerned with punishing people who deviate from the norm? The greater the tendency for people to be self-motivated and to be valued for performance the more theory Y the human-cultural subsystem can be said to be.

Structural subsystem: mechanistic or organic

Is the organization structured along bureaucratic lines with a tall hierarchy, many rules and tightly prescribed roles? Or is the structure more organic with a flatter hierarchy and less clearly defined roles and rules?

Managerial subsystem: autocratic or democratic

Do managers believe in consultation and collaboration or do they prefer to tell people what to do? To what extent are informal communications encouraged, both vertically and horizontally? Is there an emphasis on involving staff in important decisions?

Within the scheme shown in Figure 6.3 the organization is broken down into five subsystems but importantly these subsystems are located in the wider environment. An organization can be analysed in terms of the five subsystems which are described in Table 6.1. The easiest way to do this is to think of each subsystem as a continuum. Establish which end of the continuum most closely describes the organization being analysed and position the organization accordingly. Think about an organization you are familiar with. Read each of the descriptions given in Table 6.1 and then plot your organization on the grid lines in Figure 6.3. Does it show congruence (are all the subsystems in a straight line as in lines A, B and C in Figure 6.3?) or incongruence (are some of the subsystems out of alignment with others as in line D)?

As Figure 6.3 shows, organizations A, B and C show *congruence* between their subsystems. This means that each subsystem complements the other, making it likely that the organization will function well. Conversely, organization D shows *incongruence* between its subsystems with the strategic, technological, structural and managerial subsystems 'out of sync' with the environment and the human-cultural subsystem.

Read the case illustrated in Reflection Box 6.4 and analyse it using Burrell and Morgan's system. Compare your analysis with the one on page 140.

Analysis of Paperless Inc. (see Reflection Box 6.4 and Figure 6.4)

The environment is moderately turbulent in the sense that the market is uncertain and the technology used by Paperless Inc. is very new and susceptible to rapid change.

The strategic subsystem is tending towards the defensive end of the continuum. Paperless Inc. do not appear to have a coherent marketing strategy that would enable them to target potential customers more effectively.

The technological subsystem appears to be more towards the routine and of the continuum because, although Paperless Inc. uses leading-edge technology to perform its core task, the systems that support the core tasks do not seem to be very flexible – Diane Albert appears to control most of the systems leaving little discretion to her staff.

The human-cultural subsystem is towards the theory X end of the continuum because, as we can see from Reflection Box 6.4, staff appear to be concerned with pay and there are limited job opportunities which means that dissatisfied employees are less likely to leave.

The structural subsystem is difficult to analyse in this case because the business is so small.

Finally, the managerial subsystem is towards the autocratic end of the continuum because of Diane Albert's attitudes towards staff management.

Reflection Box 6.4 Paperless Inc.

Paperless Inc. is a business that provides organizations with an electronic-document-storage service. They scan documents of any type or size on to a compact disk, so saving acres of storage space and allowing, through a sophisticated indexing system, a fast and efficient means of retrieval.

Paperless Inc. is owned and managed by Diane Albert who employs five people on full-time permanent contracts. These include a sales manager, two computer-scanner operators, a computer technician and an administration assistant. They have no real marketing budget, relying on word of mouth, cheap 'flyers' and 'cold calling' to advertise their services. There are a couple of local competitors, though these are not based in the same town.

Although most companies express a real interest in the service, the company is having difficulty getting potential customers to commit to buying the service. All the staff employed by Paperless Inc. are under 25 years old, with the exception of the Managing Director who is in her 40s. She runs a tight ship because, as she says, "You need to keep on top of these young ones to get them to work hard." The wages are low and the staff frequently complain about this but, unfortunately, jobs in the area are scarce. A big problem for Paperless Inc. is that when they do get work in, the customer usually wants it done quickly and this relies on getting the scanner operators to be more productive. This can be difficult when there is little in the way of bonuses on offer.

Before you look at the analysis on the facing page make a few notes about some of the problems you feel this company has. How would you resolve them? Now, compare these with the analysis. Are your conclusions similar?

From this analysis, therefore, it appears that all the subsystems are incongruent with the environment in which Paperless Inc. operates and that a number of changes would need to be made to the strategic, technological and human/cultural subsystems in particular.

Socio-technical systems

One of the most influential typologies to influence systems approaches to organizations is the socio-technical system approach developed by Trist and Bamforth (1951). Trist and Bamforth based their approach on research done on coal mining in Durham. The coal mines in this area changed their method of coal mining in the 1950s and the new technology that was introduced caused problems with productivity, which did not improve as

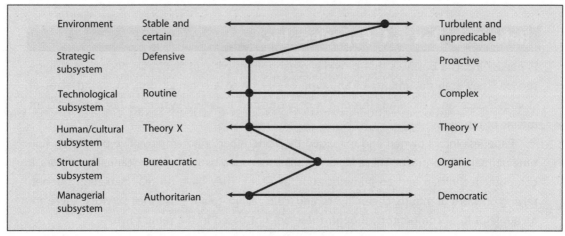

Figure 6.4   Analysis of Paperless Inc. using Burrell and Morgan's scheme.

had been anticipated. Trist and Bamforth concluded that the lower-than-expected productivity was caused by the new coal-cutting machines that disrupted the social relations between the miners.

The term **socio-technical system** denotes the idea that *social* relations between employees are a major subsystem that is totally interdependent with the *technical* subsystem (the methods used to achieve the organization's tasks). This research was viewed as highly important at this particular point because technological advances were occurring at a great rate and many trade unions were warning that not only would people's jobs be considerably deskilled by new technology but also that very many jobs would be lost throughout the manufacturing industry. Thus, Trist and Bamforth's work was taken up enthusiastically by those who wished to represent the interests of manufacturing workers because it emphasized the importance of the human operator. Machines and people are dependent on each other.

The pros and cons of the systems metaphor

Systems approaches are still considered an extremely useful method of organizational analysis today. As we have seen, unlike the machine metaphor systems approaches recognize and deal with the fact that organizations exist in, and in relationship to, an environment. They also recognize that organizations are composed of more than just methods of production – people are involved with their own sets of needs and motivations and have an enormous impact on the way an organization runs.

Systems thinking also draws our attention to the fact that the various parts of an organization cannot be analysed or understood in isolation. Each part is interdependent. Each affects and is affected by the others. Finally, systems approaches are particularly useful for looking at an organization's response to changes in the external environment because they draw attention to those subsystems that may not be congruent with the changing demands of the environment.

Systems approaches do have flaws, however. First, the approach is highly *rational*. So, while it is useful for systematically locating and identifying problems, it tells us little about how the problems might be solved. For example, in the Paperless Inc. case our analysis led us to conclude that the problems are related to the incongruence between the environment and its subsystems but it doesn't help us resolve them.

Second, the approach tends to treat organizational subsystems as if they are naturally intended to work together harmoniously. However, some theorists take the view that employees in any organization will always experience some sense of conflict with the managers or owners of the company because of the power differences that exist between the two groups. Thus, the systems approach can downplay or even neglect issues of conflict that may in fact be more natural in organizations than the harmonious picture painted by systems theorists.

Can you think of any other disadvantages or advantages?

6.4 Structure or systems? Which is more appropriate for analysing contemporary organizations?

Some commentators have argued that most organizations are now structured along **organic** principles since this is the best way to be organized in the extremely turbulent global economy. Whether organizations that would claim to be 'organic' really are, however, is questionable. Organizations are certainly flatter. They have fewer hierarchical levels but, arguably, these have evolved largely because of redundancies. It is also certainly the case, as we have seen, that many organizations now utilize a wide array of flexible working practices.

However, it is less clear whether the spirit of organic organizations is present in those who would claim that status. Most power remains firmly at the top of the organization and is not dispersed among the rank and file in the way that scholars suggest it should be (Wilmott, 1993). Additionally, the commitment of employees is questionable in an economic climate in which many people believe their employers treat them as commodities (Jermier *et al.*, 1994).

6.5 Complexity theory: a new metaphor?

A new way of thinking about organizations that focuses not only on the human and structural features of organization but also on the business environment is **complexity theory**. Complexity theory was originally developed to explain the behaviour of complex and apparently unpredictable systems, such as ant colonies. An ant colony appears to behave in an extremely purposeful and organized way, achieving highly intelligent goals. However, there is no single 'head' ant in charge of the colony. Rather, it is the coordinated and competitive behaviour of each individual ant that results in the ordered pattern we see in the behaviour of the whole colony. In complexity theory this phenomenon is called **emergent order**.

Another feature of complex systems is that they are **radically unpredictable**. Small changes in the system can lead to unforeseeable results. The weather is an example of a complex system that shows radical unpredictability. Knowing what the weather is like today does not enable us to predict with much confidence what it will be like in 3 days' time!

A final and important feature of complex systems is that they are **chaotic**; there are inherent irregularities in the behaviour of the system but, paradoxically, it is these which enable it to survive. For example, our circulatory system is coordinated partly through the beating of the heart. Research shows that in healthy individuals the interval between heartbeats is irregular; the intervals vary in an unpredictable way. If the heartbeat is too regular it may be a sign of ill health.

The application of complexity theory to organizations is a very recent development. However, it is clear that organizations possess all the features of a complex system and that complexity theory offers a means of analysis that embraces the inherent unpredictability of organizational life. This is a radical departure from the types of analysis we have discussed so far in which the focus has been on *prediction* and *control*.

According to Storr (1999), an organizational psychologist specializing in complexity theory, "Organizations cannot be understood in terms of some or other blueprint." She argues that organizations cannot be controlled from the top and should instead embrace the principles of a complex system. One example is the Brazilian manufacturing organization, Semco, who have used complexity theory to inform their organizational design (Semler, 1994). The structure is based on small business units of approximately 10 people who are self-managed and totally responsible for their own area of work. Teams select their own leaders and decide their own pay and everyone in the team is fully informed about the performance of their business unit. The team also takes responsibility for their unit's profitability. Semco is both an economic success and the most popular workplace in Brazil (Storr, 1999).

6.6 Summary

In this chapter we have looked at two metaphors that can be used to analyse organizations. The **structure metaphor** focuses on the roles, goals and functions of the organization. It is very useful for providing a *visual* picture of the organization via the structural diagram, which most organizations produce. This helps us to understand the lines of control and communication and to understand the different components of the organization and how they are positioned relative to one another.

As we have seen, some scholars and practitioners once believed that all organizations should be organized bureaucratically. However, as the capitalist world grew more complex it was clear that bureaucracy could render an organization 'blind' to its environment and unable to adapt to change. We looked at the distinction between **mechanistic** and **organic** forms of organization. The mechanistic or machine bureaucracy is best suited to a stable environment in which little flexibility is required and the organic organization is best suited to a turbulent environment. The organic organization differs from classic bureaucracy in that it has fewer levels in the hierarchy and its functions and roles are less tightly defined.

A greater focus on the relationship that an organization has with its environment led to the development of **contingency theories**, which suggest that structure depends on the nature of the environment and that an organization may need to change its structure to adapt to changes in the environment. We concluded this section by looking at the flexible firm, an organizational form that has emerged to deal with an increasingly complex economic and technological environment.

We moved on to look at the **systems metaphor** which develops this concept of organization/environment interdependency at greater depth. Systems approaches view the organization as composed of subsystems that act interdependently. The systems approach emphasizes the importance of *congruence*. Subsystems need to be congruent with each other and with the environmental subsystem if the organization is to function effectively.

We concluded the chapter by taking a brief look at complexity theory and how this can be used to perform organizational analysis. We argued that the key ideas from complexity theory are especially relevant to contemporary organizations that need to learn how to adapt quickly in a highly competitive environment.

Questions

Self-test questions

1   List the main features of bureaucracy.
2   To what sorts of environmental conditions is a bureaucratic structure most suited?
3   List the main features of an organic organization and describe the environment to which it is most suited.
4   What are contingency theories?
5   Describe any four organizational subsystems.
6   What does the term congruence with reference to the systems approach to organizational analysis mean?
7   List the strengths and weaknesses of both the systems and structure approaches to organizational analysis.
8   List some of the key features of a flexible firm.
9   Briefly describe the features of a complex system and explain why these are useful to consider in an organizational analysis.

Discussion questions

1   What is the value of organizational analysis?
2   Organizations are far too complex to enable any single metaphor to be truly useful. To what extent is this statement true?
3   Is hierarchy an inevitable feature of organization?
4   Flexible firms make the analysis of structure almost impossible. Discuss this hypothesis.

References and bibliography

Burns, T. (1984) Mechanistic and organismic structures. In Pugh, D. S. (ed.) *Organisation Theory*, Harmondsworth: Penguin.

Burrell, G. and Morgan, G. (1979) *Sociological Paradigms and Organisational Analysis: Elements of the Sociology of Organisational Life.* London: Heinemann Educational.

Chandler, A. D. (1962) *Strategy and Structure: Chapters in the History of American Industrial Enterprise*, Cambridge, MA: Massachussetts Institute of Technology.

Ferguson, K. E. (1984) *The Feminist Case Against Bureaucracy*, Philadelphia, PA: Temple University Press.

Jermier, J. M. *et al.* (1994) (eds) *Resistance and Power in Organisations*, London: Routledge.

Lawrence, P. R. and Lorsch, J. W. (1984) High-performing organisations in three environments. In Pugh, D. S. (ed.) *Organisation Theory*, Harmondsworth: Penguin.

March, J. G. and Simon, H. A. (1984) The dysfunctions of bureaucracy. In Pugh, D. S. (ed.) *Organisation Theory*, Harmondsworth: Penguin.

McGregor, D. (1960) *The Human Side of the Enterprise*, New York: McGraw-Hill.

Merton, R. K. (1968) *Social Theory and Social Structure*, London: Collier Macmillan.

Presthus, R. (1962) *The Organizational Society*, New York: Alfred A. Knopf.

Semler, R. (1994) Why my former employees still work for me, *Harvard Business Review*, **72**(1), 64–72.

Simon, H. (1984) Decision making and organisational design. In Pugh, D. S. (ed.) *Organisation Theory*, Harmondsworth: Penguin.

Storr, F. (1999) That's another fine mess you've got me into: The value of chaos in organisational analysis. Paper presented to the *British Psychological Society Occupational Psychology Conference, January, Blackpool*.

Stredwick, J. and Ellis, S. (1998) *Flexible Working Practices, Techniques and Innovations*, London: Institute of Personnel and Development.

Trist, E. L. and Bamforth, K. W. (1951) Some social and psychological consequences of the longwall method of coal-getting, *Human Relations*, **1**, 3–38.

Weber, M. (1984) Legitimate authority and bureaucracy. In Pugh, D. S. (ed.) *Organisation Theory*, Harmondsworth: Penguin.

Whitlam, P. and Hale, R. (1998) Viewpoint: The concept of the virtual organisation, *International Journal of Retail and Distribution Management*, **26**(4–5), 190–191.

Willmott, H. C. (1993) Strength is ignorance; slavery is freedom: managing culture in modern organisations. *Journal of Management Studies*, **30**(4), 515–552.

7

Organizational analysis: culture, power and conflict

Contents

Objectives

By the end of this chapter you should be able to:

- distinguish between unitarist and pluralist perspectives on organizations and use them as a framework for analysing different approaches to organizational analysis
- explain what is meant by organizational culture
- differentiate between functional and interpretive approaches to cultural analysis
- describe Schein's typology for interpretive cultural analysis
- itemize the strengths and weaknesses of cultural analysis
- dene power and explain how this concept can be used to understand why groups in organizations may have different perspectives or interests
- appreciate how new forms of organization have affected the way that power and conflict are manifested
- discuss different ways in which conflict can be manifested and managed

7.1 Introduction

In this chapter we develop some of the ideas introduced in Chapter 6. In particular, we will focus explicitly on analysing culture, power and conflict in organizations. These types of analyses are particularly relevant to large organizations that consist of a diversity of groups and departments.

Using the concept of culture to analyse organizations can be very useful for focusing on the more behavioural and attitudinal aspects of organizational life. Culture takes as its focus those *shared aspects of behaviour and thinking that bind the members of an organization together*. As we shall see, however, this feature of cultural analysis can lead us to play down or even neglect the extent to which people differ in their beliefs and behaviours.

Analysing an organization in terms of power and conflict addresses some of the limitations of cultural analysis. First, analysis of power and conflict assumes that organizations are inherently **plural**, not **unitarist** (Fox, 1973); that is, organizations consist of groups whose interests probably diverge: not everyone is working for the same reasons nor share the same beliefs or value systems. Second, conflict is not seen as something to be avoided at all costs but as a potential source of organizational learning. Third, the inherently unstable and unpredictable aspects of organizational life are more explicit in these analyses. Power shifts and conflicts cause change.

We begin the chapter by exploring what the concept of organizational culture actually means before moving on to examine a typology developed to enable us to undertake cultural analysis. The benefits and drawbacks of this type of analysis are discussed.

We then move on to consider power. To begin with we try to define what power is before moving on to look at how power is acquired. We shall be focusing on power bases in this section of the chapter – those features of groups that enable them to acquire power. We will then move on to consider the differences between possessing power and exercising it. We then consider whether analysing power in contemporary organizations is as relevant as it might have been 20 years ago when power differences were more apparent because of the dominance of trade unions.

We then consider conflict in organizations, exploring the sorts of factors that can lead to conflict and briefly consider how to manage it. We then look at the concept of resistance. Some differences in power will be manifested not in conflict but in more subtle ways. We conclude the chapter by taking a brief look at some of the more recent research in this area.

7.2 Organizational culture

Cultural explanations of behaviour at work have developed from studies by anthropologists and sociologists who have looked at the ways that small societies develop and evolve. Such studies have examined a society's values and norms, taboos, rituals, stories and customs, and used them to explain the behaviour of its individuals.

Emile Durkheim (1858–1917), a French social theorist, was one of the first industrial sociologists to use this concept within a working society. He talked about the importance of common values, such as religious beliefs, in regulating social relationships. Durkheim argued that religious and moral values were the 'glue' that bonded a society together and further suggested that the mobility associated with modern-day societies tended to break down traditional values, such as those concerned with families and communities. Such a breakdown would lead to a feeling of rootlessness, not belonging or lacking a distinct social identity, and this would have concomitant antisocial effects on levels of suicide and crime.

In the 1970s the concept of culture gained in popularity and became a focus of research into organizational behaviour, apparently because of the growing concern in the United States about Japanese competition. Various studies were conducted comparing Japanese companies with their American counterparts. These studies found that the causes of Japanese success were not related to expected factors – the size of the enterprise, its structure or technology – but to the nature of the social relationships that exist in Japanese companies. Moreover, these relationships were reinforced by the national culture.

These early findings stimulated a flurry of research activity into culture. Probably the best known and most influential of subsequent publications was the book of Peters and Waterman (1982), *In Search of Excellence*. They claimed to have identified eight basic principles underpinning the culture of their 'excellent' organizations. Among these were ideas which have now permeated 'manager-speak' throughout the world – 'a bias for action' and 'close to the customer'.

Peters and Waterman popularized the notion that culture is something which can be managed. In other words, managers can *change* cultures. However, despite the promise that culture approaches appear to offer, reality suggests that organizational culture cannot be changed by individual managers. And, it has to be said, many of the 'excellent' companies in the original Peters and Waterman research are now not so excellent; in fact they are doing pretty badly.

However, despite the fact that culture can be construed as yet another management fad, it does provide another way of analysing an organization. The approaches to culture that typified the 'excellence' literature have been labelled **functionalist**; that is, they *are concerned with what culture can do and how it can be managed* (Smircich, 1983). The approaches we are going to focus on here can be called **interpretive**; that is, culture is used to analyse *what an organization is* (ibid.). How can such a task be achieved?

7.3 Using the concept of culture to analyse organizations

One of the most comprehensive attempts to analyse organizations using the concept of culture was that of the American academic Schein (1985). Schein was concerned to describe and explain clearly what culture is and how it can be used to understand what an organization is like. Schein's definition of culture is that it is those sets of attitudes, values and beliefs that exist in any given organization and which serve as 'guides for action' for employees (Schein, 1990). What does this mean?

Defining culture

An attitude can be defined as a certain 'regularity of an individual's feelings, thoughts and predispositions to act towards some aspects of his environment' (Secord and Backman, 1969). Attitudes are often said, on the basis of this definition, to contain a cognitive component (beliefs) and a behavioural component. For instance, I might believe that fox-hunting is wrong (cognitive component), which therefore causes me to go on anti-hunt marches (behavioural component). In addition, attitudes are usually evaluative in that they tend to be either positive or negative. For instance, in the example just given it is clear that I have a negative attitude towards fox-hunting (see Chapter 2 for a further discussion of attitudes).

Values are higher-order attitudes that encompass a broad range of beliefs. For example, I may value the sanctity of all life on earth, which causes me to believe that fox-hunting is wrong, and to believe that I ought not to eat meat, and that I ought to spend time campaigning on a variety of animal-rights issues.

Every society has values, attitudes and beliefs that have a major influence on the ways members of that society behave. Thus, in many Western societies freedom of speech is greatly valued and many of us will have negative attitudes towards anything that denies us that facility. Similarly, we believe that people have the right to be safe in their own homes, which causes us to have a negative attitude towards intruders. We also believe that people have a right to remain healthy, which causes us to value subsidized health services. Organizations also have values, attitudes and beliefs about a range of things which have a fundamental effect on the way people behave at work. Schein's typology is an attempt to define, quite systematically, the types of things in any organization about which people hold values, attitudes and beliefs.

Schein, along with other authors, has suggested that culture may be analysed at three levels – surface knowledge, daily enactment and basic assumptions.

Surface knowledge incorporates the more tangible features of culture, such as the methods of communication used, the arrangement of the building, dress codes and so on. Daily enactment is related to the 'way things are done around here' and is concerned with the language used, the behaviours that are seen as appropriate or acceptable and the ways people typically relate to one another. Basic assumptions incorporate the less tangible aspects of culture, such as basic beliefs about how the tasks should be done, the nature of external reality and the nature of people. It is these basic assumptions which act as the strongest guides to action and it is argued that these are so 'deeply embedded' within the culture that they are taken for granted by organizational members and over time will cease to be questioned or challenged.

Schein's typology

Schein (1990) developed the typology shown in Table 7.1 for cultural analysis. Each dimension, described in detail below, is concerned with specific sets of beliefs that organizations have.

1. *The organization's relationship to its environment (beliefs that relate to the broader environment)*

Some organizations believe they are very important and are capable of dominating the environment, whereas others believe that they have a limited niche which they need to keep and protect if they are to survive.

Table 7.1 *Schein's typology for analysing organizational culture.*

- The organization's relationship to its environment
- The nature of human activity
- The nature of reality and truth
- The nature of human nature
- The nature of human relationships
- Homogeneity versus diversity

We might perhaps class Virgin as an example of an organization with the former belief and many small businesses as examples of the latter.

Such beliefs strongly influence the organization's strategic behaviour. Those who believe they are dominant will be prepared to 'boldly go' into new markets, new products and services or even to acquire smaller organizations. Those who believe they have a specific niche will be concerned to protect their market share, to compete effectively and to stay within their field of knowledge and competence.

2. The nature of human activity (beliefs about what the core activity of the business should be)

In larger organizations there is likely to be a lack of consensus on what the core activities should be. Different departments tend to view their own tasks as being the most important or have strong ideas about what other departments should be doing. Groups may also differ in their beliefs about how the organization should achieve its goals. For example, Langan-Fox and Tan (1997) studied culture change in a public-sector organization. The organization was attempting to become more customer oriented, in contrast to its current emphasis on administering policies and procedures. They found that organizational members could be grouped into three categories – those who had adopted these beliefs, those who were trying to and those who hadn't.

3. The nature of reality and truth (the methods used to establish 'facts' and what are perceived as relevant facts)

Most organizations operate in conditions of relatively high ambiguity and uncertainty. It is often difficult to tell what the immediate future holds and what any given set of information might mean. Organizations often have preferred methods of establishing facts. For instance, in the organization researched by Langan-Fox and Tan facts were often established by checking policy documents or getting the opinion of a senior manager. What the organization was hoping to move to was a situation where facts were established through measurable criteria, such as the extent of customer satisfaction or the extent to which organizational goals had been achieved. So, for example, if a customer complained this should ideally be treated as a sign that the organization was not functioning as it should be, rather than a sign that the customer was being unreasonable.

Organizations may also have strong beliefs about what counts as relevant facts. For example, Alvesson (1994), in his study of a Swedish advertising agency, discusses how advertising professionals would often dismiss their client's ideas for advertising campaigns on the basis that they lacked expertise. In Alvesson's study 'facts' about the product were determined by the advertising agency and not the client.

4. *The nature of human nature (beliefs about what people are like)*

Some organizations have theory X beliefs about people (see Chapter 6), believing that the carrot and the stick is the only way to get people to work. Others might believe more along the lines of theory Y, believing that people come to work for more reasons than pay. Such beliefs will underpin the management style in an organization. For instance, in many disciplined organizations, such as the police and army, theory X beliefs are pervasive and manifest in the giving of orders and the 'discipline codes' that set out tightly prescribed codes of conduct. Conversely, in the advertising agency studied by Alvesson there was strong 'anti-bureaucratic' belief which emphasized the importance of the skill and autonomy of each individual employee.

5. *The nature of human relationships (beliefs are about how people should relate to one another both hierarchically and horizontally)*

Some organizations believe in extremely formal relationships in which everybody – the boss, colleagues and subordinates – are called by their surnames and an appropriate title (Miss, Mr, Ms) and people keep their distance from each other. Some companies have separate dining areas for management and shop-floor staff. Other organizations are highly informal. Everyone is on first-name terms and go out together socially. Some organizations may emphasize the importance of teamworking while others may value individuality.

6. *Homogeneity versus diversity (beliefs about how similar or diverse the workforce should be)*

Does the organization expect everyone to have similar attitudes and behave in similar ways (homogeneity) or welcome differences between people (diversity)? There is evidence that many organizations prefer the former state. A study by Covaleski *et al.* (1998) into accountancy firms in the US reported that the pressures on employees to conform to the organization's expectations were so intense as to result in the production of 'corporate clones' – people who were not only similar in beliefs and attitudes but also in looks, dress and hobbies.

The pros and cons of cultural analysis

Schein's typology is one way among many of analysing an organization's culture but it has the advantages of being reasonably systematic and yet comprehensive enough to enable its application to almost any organization, whatever its size. Additionally, the typology is extremely useful for understanding the way an organization behaves both on the macro-level (that is, as a whole) and the micro-level (that is, how individuals act).

Unlike functionalist approaches, interpretive approaches like Schein's are not concerned with trying to change or manage culture (a highly dubious set of claims in any case) but with attempting to understand the organization at quite a fundamental level. It is similar to trying to understand a person in some depth. Understanding what makes someone tick is not necessarily going to enable you to make that person do what you want them to but is likely to help you to be able to predict some of their behaviours in some circumstances.

One of the drawbacks of cultural analysis is that it does not explain how culture affects the behaviour of individuals. First, what is the process through which the norms, values and attitudes in any organization are learned or acquired? And how do we account for individual differences in the extent to which people conform to these rules? These questions are important given that an analysis of culture is so focused on behaviour and attitudes.

Second, where do the values and attitudes that configure an organization's culture come from? Some scholars believe that values and attitudes are developed by the founder of the organization and are then continued or modified by the employees who follow the founder (Trice and Beyer, 1991). However, while this point of view may have some validity, it is clearly the case that many organizations share aspects of culture in common (Hofstede *et al.*, 1990). Many organizations in the 1990s tended to have strong theory Y beliefs, for example (Rose, 1990). Such similarities show us that organizational culture is probably influenced by broader social conditions. Thus, another weakness of cultural analysis can be its insularity: it is too inwardly focused. Another weakness is that it can sometimes assume that an organization's culture is homogeneous; that is, it is the same in every department. Clearly, however, if the organization is large enough different departments have different cultures or subcultures (Riley, 1983; Moch and Bartunek, 1990). While some of the culture literature does address this issue, in general cultural analysis downplays differences between groups in organizations.

Finally, cultural analysis is very useful for examining the ways in which individuals and groups differ or agree about the beliefs and values in an organization but does tend to play down the influence of the environment or society more generally on such beliefs and attitudes.

7.4 Analysing organizations using the concept of power

Analysing power in organizations emphasizes the idea that organizations are composed of diverse groups of people, not all of whom share the same interests or views on life. This encourages us to think about the ways in which people at work acquire and use power and how this affects relationships and working practices. Analysis of power is concerned with understanding the differences that exist between different groups in organizations, the reasons why such differences exist and the effects that such differences have on the way the organization functions. Before we look at how power can be used in organizational analysis, let's look at some definitions.

Some definitions of power

Power is the probability that one actor within a social relationship will be in a position to carry out his own will despite resistance.

(Weber, 1947)

A has power over B to the extent that he can get B to do something that B would not otherwise do.

(Dahl, 1957)

Power is defined as the capacity to effect (or affect) organizational outcomes.

(Mintzberg, 1983)

There are many other definitions, but these three provide the general flavour. What do these definitions tell us about power?

First, each definition assumes that power is a commodity or resource in the possession of some or other person. As we shall see at the end of this section this view can be challenged but for now we will stick with it. Second, there is an idea that power can be used to influence people or outcomes in some way. Or, more simply, that power can be used to bring about changes in behaviour. Third, each definition shows us that power works within a relationship between two or more people. So, although we might, for instance, describe the President of the United States as a powerful man, the effects of his power can be shown only within specific relationships he has, for instance, between himself and the staff of the Oval Office.

Bases of power

What enables people or groups to take possession of power? One useful approach to answering this question comes from the work of Pfeffer (1981), of Stanford University in the United States, who has identified several ways in which groups in organizations can acquire power. These organizational power bases include:

- providing resources;
- coping with uncertainty;
- being irreplaceable;
- affecting decision processes;
- being central.

1. Providing resources
Groups in organizations can acquire power if they are able to provide an important resource that creates dependency on the part of other groups. Resources can be any expendable commodity – money, time, expertise, technology, skills, knowledge or authority. Looked at in this way every group in every organization has some power, though clearly some groups have resources that are more highly valued than others. Managers are often the most powerful groups in organizations because

they possess money in the form of budgets and the authority to determine how those budgets should be allocated.

2. Coping with uncertainty

As we saw in the previous chapter many organizations operate in conditions of high uncertainty and find it difficult to predict what is going to happen or interpret what is going on. Groups that are able to reduce any of the uncertainties an organization might face are likely to acquire power. For example, in organizations planning downsizing (redundancies) the human-resource department may acquire power because it will have knowledge about where redundancies are likely to occur.

3. Being irreplaceable

Groups and departments that have knowledge and expertise that are exclusive to them can often be powerful. Departments that possess complex technical skills fit into this category. One can think of engineers, computer technicians and systems analysts and, of course, accountants. The skills that these groups provide cannot be acquired readily by others and working life can become difficult for everyone if these experts are not available. If something goes wrong with your computer or car you may not have the expertise to put things right and become totally dependent on experts.

4. Affecting decision processes

People are also powerful if they have some say about what happens in an organization. Morgan (1986) suggests there are three ways in which people can influence organizational decision making – by controlling decision *premises, processes* or *issues.* Controlling decision premises involves influencing the issues that the organization perceives as important. One way of doing this is to direct attention away from the goal the group is trying to obtain. For instance, a department campaigning for an increase in staff numbers might achieve this goal by default by directing attention to an increase in customer complaints, for example.

Controlling decision processes is a more direct influence tactic, where a group will attempt to influence how the organization makes its decisions. For instance, a department might insist it is invited to policy meetings from which it has been hitherto excluded.

Finally, controlling decision issues can be achieved by presenting information in specific ways. For instance, reports that will influence decision making can be written in ways that emphasize some issues and gloss over others.

5. *Being central*

People at the operating core of an organization are also likely to be powerful. The operating core is that group of people responsible for conducting the organization's main business – the manufacture or the production of goods and services. In times of industrial unrest, for instance, the power of core groups was used to improve conditions of employment. A study by Robinson and McIlwee (1991) showed that in US engineering companies professional engineers were central when companies were structured organically but not when they were structured bureaucratically (see Chapter 6 for explanations of these structural forms). They further found that when engineers were central, female engineers were far less likely to be promoted than their male counterparts. Robinson and McIlwee concluded that this was because the power base of the engineers enabled them to emphasize masculine aspects of the role, such as 'tinkering with machinery'. Chapter 8 deals with these issues at some depth.

Power bases and differences of interest

Many of the disagreements between groups in organizations stem from attempts to secure a power base or render an existing one more secure. These attempts cause groups and individuals to jockey for position as they attempt to prove that they are central or irreplaceable. Some groups deliberately make themselves irreplaceable by not committing any of their expertise to paper but keeping it inside their heads. At other times conflicts occur because groups are fighting to protect their position and stop others moving in. What power bases are apparent in **Case Study 1 'Building a flexible organization: British Gypsum'**? How are these being threatened by the change in working conditions?

Of course, what has probably struck you already is that having a power base does not necessarily mean that you will be able to exercise any power. Expressing power depends on a number of things, including the realization of power and its mobilization (Batstone *et al.*, 1978). For power to be exercised by any specific group they need first to recognize that they actually *possess* power and, second, that they have the means to collectively mobilize that power. Realizing power is one thing but mobilizing power is quite another.

Rewards and sanctions

At least one important factor in the decline of strikes in the UK as a manifestation of industrial conflict was the legislation passed by the governments of 1979 to 1997 that aimed to curb the power of the trade unions. This legislation rendered illegal certain types of strike-related behaviour, such as the practice of secondary picketing, which means carrying on the dispute at a place other than one's own place of work. It also enabled employers to take legal action against unions that were deemed to be breaking these new laws. Thus, the mobilization of power is dependent upon what the group perceives to be the likely costs and benefits of mobilizing their power. A group that perceives it has more to lose than to gain is unlikely to be willing to take any action even if it believes its power base is very strong. Thus, the mobilization of power is highly dependent on whether the rewards of taking action (say, gaining a pay rise) are more likely to be realized than potential sanctions (say, being sacked).

The reward and sanction elements of power are the means through which power yields its effects. We do what the boss tells us because he or she has the ability to reward us or impose sanctions if we do not.

7.5 Power in contemporary organizations

All human relationships embody an element of power. Boyfriend/girlfriend, brother/sister, parent/child, team member/team leader all have to determine where the power lies. Some would argue that the ideal situation is a balance of power so that no one party can dominate the other. Mature relationships might even allow power to shift between parties in accordance with who is the most appropriate person to hold the power.

In any organizational setting power relations are crucial in determining the way managers and subordinates work together. When power is held totally in the hands of the manager or owner, because they have ultimate power to employ or dismiss or they control all the resources that employees use, the temptation to employ a dictatorial style of management will be strong. At the other extreme, if employees have organizational power through their ownership of intellectual skills, information or ability, a more consensual or partnership style of management would be more appropriate.

Table 7.2 *The power of organizational stakeholders.*

- Employee groups (on-site, off-site)
- Owner groups (shareholders, institutional shareholders, founders)
- Environmental groups (local and national)
- Customers (past, present and future)
- Industry bodies, trade associations
- Buyer groups (supply-chain coordinators)
- Competitors/collaborators
- Professional bodies (e.g. legal/financial)
- Local residents
- Government legislative and regulatory bodies (local, national and international)

The concept of the organization **stakeholder** has recently been coined to explain the view that organizations must recognize a number of connected interest groups and take account of their requirements (Mintzberg, 1983). The traditional view that organizations had only two sets of members, the owners and the workers, is now widely recognized as being dated and naive. A **stakeholder** can be described as anyone who has an interest, commercial or otherwise, in the organization. Table 7.2 illustrates the range of possible stakeholders.

Using a technique like **forcefield analysis** (Lewin, 1947) allows an organization to gauge the power of each stakeholder group and predict the level of support likely for planned organizational changes or decisions. Figure 7.1 shows a simple application of forcefield analysis to gauge stakeholder reaction to relocating a plant.

Figure 7.1 shows the typical way in which such a decision is supported by some stakeholders but resisted by others. In the case of the new location residents, mixed feelings of support and resistance are likely to be experienced (some will welcome the job opportunities and others will be fearful of the traffic and other nuisance factors). The force or strength of each of these factors, represented by the length of each line, will need to be considered by the managers responsible before coming to the final decision. Evidence will need to be gathered to make the length of the lines a true reflection of the strength of feeling. For example, surveys, questionnaires, interviews and written communication with all stakeholders will give an idea of what support and resistance is likely to the change.

The force-field analysis will give managers more guidance when it comes to making the decision and warn them of what preparatory work may be required.

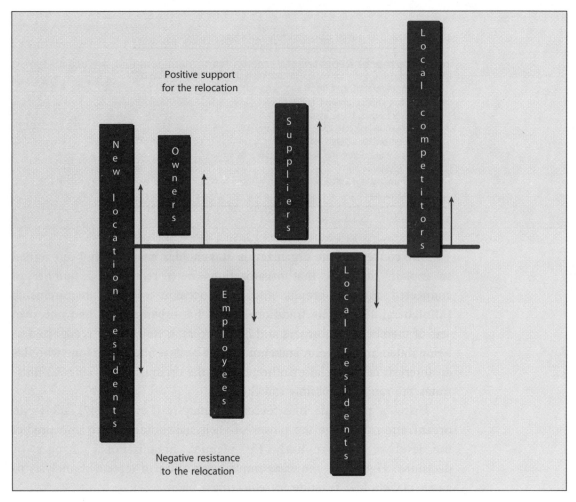

Figure 7.1   Force-field analysis of plant relocation.

7.6 Power and conflict

As we have seen, organizations are generally flatter today and there is a general trend in larger organizations to utilize functional flexibility. In other words, there is less emphasis on separate roles and departments and greater emphasis on multi-skilling so that people can be grouped together into temporary project teams. Clearly, if this is the case some of the power bases identified by Pfeffer (1973) are less relevant today. For instance, the extent to which groups can make themselves irreplaceable or become absolutely central is limited in organizations that rely heavily on functional flexibility.

Some organizations talk of the family structure of their business. Employees can be told repeatedly that they are part of a partnership or team approach. Repeated statements from managers that 'we are all in this together' or that 'employees are all part of the XYZ company team' are often intended to reinforce this view. Such statements appear to be underpinned by the assumption that organizations are fundamentally **unitarist** in their composition: most people are there for the same reasons and want the same things. The implication is that no material difference exists between members whatever level they operate at. The highest level managers and the lowest level employees must share the organization's goals and objectives and work together to achieve them.

The reality of organizational life is more likely to reflect the fact that employees differ from managers in many ways. In other words, organizations are fundamentally **pluralistic** in their composition. Employees and managers are, even today, likely to come from different social backgrounds and have different social, economic and cultural norms and values. They will belong to different peer groups and are consequently likely to have widely differing goals and objectives. It is because of these differences that many organizations operate in an uneasy environment of tension and dispute. See Chapter 4 for a further discussion of conflict between teams.

The imbalance of power in organizations means that all people who work in them will sooner or later experience or witness conflict. Some people argue that a limited amount of conflict is actually a healthy thing. It might stimulate competition, encourage innovation and keep people from getting bored. Where the conflict is too great, however, it spills over into aggression or even sabotage, and the manager's job is often first to quell the conflict and then trace the sources of the trouble (see Reflection Box 7.1).

Types of conflict

According to Champoux (1996) conflict can be classified into the following categories:

- Intraorganizational conflict occurs between functions or departments, often over resource or responsibility disputes.
- Intragroup conflict – members of the same group or team disagree.
- Intergroup conflict – one part of the organization has a dispute with another.

> ### Reflection Box 7.1 What should be done about conflict in organizations?
>
> Conflict can manifest itself in different ways: from doubt or questioning of instructions or ideas through to outright opposition. In severe conflicts one party might be seeking to prevent another one from achieving its goals thereby developing an antagonistic interaction. But at the lighter end of the scale some conflict might be useful in testing assumptions, generating new ideas and sparking innovation. Some would argue that conflict is essential to organizational survival and should be encouraged. We can all use our experience to imagine the potential for conflict that exists in many organizations. Others do not like to see conflict and see it as a sign that things are not well.
>
> The level of conflict in an organization might therefore be something that cannot be eradicated and therefore needs to be effectively managed.
>
> Is conflict inevitable in organizations? Can you think of any of your own personal experiences where conflict has proved useful?

- Interpersonal conflict – between a customer and a salesperson, for example.
- Intrapersonal conflict occurs within an individual because of a threat to personal values or beliefs, or a feeling of unfairness.

Robbins (1990) offers an alternative categorization suggesting that the most frequently cited sources of organizational conflicts are:

- Mutual task dependence: forced interaction means that extra pressure is placed on working relationships.
- One-way task dependence: the power balance has been shifted in favour of one party.
- High horizontal differentiation: the higher the level in the hierarchy the more chance there will be for employees to be working to different views of urgency, resource usage and priority.
- Low formalization: few rules and procedures and ambiguity can lead to misunderstanding but, just as in a game of football, the presence of rules does not stop people breaking them.
- Dependence on common scarce resources: fights can often break out over the sharing of labour, space or equipment.

- Differences in evaluation criteria and reward system: different groups are rewarded differently for separate performance rather than combined efforts.
- Participative decision making: joint decision making allows airing of disputes and disagreements to arise.
- Heterogeneity of members: personal differences such as education, background and beliefs all lead to less common ground and more potential for dispute.
- Status incongruence: White's (1948) study of waitresses and cooks in the restaurant industry provides evidence that when low-status employees give orders to high-status ones this often leads to conflict.
- Role dissatisfaction: employees may be unhappy with their position, possibly believing that they should have been moved or promoted.
- Communication distortions: information gets distorted as it is passed around an organization causing undue alarm.

Conflict can arise between individuals for a number of reasons. It can be a simple matter of a clash of personalities if two people simply do not get on but a far more serious form of conflict occurs when organizational groups come into conflict. Typically, one department or division will quarrel with another if one group feels it has been given an unreasonably low allocation of resources or that it has in some other way been discriminated against. Conflict can also occur when two work groups have goals or objectives which work against each other (see Reflection Box 7.2).

Managing conflict

Some authors believe that conflict can be an important mechanism for bringing about change in organizations (Chamberland and Kund, 1965). Many organizations, however, would rather avoid conflict altogether. Given the degree of diversity that exists in organizations some conflict is inevitable.

Research shows that organizations can manage conflict in a number of ways: negotiation is one tactic; the conflicting parties communicate in an effort to find a mutually agreeable solution (Putnam and Poole, 1987). Mediation is another possibility. A neutral third party will listen to the grievances and concerns of those involved in the decision and make suggestions for their resolution (Kochan and Katz, 1988).

Reflection Box 7.2 Conflicting goals

Imagine the sales and service departments of an organization seeking to improve their customer-care ratings. One of the best ways of doing this would be to offer a quick efficient service. In order to achieve it they would have to ensure that the firm keeps a large stock of spares and components so that repairs can be carried out quickly. But the stock control and spares department may actually be seeking to *minimize* the amount of stock they hold to keep the cost of inventory, insurance and use of storage space all down to a minimum. Typically this is known as a 'just-in-time' (JIT) stock-control system. So anyone from the sales and service departments who required parts for a customer might be held up while the non-stocked parts could be sourced and delivered. Clearly these two sets of goals, both equally valid for the group members concerned, will lead to conflict sooner or later.

How might organizations manage such processes to prevent conflict from damaging the relationship and performance of the two departments?

Conflict is not always manifested in overt ways, however, and may not therefore be amenable to direct management. Increasing attention is being focused on resistance, a more subtle expression of conflict.

7.7 Power and resistance

As we saw at the beginning of this section, power can be exercised only within specific relationships. In fact, some theorists, particularly the French social philosopher Foucault (1977), have argued that power is not in fact a *possession*, as is commonly assumed; it arises out of relationships between two or more people. So it is nonsense to talk of someone being powerful; they are only powerful in the sense that the various people with whom they have relationships allow them to have their own way.

According to Foucault, in any relationship where power is being exercised there will also be resistance. Resistance need not necessarily mean an outright refusal to comply but can be thought of as any act that tries to subvert the power relationship. In other words, it can be anything that allows the person who is the target of an exercise of power to feel that, in reality, he or she is the one who is exercising power.

Robert Bruno (1998) examined the ways that American steelworkers resisted their managers without taking any direct action. He suggests that workers resist management in many ways, including holding disparaging attitudes towards their supervisors (who were generally thought of as 'useless') and engaging in petty theft. Other researchers have argued that modern workplaces are full of such examples of resistance. Jermier *et al.* (1994) argue that the tendency for businesses to treat staff as commodities (e.g. making them redundant at a moment's notice), while it reduces the likelihood that people will engage in acts of overt resistance, increases more covert acts of resistance such as those identified by Bruno.

The pros and cons of analysing organizations using the concept of power

Using the concept of power to analyse organizations is helpful in getting us to think about organizations as diverse groups of people who may not necessarily be in pursuit of the same goals. Marx (1964) pointed out that the inherent conflict of interest between people who own businesses and those who work in them exists because, put simply, the owners want the workers to work as hard as possible for as little as possible and the workers want the reverse.

Conflicts of interest also occur between various groups and departments, usually because they are in pursuit of some or other power base. An analysis of power helps us to understand what it is that people are trying to obtain and why this creates conflict. Contemporary organizations, because of blurring of boundaries between roles and departments, may have reduced or even removed some of the bases of power that were more actively pursued in bureaucratic forms of organization (Jermier *et al.*, 1994). However, it would be a mistake to assume that conflicts of interest have been eradicated. The form and manifestation of conflict have shifted but have not gone away.

A great deal of attention is focused on resolving conflict and overcoming resistance. However, Foucault suggests that power and resistance are an inevitable consequence of any disciplined social structure. So the problems are not necessarily conflicts of interest in themselves but are to do with the way organizations themselves are organized.

In any hierarchical system power is exercised by those at the top and resisted by those at the bottom (Ferguson, 1987 and see Reflection Box 7.3). For this reason conflicts can never be truly resolved or resistance overcome. Both will be manifested in some way or other. A further problem with analysing organizations using the concept of power is that, like cultural analysis, it is very much focused *inside* the organization and plays down the effects of the wider organizational context. It is notable, for

Reflection Box 7.3 Discourses of dissatisfaction in a bureau-cratic organization

Bureaucracy as a system of organization produces a patterned behavioural response in some employees. This is upward mobility (Presthus, 1962) – the desire for promotion. However, in any hierarchical organization the opportunities for promotion are always limited: by default there are more people in the lower parts of the hierarchy than at the higher levels. When people are frustrated in their promotion attempts they need to be able to explain this in ways that do not compromise their own self-esteem. This might be due to the self-enhancement motive (Snyder *et al.*, 1978) – the idea that people try to protect their self-esteem – or because of the effects of discourse – social norms that suggest we should try to always feel good about ourselves (Potter and Wetherell, 1987). The fundamental effect is, however, that people who are frustrated will tend to blame other people rather than themselves. More importantly, bureaucracy or hierarchy is never blamed because, as Ferguson points out, hierarchy is so completely taken for granted that nobody ever questions it. The following extracts are taken from research into upward mobility conducted on a UK police force (Dick and Cassell, 1999).

Extract 1

Dave (Inspector): I hadn't been shafted then. I was on the verge of becoming a Chief Inspector. You get treated badly don't you? The last two years I've been treated very badly – ACPO people. We have these supposedly objective assessment centres where we all assess each other and that . . . Of course, when I was in favour . . . we all went up there and I came second . . . but another bloke, just as competent (as me) came last. And they pretend it's fair, all above board, all about equal ops.

Extract 2

Peter (Sergeant): Probably when I joined I was very quiet in interviews. But now, you don't get on in this job unless you actually speak and tell them what they want to hear – you know, even if it's not always what you think, you've got to tell them what the party line is or else you'll never get on.

As the extracts show, Dave and Peter, both of whom have been unsuccessful at their last promotion board, express cynicism about the organization's promotion system. Such cynicism was expressed by most officers whose upward mobility was frustrated. However, as Ferguson points out, it is the organization itself that causes both upward mobility and its frustration. If there was no hierarchy then people would not struggle to climb it.

Is upward mobility truly inevitable? Could employees in hierarchical organizations be persuaded to consider alternative forms of reward to promotion?

instance, that when an organization faces a real crisis, such as whether it can actually survive the next month, conflicts often disappear overnight.

7.8 Summary

Organizations can be thought of as essentially **unitarist** or **pluralist**. On the whole, cultural analyses of organizations tend to take a unitarist view, focusing on the extent to which organizational members share the same beliefs, attitudes and values (though there are exceptions to this view in the literature). **Functionalist** approaches to cultural analysis focus on how such beliefs and values can be managed and changed in order to facilitate organizational performance. Conversely, **interpretive** approaches focus instead on the *content* of the beliefs and attitudes that people share to create a better understanding of the actual nature of the organization. We used Schein's typology to show how interpretive analysis of culture might be performed.

We noted that while culture is very useful for a clearer understanding of the behavioural aspects of organizations it does tend to play down both the effects of the external environment and the extent of heterogeneity in beliefs and values within an organization.

Analysing organizations using the concept of power is based on the assumption that organizations are essentially **pluralistic** in composition. Many conceptualizations of power involve the idea that power is a *commodity* that is in the *possession* of one or more individuals or groups.

Power has to be realized and mobilized to be effective. Furthermore, the exercise of power depends upon **perceived rewards** and **sanctions**. Power is exercised only if the benefits of doing so outweigh the costs. Historically, power shifted between workers and managers dependent on economic conditions. Today, there is a greater degree of interdependency between groups, including managers and workers. We discussed the concept of **stakeholders** as a way of conceptualizing these new relationships.

Conflict is one manifestation of power differences between groups. We looked at the factors that can lead to conflict, noting that not all conflict is dysfunctional or undesirable. We then looked briefly at ways of managing it. **Resistance** is another manifestation of power differences. We noted that resistance can often be a far more subtle reaction to power differences than outright conflict, because it enables individuals and groups to retain a sense of control in unbalanced power relationships.

Questions

Self-test questions

1 Describe what is meant by unitarist and pluralist views of organization.
2 How can organizational culture be defined?
3 What is the difference between functionalist and interpretive approaches to organizational culture?
4 Describe two of the dimensions along which culture can be analysed according to Schein's typology.
5 What are the chief disadvantages of a cultural analysis?
6 Name two features of a typical definition of power.
7 List Pfeffer's bases of organizational power.
8 Explain why the possession of power alone will not guarantee its expression.
9 What is meant by stakeholder analysis and what is its value?
10 What might cause conflict in an organization and what steps can be taken to manage it?

Discussion questions

1 Is it possible to identify the difference between the values and attitudes that members of organizations say they have and those they *really* have? Does it matter?
2 In what circumstances might a cultural analysis be useful and why?
3 As increasing numbers of organizations introduce more flexible structures and practices, will an analysis of organizational power become less relevant?

References and bibliography

Alvesson, M. (1994) Talking in organizations: managing identity and impressions in an advertising agency, *Organization Studies*, **15**(4), 535–563.

Batstone, E., Boraston, I. and Frenkel, S. (1978) *The Social Organisation of Strikes*, San Francisco: Jossey-Bass.

Bruno, R. (1998) Working, playing and fighting for control: steelworkers and shopfloor identity, *Labor Studies Journal*, **23**(1) 3–22.

Chamberland, N. W. and Kund, J. W. (1965) *Collective Bargaining*, New York: McGraw-Hill.

Champoux, J. (1996) *Organisational Behaviour: Integrating Individuals, Groups and Processes*, New York: West Publishing Company.

Covaleski, M. A., Dirsmith, M. W., Heian, J. B. and Samuel, S. (1998) The calculated and the avowed: techniques of discipline and struggles over identity in Big Six public accounting firms, *Administrative Science Quarterly*, **43**(2), 293–327.

Dahl, R. A. (1957) The concept of power, *Behavioural Science*, **2**, 201–215.

Dick, P. and Cassell, C. (1999) Talking cop: Discourse, identity and diversity in a UK police force. Paper presented to the *British Academy of Management Conference, September, Manchester*.

Durkheim, E. (1951) *Suicide*, New York: Free Press.

Ferguson, K. E. (1987) Work, text and act in discourses of organisation, *Women and Politics*, **7**(2), 1–21.

Foucault, M. (1977) *Discipline and Punish: The Birth of the Prison*, London: Allen-Lane.

Fox, A. (1973) Industrial relations: A social critique of pluralist ideology. In Child, J. (ed.) *Man and Organization*, London: Allen & Unwin.

Hofstede, G., Neuijen, B., Ohayv, D. D. and Sanders, G. (1990) Measuring organizational cultures: a qualitative and quantitative study across twenty cases, *Administrative Science Quarterly*, **35**, 286–316.

Jermier, J. M., Knights, D. and Nord, W. R. (1994) (eds) *Resistance and Power in Organisations*, London: Routledge.

Kochan, T. A. and Katz, H. C. (1988) *Collective Bargaining and Industrial Relations*, Homewood, IL: Irwin.

Langan-Fox, L. and Tan, P. (1997) Images of a culture in transition: Personal constructs of organizational stability and change, *Journal of Occupational and Organizational Psychology*, **70**(3), 273–294.

Lewin, K. (1947) Frontiers in group dynamics, *Human Relations*, **1**, 1–14.

Marx, K. (1964) *Early Writings* (translated and edited by Bottomore, T. B.), New York: McGraw-Hill.

Moch, M. K. and Bartunek, J. M. (1990) *Creating Alternative Realities at Work: The Quality of Work Life Experiment at FoodCom*, New York: Harper Business.

Morgan, G. (1986) *Images of Organization*, London: Sage.

Mintzberg, H. (1983) *Power In and Around Organizations*, Englewood Cliffs, NJ: Prentice-Hall.

Peters, T. and Waterman, R. H. (1982) *In Search of Excellence*, New York: Harper and Row.

Pfeffer, J. (1981) *Power in Organizations*, Marshfield, MA: Pitman.

Potter, J. and Wetherell, M. (1987) *Discourse and Social Psychology: Beyond Attitudes and Behaviour*, London: Sage.

Presthus, R. (1962) *The Organizational Society*, New York: Alfred A. Knopf.

Putnam, L. L. and Poole, M. S. (1987) Conflict and negotiation. In Jablin, F. M., Putnam, L. L., Roberts, K. H. and Poret, L. W. (eds) *Handbook of Organizational Communication*, Beverley Hills, CA: Sage.

Riley, P. (1983) A structurationist account of political culture, *Administrative Science Quarterly*, **28**, 414–437.

Robbins, S. (1990) *Organisation Theory*, New Jersey; London: Prentice Hall International.

Robinson, J. G. and McIlwee, J. S. (1991) Men, women, and the culture of engineering, *The Sociological Quarterly*, **32**(3), 403–421.

Rose, N. (1990) *Governing the Soul: The Shaping of the Private Self*, London: Routledge.

Schein, E. H. (1985) *Organisational Culture and Leadership*, London: Jossey-Bass.

Schein, E. H. (1990) Organization Culture, *American Psychologist*, **45**, 109–119.

Secord, P. F. and Backman, C. W. (1969) *Social Psychology*, New York: McGraw-Hill.

Smircich, L. (1983) Concepts of culture and organizational analysis, *Administrative Science Quarterly*, **28**(3), 339–358.

Snyder, M. L., Stephan, W. G. and Rosenfield, D. (1978) Attributional egotism. In Harvey, J. H., Ickes, W. and Kidd, R. F. (eds) *New Directions in Attributional Research* (second edition), Hillsdale, NJ: Erlbaum.

Trice, H. M. and Beyer, J. M. (1991) Cultural leadership in organizations, *Organization Science*, **2**, 149–169.

Weber, M. (1947) *The Theory of Social and Economic Organisation*, Glencoe, IL: Free Press.

White, W. (1948) *Human Relations in the Restaurant Industry*, New York: McGraw-Hill.

8

Understanding and managing diversity

Contents

Objectives

By the end of this chapter you should be able to:

- explain what is meant by workforce diversity
- understand the ways in which organizational culture can impede the career progression of minorities
- recognize the ways in which socialization influences career choice and progression
- outline the concept of embodiment and discuss how this can be used to explain why minorities may rule themselves out of certain occupations
- discuss ways in which organizations can prevent discrimination against minorities during the selection process
- describe different approaches to diversity management and outline the conditions that support each approach
- identify some of the weaknesses of managing diversity approaches

8.1 Introduction

One of biggest challenges facing organizations is how to increase and manage workforce diversity. Before we look at this issue in detail, however, we need to understand what workforce diversity means and why it is important for organizations to think about it.

Diversity, in organizational-behaviour terms, means differences between working individuals, such as gender, ethnicity, colour, sexuality, religion, disability, age, background, education, personality, work style and skills. Gender and race have attracted most attention largely because of legislative requirements that organizations have to meet (the Sex Discrimination Act, 1975 and 1986; the Race Relations Act, 1976 and the Disability Discrimination Act, 1995).

The Stephen Lawrence Inquiry (1998) drew attention to the fact that, despite being a multiracial and multicultural society, racism in the UK is 'institutional'. In other words, negative attitudes towards people of different races are taken for granted. Most people do not believe themselves to be racist but statistics show that if you belong to certain racial minorities in this country your life is probably going to be far more difficult than if you are white. For example, the Labour Force Survey (1988) carried out by the Department of Employment showed that of the 5 per cent of the working population that were of African, Asian or Afro-Caribbean origin significantly greater numbers were unemployed compared with their white counterparts. Black men are about three times as likely as any other group to be stopped by the police, whether walking or driving, and black women earn significantly less than white women (Bhavnani, 1994).

In terms of gender, the explosion in the service sector of the economy has brought many more women into employment. But women tend to be concentrated in low-skill low-status low-pay jobs and are hugely under-represented in managerial jobs (Dickens, 1997). Even in female-dominated occupations, such as nursing, there is hierarchical segregation. Women are concentrated towards the bottom of the hierarchy and men numerically dominate the higher levels (Reskin and Hartmann, 1986). There is also evidence to suggest that women face difficulties in career advancement because of covert discrimination – the so-called 'glass-ceiling' (Marshall, 1984).

Governments throughout Europe and North America are encouraging workplaces to increase workplace diversity, largely because members of minorities who face the sorts of discrimination outlined above lobby for these sorts of changes. For example, the disabled lobby and civil liberties lobby in North America are particularly strong, putting considerable pressure on the Government to legislate for greater workplace diversity (Dass and Parker, 1999). In the UK, public-sector organizations, such as the police, face particular problems; in inner London an overwhelmingly white workforce is expected to police a black-majority community. The Home Office has recently issued new targets for the police to increase the numbers of officers from different ethnic and racial groups. And women are increasingly frustrated and dissatisfied with their lot at work when they compare themselves with their male counterparts.

Organizations are less interested in diversity because they tend to be most concerned about issues that directly affect their business performance. Comer and Soliman (1996), for instance, suggest that a major factor in encouraging some organizations to think about diversity is their public image. Some organizations are keen to increase diversity not because of any particular ethical imperative but because they believe it may win them new customers. The assumption that organizations need to be persuaded to think about workforce diversity is clear in much of the literature, in which a 'business-case' for increasing workforce diversity is often set out (Kandola and Fullerton, 1998).

We will examine workforce diversity in some depth, focusing on two principal concerns: how to increase workplace diversity and how to manage it.

In the first section we will examine some of the work that has been done on increasing workplace diversity. We will consider gender mainly because this has been the focus of a large amount of research. However, the concepts we will discuss apply to any minority group. In the first section we will therefore look at some of the difficulties minorities face in trying to enter certain occupations and also examine the problem from the organizational perspective – the difficulty in attracting applications from certain groups in the first instance.

In the second section we will examine how organizations attempt to manage diversity and look at some of the (sparse) literature on this topic. The final section is a critique of some of the approaches to diversity management.

8.2 Discrimination in the workplace

Under the banner of equal opportunities many companies claim not to discriminate against employees on the grounds of race, gender or any other such characteristic. However, as we have already noted, there is plenty of evidence that certain groups are relatively disadvantaged.

The 'glass ceiling'

The **'glass ceiling'** is a phrase coined to illustrate the fact that many working women are able to see promotion opportunities but fail to secure them. Arguments about why this should be fall into two groups: barriers to women's progression are located in **organizational culture**; and **socialization** encourages men and women to take up certain roles. We will look at each of these approaches in turn.

Barriers to women's progression are located in organizational culture
During the 1980s a great deal of literature emerged which suggested that women's lack of career progression relative to men was the result of organizational culture (a concept we covered in Chapter 7 and which you should revisit if you are unfamiliar with it). The basic argument is that because men numerically dominate organizations (at least in the most powerful positions) the culture reflects male ways of thinking and behaving which, in turn, makes it difficult for women to either be perceived as competent or to feel as if they fit in.

Studies from both the UK and North America have provided considerable support for this argument. For example, several studies have suggested that being promoted is in many organizations at least partially based on networking with the 'right' people (e.g. senior managers). Such networking often occurs on the basis of shared social interests, such as golf or football. It is argued that because women tend to be less interested in these sorts of activities they find it difficult to get noticed or feel accepted (Crompton and Jones, 1984).

Other studies have argued that the informal communication processes in organizations favour men because the sort of language used reflects male interests. Organizational performance is discussed in terms of metaphors; for example, *We haven't got enough team players* or *We're battle weary in this department.* It is argued that the use of such language bolsters male dominance and makes it more difficult for women to communicate (Riley, 1983).

There is work that suggests that in some occupations the culture emphasizes those aspects of the job that men prefer. For instance, one study found that male engineers tend to emphasize the importance of playing about with machinery and getting dirty (Robinson and McIlwee, 1991) and another suggested that the police overemphasize the physical aspects of the role, such as dealing with violence (Morash and Greene, 1986). This research indicates that women, who are less likely to enjoy such aspects of their roles, are simply not perceived as being as competent as their male colleagues.

Finally, there is research to suggest that women find it difficult to know how to behave in male-dominated environments. For example, Sheppard (1989), a Canadian researcher, found in her study of female managers that many women struggled to strike a balance between maintaining their femininity and appearing competent. By being perceived as too feminine they ran the risk of not being taken seriously while if they were not feminine enough they ran the risk of being perceived as 'uncomfortably' masculine.

According to these studies, the answer to the problem of discrimination is to increase the number of women in managerial posts so that the culture can start to reflect 'female' ways of behaving. Raising awareness of the sorts of issues we've looked at is also seen as important, as well as allocating mentors to women so that they can be encouraged to progress within their careers and be supported at the same time. More recently it has been suggested that demands for quality and service will push to the fore the necessity of behaving in more traditionally feminine ways – supporting, nurturing and facilitating (Kerfoot and Knights, 1996). This argument suggests that women will progress more easily as their skills and characteristics become more consistent with evolving business demands.

Socialization

Another set of ideas suggests that women and men are socialized from a young age to develop certain expectations about how they should behave, what they should be good at and, most importantly for our purposes, what sorts of jobs they should do. Statistically, there is evidence to support this argument. Women are more likely to be found in jobs which mirror their domestic roles, such as nursing, cleaning and teaching, whereas men are more likely to be found in manufacturing and craft jobs (Labour Market Trends, 1996). The literature, while it accepts that organizations need to do more to encourage men and women into non-traditional jobs, argues that a major part of the problem is the way that women and men perceive themselves and each other.

Several studies, for example, show that women are more likely than men to attribute their success to luck and their failures to themselves and that this is a consequence of childhood socialization (Rosenthal *et al.*, 1996). Other studies have shown that women are more likely to under-estimate their abilities relative to men (Deaux, 1976). These studies imply that part of the problem in attracting women into non-traditional roles is their lack of confidence. Women are much more likely than men, it seems, to convince themselves that they won't be able to do certain jobs. Other studies suggest that women, because of their relative lack of self-confidence, are less likely to promote themselves in ways that would facilitate their career progression (Hackett and Betz, 1981).

There has been much research on men's and women's work styles, focusing particularly on leadership style. Some researchers have suggested that women have very different leadership styles from those of men and are particularly good at interpersonal relations and communication (Grant, 1988; Rosener, 1990). However, Eagly and Johnson (1990) in a study that examined the results of previous research into gender differences in leadership style concluded that there were no significant differences between men and women. However, there does appear to be a taken-for-granted assumption in some of the literature that women are better at relationships than men (Osland *et al.*, 1998).

There is also research to suggest that people of both sexes, when making interpersonal judgements, are influenced by the gender of the individual concerned. For example, laboratory studies have shown that male interviewees tend to be rated more favourably than females (Hitt and Barr, 1989). However, a more recent study that looked at the way people judged each other in real interviews showed that male interviewers did not judge male or female applicants any differently and that female interviewers made more favourable judgements of female interviewees (Graves and Powell, 1996). So, the evidence on this point is rather mixed.

Finally, there has been much research into **sex-role stereotypes**: the notion that certain attributes belong to all women or men. Schein (1973; 1975), for instance, has repeatedly shown that characteristics thought to best describe managerial roles are also those that are judged to be more representative of men as a group than women as a group. Thus, the typical manager is expected to possess masculine characteristics.

Similarly, a study by Brown *et al.* (1992) showed that policewomen were more likely to be deployed to situations involving children because, they argue, women are stereotyped as being 'good with children'. These studies suggest that women may find it difficult to gain entry to certain occupations because they will be perceived not to possess the characteristics that are assumed to be necessary for successful performance.

Socialization approaches argue that stereotypes need to be broken down by disrupting the socialization process. For instance, it is argued that bringing female role models into senior jobs will encourage other women (Kanter, 1977), though other authors have argued that increasing the numbers of women in traditionally male-dominated jobs may result in a backlash from the male dominants in the form of sexual harassment, wage inequalities and limited opportunities for promotion (Yoder, 1991).

Dual commitments

Because women are generally perceived, and perceive themselves, to be the primary homemaker and carer in the family, women are under more pressure to take career breaks when they have children and to return to work only on a part-time basis. There is some evidence to suggest that this disadvantages women relative to men and that they find it harder to re-establish their careers in these circumstances (Maitland, 1998).

However, some service-sector organizations, notably banks, have realized the value of retaining women and enhancing their careers because of the costs of recruitment and training (Wise, 1988). In such organizations many flexible working practices have been introduced, such as homeworking, flexitime, job-share schemes and work-based crèches. It is likely that where women dominate an industry an increasing number of organizations will respond positively to encourage women returners.

Other minority groups

The organizational-culture approach offers most promise in understanding why members of other minorities find it difficult to gain entry and acceptance into many occupational roles and professions. It appears, on balance, that getting on in most occupations is facilitated by being a white middle-class man (Kanter, 1977). However, the specific difficulties faced by minority groups other than women is an under-researched area.

Anecdotal evidence suggests that individuals who do experience discrimination at work on the grounds of race are not always willing to take the organization to an industrial tribunal because they believe that they will find it difficult to return to work in the same organization and are likely to be seen as 'high risk' by potential employers.

It is also difficult for individuals to prove that they are being treated differently because of their gender, race or other factor. Additionally, research suggests that members of minority groups often do not believe they are treated any differently at work, despite the statistics that suggest otherwise; for example, under-representation in senior management positions (Sheppard, 1989).

The organizational perspective – "They just don't apply!"

The police and other organizations despair of trying to recruit more females and ethnic minorities because they find that these groups do not apply in sufficient numbers to enable adequate representation to be achieved. Why?

A study by Kandola and Keane (1998) suggests that at least part of the problem might be company image. Some organizations, such as the police, have a reputation (fairly or unfairly) for being sexist and racist and it is argued that this might deter minorities from applying. The sorts of strategies discussed above, such as positive role models, might be useful in these cases. The police are now advertising for recruits in parts of the press that minority groups are likely to read and find accessible.

Embodiment

A potentially fruitful line of research for understanding why it is difficult to attract minority groups into certain occupations is the concept of **embodiment**: the idea that a person's identity is more than their psychological make-up. Identity is also heavily inscribed on a person's body in the way they walk, talk, move and look. For example, being a woman is more than possessing the obvious physical characteristics; it is also associated with a certain way of walking, talking, sitting and looking. Class is another major variable that researchers suggest is embodied. Upper-class people look and sound different from those in the lower socio-economic classes. Research has shown that people are extremely proficient at judging class member-ship simply from photographs (Bourdieu, 1984).

Recently this concept has been used to examine embodied occu-pations: those jobs that require a person to look the part. A study by Cassell (1996), an American researcher, looked at the concept of embodi-ment as it applied to surgeons working in American hospitals. She found that women found it much more difficult to look the part of a surgeon than did their male counterparts and this was largely because of the way their work colleagues reacted to them. Male surgeons who behaved in an obstructive or unpleasant manner were perceived positively by both nursing staff and patients, whereas a female surgeon behaving in the same way was seen as a 'bitch'. Such women were also likely to face difficulties in their relations with nursing staff, who were less likely to cooperate with them. Another female surgeon advised a female colleague never to go into theatre without wearing lipstick in case people mistook her for a lesbian.

Cassell also documented the effects of being unable to adequately 'embody' a professional identity, which was basically experienced as being very uncomfortable. Cassell argues powerfully that embodied occu-pations (like surgery) will find it difficult to attract certain minorities simply because they are the 'wrong body'.

The important message from Cassell's research, however, is that people *do* differ because of their gender, their class, their religion or their ethnicity. These differences will not be experienced in the same way by everybody but, as a group, minorities may find it difficult to anticipate belonging to occupations which embody identities that they simply cannot assume. This situation will change only when, as Cassell argues, we do not ignore these differences or pretend that they do not exist but actually welcome the diversity that membership of a minority can bring to an occupation. And this, in turn, can only happen when it becomes easier for minorities to gain acceptance in non-traditional roles.

One of the real difficulties is that social conventions demand that we look the part when doing certain jobs. Managers are expected to look and dress smartly and people are expected to make an effort with the way they look when attending an interview. However, Cassell's work suggests that this may be a problem in itself. If we truly want to value difference then we need to relax about our expectations of what people should look like.

8.3 Methods of increasing workplace diversity

In the next part of the chapter we will examine methods organizations can use to increase workplace diversity before we move on to consider the more problematic area of managing diversity.

The methods organizations can use to increase workforce diversity can be grouped under two main headings: methods of attracting more members of minority groups; and methods of preventing discrimination against minority groups during recruitment and selection.

Methods of attracting minorities

Positive discrimination
One potentially fruitful means of increasing the numbers of members of minorities in occupations is through having all-minority shortlists. For instance, all women or all black women or all gay or whatever. However, this type of positive discrimination is often opposed by organizations and minorities alike, who argue that jobs should be obtained through merit and not any other characteristic (Holzer and Neumark, 1999).

This argument sounds very plausible but makes a fundamental assumption that is probably untrue: that on the whole selection decisions *are* based on merit. Research suggests that interviewers tend to select people who are like themselves: they recruit in their own image (Cook, 1998). Furthermore, selection decisions are often more irrational than arguments about merit judgements suggest (Herriot, 1989).

Flexible working practices
Flexible working practices are very important for attracting women and individuals whose religious beliefs mean they need to attend regular prayer or other meetings (Cooper and Lewis, 1998). There are several means of introducing flexible working, including flexitime and annualized hours. Flexitime is where the individual can start and finish work within a set of parameters that allow greater flexibility (e.g. start between 7 am and 10 am and finish between 3 pm and 6 pm).

Annualized hours differ in definition from one organization and industry to another, but in Germany, for example, in clerical jobs (which typically attract females) the individual is given the total amount of hours in a year that they have to work (say 450) and they can then choose (within limits) how to work these hours. So they could choose to work completely within school hours when it is term-time and not come in at all during school holidays.

Homeworking is becoming more and more feasible as technology advances into the home at an ever-increasing pace and as the service industry continues to expand, particularly the types of service that can be performed by homeworkers, such as financial, sales and marketing.

Methods of preventing discrimination against minority groups at selection

Equal-opportunities policies

An equal-opportunities policy is a method an organization can use to help prevent discrimination during recruitment, selection and employment. It is a written statement that outlines the organization's commitment to eradicating discrimination against individuals on the basis of membership of a minority and sets out the processes through which it intends to prevent discrimination and the steps any individual can take if they suspect that they or any one else is being discriminated against. Figure 8.1 shows a typical example of an equal-opportunities statement.

As you will appreciate, having a successful equal-opportunities policy needs more action than the sort of statement illustrated in Table 8.1. It also needs to be disseminated throughout the organization. Many organizations provide training in equal opportunities to members of the human resource or personnel department, who are then given responsibility for communicating the policy to the rest of the organization, often using workshops or team briefings. Reflection Box 8.1 is an example of how this was done in a public-sector organization and shows what a lengthy task this can be. Even if the policy is well thought through and implemented carefully, it is still not guaranteed to work (see Reflection Box 8.1).

Selection training

Selection training is usually carried out in conjunction with the implementation of an equal-opportunities policy. Selection training is concerned with raising awareness of processes that lead to discrimination. It is usually targetted at people who are involved in selection and focuses on a number of issues, such as avoiding both direct and indirect discrimination when compiling job advertisements and application forms; using structured interviewing techniques (in which every interviewee is asked the same questions); designing interview questions so they do not indirectly

Confidential Monitoring Questionnaire

1　**Name in full** . . . .

2　**Date of birth** . . . . **Age** . . . .

3　**Gender** (please tick box)

Male [　] Female [　]

4　**Marital status** (please tick box)

Married [　] Divorced [　] Separated [　]

Single [　] Widowed [　]

5　**Would you describe yourself as having a disability?**

Yes [　] No [　]

If yes, are you registered disabled?

Yes [　] No [　]

6　**Please tick the box from the following list which best describes the ethnic category to which you belong:**

White British [　] Black Caribbean [　] Pakistani [　]

White Irish [　] Black British [　] Bangladeshi [　]

White other [　] Black other [　] Chinese [　]
(please specify) (please specify)

Black African [　] Indian [　] Other [　]
(please specify)

7　**Are you employed/unemployed?** (please tick box)

Employed [　] Unemployed [　]

8　**Do you require/have a work permit?** (please tick box)

Yes [　] No [　]

Signature . . . . Date . . . .

Figure 8.1　　　An equal-opportunities – monitoring form.

Table 8.1 *Example of an equal-opportunities statement.*

1   Employees and applicants for employment of both sexes and of all racial groups have a right to equal opportunity of employment. The purpose of the following statement is to reinforce the awareness of all personnel of their duty to comply with the law on sex and race discrimination and to encourage a positive attitude towards fairness of treatment and opportunity. The Authority has adopted policies to prevent unlawful discrimination and promote equal opportunity in employment. The following statement of policy should be read carefully and fully observed at all times. The Authority will aim to ensure that no job applicant or employee receives less favourable treatment than another on the grounds of sex, marital/parental status, race, colour, ethnic or national origin, nationality, creed, religion, trade union or political beliefs, sexual orientation, age (within the context of normal retirement age and Home Office Regulations), disability or any other requirements which cannot be shown to be justified. The Authority is also committed to a working environment where personnel are free from harassment at work. This incorporates: sexual harassment, racial harassment, harassment of a general nature (i.e. bullying).

2   The Chief Fire Officer/Chief Emergency Planning Officer have responsibility for the implementation and monitoring of this policy. As part of this process, policies and practices within the Authority will be continually monitored and revised. The intention is to ensure that managers and other relevant decision makers understand their position in law. Within the Authority's policy, training and guidance will be provided.

3   The law requires that individuals shall not unlawfully discriminate or help others to do so. Eliminating discrimination and providing equality of opportunity depends upon personal commitment and all members of the Authority without exception must observe the requirements of the Equal Opportunities Policy and apply its principles.

4   Discrimination is not always intentional or overt. Practices and policies within the Authority will be consistently monitored to ensure that the Equal Opportunities Policy is being properly implemented and where barriers to equal opportunity are identified, necessary changes will be made.

5   Apart from consideration of equality of opportunity and strict compliance with the law, the efficiency of any organization will clearly be improved if it seeks to develop the skills and abilities of all employees.

discriminate (e.g. asking about child-care arrangements); and raising awareness of the sorts of personal bias that influences judgements. See Reflection Box 8.2 for an example of the type of technique used.

Legal definitions of sex and racial discrimination

The Sex Discrimination Acts make it unlawful to discriminate against a person directly or indirectly on the grounds of sex and/or marriage.

Direct sex discrimination occurs when a person of one sex is treated less favourably on grounds of sex than a person of the other sex would be in the same circumstances (e.g. advertising for a handyman rather than a handyperson).

Indirect sex discrimination consists of applying requirements or conditions which, whether intentional or not, adversely affect a considerably larger proportion of one sexual group than another which cannot be justified (e.g. demanding technical qualifications which few women possess and which are not

Reflection Box 8.1 Trying to improve equality of opportunity in the Fire Brigade

A municipal UK Fire Brigade services an area of 500 square miles, with 12 fire stations and employs a total of 113 firefighters. Like all fire brigades in the UK it employs very few female, black or Asian fire fighters. (The London Fire Service has a much better record than any other.) Like all public service providers the Brigade is inspected from time to time by Her Majesty's Inspectorate (HMI), a body responsible for commenting on all aspects of an organization's performance. Like many others the Brigade here has been criticized for its failure to improve the profile of its employees in respect of race and gender.

In an attempt to improve this situation the Brigade decided to put on in-house workshops to promote the idea of equal-opportunities. These workshops were designed and delivered by a female personnel officer in conjunction with a member of the fire brigade's Union. The workshops consisted of an outline of the Brigade's equal-opportunities policy, an explanation of its importance and an opportunity to discuss concerns and issues. The main aim of the workshops was to improve knowledge of equal-opportunities legislation and to clear up any misconceptions firefighters might have, such as what constitutes 'unreasonable behaviour' in terms of sexual or racial harassment or discrimination.

Initially, the workshops were greeted with scepticism and cynicism. Firefighters opposed the idea of female fighters because of issues such as sleeping arrangements (watches of firemen generally share a dormitory during night shifts); swearing (they would have to stop using bad language if women came into the service) and marital issues (their wives and partners would not like them virtually 'living with another woman' during their time on duty).

The personnel officer and the union official were able to discuss many of these issues to the point where, in the personnel officer's view, the majority of firefighters saw the reasonableness of bringing more females into the brigade. She said 'There are still a few bigots around but, on the whole, things seem to be moving in the right direction.' The HMI during their last visit expressed delight with the amount of knowledge about the Brigade's equal-opportunities policy and firefighters' knowledge of their own responsibilities with respect to it. The HMI suggested, however, that there was still a considerable attitudinal mountain to climb and that it was still necessary for the Brigade to win hearts and minds.

The personnel officer feels that attitudes have altered since the first round of training almost 3 years ago. She feels that people are much more welcoming and accepting of diversity; some gay firefighters having recently come out and been supported by their colleagues; the Chief Fire Officer has insisted that all personnel stop using the term firemen and only use the term firefighters and two female recruits have recently been employed, the first ever in the history of this brigade.

How would you judge whether attitudes were changing? Is the evidence being used by this fire brigade sufficient to suggest that there is reason for optimism? Would you like to be the only female firefighter on a watch? What could be done to encourage more females to apply?

necessary for the job would be indirect discrimination against a woman who did not possess those qualifications).

The Race Relations Act makes it unlawful to discriminate against a person directly or indirectly in the area of employment.

Direct discrimination consists of treating a person on racial grounds less favourably than others are, or would be treated, in the same circumstances. Segregating a person from others on racial grounds constitutes less favourable treatment (e.g. not considering applications from people of a specific racial group).

Indirect discrimination consists of applying requirements or conditions intentionally or not which adversely affect a

Reflection Box 8.2 Raising awareness of personal biases

A group of careers officers were asked to attend equal-opportunities training by the local authority that employed them. The training focused on legislative aspects of equal opportunities, interview techniques and the design of interviews and application forms. There were also discussion sessions and group tasks to complete that were designed to raise awareness of personal biases. Here is one of them:

A young boy is admitted to an accident-and-emergency unit at a hospital, having been involved in a serious car accident. The boy was unconscious and accompanied by his father who had been in the car accident with him but who had thankfully sustained only minor injuries. The boy was rushed to the operating theatre on arrival while his father waited anxiously for news. When the boy was wheeled into the theatre the on-duty surgeon, waiting to operate on the boy, turned visibly white and exclaimed 'My God! This is my son!'

The question is: What is the relationship between the surgeon and the boy? See the end of the chapter for the answer, if you don't know.

considerably larger proportion of one racial group than another which cannot be justified (e.g. advertising only in mainly white residential areas of the recruitment vicinity).

Minority monitoring

Again, this usually is implemented in conjunction with an equal-opportunities policy and is mainly used by large organizations that do a great deal of recruitment. Minority monitoring is a straightforward statistical check on the diversity profile of an organization. The gender, race, religion and other minority characteristics of individuals are collected from candidates who apply for employment within any given organization and the percentage of minority applicants who are actually offered posts is checked against all other applicants to ensure that there is no systematic discrimination (wittingly or unwittingly). See Figure 8.1 for a typical example of a minority-monitoring form sent to job applicants. For example, if an organization found that 5 per cent of its Asian applicants were eventually offered posts compared with 45 per cent of its white applicants they would need to scrutinize the selection process and identify whether the imbalance was occurring across the board or in specific departments or locations.

Minority monitoring is extremely useful but is only helpful if any suspect statistics are actually checked out and dealt with.

8.4 Managing diversity

Increasing the amount of diversity in an organization is simply a starting point. The biggest challenge facing organizations is how to *manage* diversity. This is the topic we are now going to address. You will probably note from the references at the end of this chapter that the majority of the research and commentary on managing diversity comes from North America. In the main this is because North America has a culturally diverse workforce and a greater number of different races make up any given workforce. For these reasons problems of managing diversity have become more apparent and attracted research there. Additionally, as we have already noted, many minority lobbies in North America are powerful and are able to put pressure on the Government to introduce legislation.

In this part of the chapter we are going to review various recommended approaches for managing workforce diversity. You might find it useful to examine the extent to which the approaches discussed here might help resolve the problems presented in **Case Study 6 'Take your mother not your lover'**. Having reviewed these approaches and some of the research into their effectiveness, we will conclude the chapter with a critique of the managing-diversity literature.

Approaches to managing diversity

In a recent review of diversity initiatives Dass and Parker (1999) suggest that diversity initiatives can be classified under three headings – episodic, free standing and systemic.

Episodic approaches

Episodic approaches are likely to be prevalent in an organization in which diversity is seen as a relatively unimportant issue, so that it experiences little pressure to embrace its problems. Problems that appear to be a consequence of poor diversity management are dealt with individually not systematically. For instance, a company might dismiss a case of racial discrimination as a 'one-off' (Rice, 1994) or might send its managers on a 1-week seminar on diversity issues (Dass and Parker, 1999).

The difficulty with the episodic approach is that issues, such as discrimination, are not examined at sufficient depth. Kandola and Fullerton (1998), for instance, argue against the use of training as a solution to managing diversity. They argue that if training is not supported by a culture that actually values diversity it is unlikely to be successful.

Free-standing approaches

Free-standing approaches are likely to be adopted by organizations that are being put under pressure to manage diversity and who think of the issue as significant but not central to their corporate aims and activities. In such organizations diversity initiatives are likely to be formal but are not related to the company's core activities. For instance, there may be formal internal training for managers about diversity issues and consciousness-raising activities in which diversity issues are brought up and discussed openly (as in Reflection Box 8.1). And there are likely to be policies about harassment and how to follow a grievance procedure if an employee believes their minority status is affecting the way they are treated at work. However, these various initiatives are not seen as central to the organization's goals and hence are not formally monitored or evaluated. We will say more about this in the next section.

Systemic approaches

Systemic approaches are likely to be found in organizations in which there is a high level of external pressure to increase and manage diversity and where the power holders in the organization perceive diversity to be a strategic issue. In such organizations diversity is closely related to the organization's strategic plan and, as a consequence, all the activities aimed at managing diversity are monitored, supported and evaluated. For example, the organization would include diversity within its corporate plan: "Company X wishes to increase the amount of Asian and black employees by 8 per cent over the next two years." Once stated in these terms the company has to set about thinking how it is going to achieve this aim and how to support, monitor and evaluate it. A company might reward managers who show they are actively able to retain and promote Black and Asian employees (support); it will monitor the amount of Black and Asian people applying and will act on any discrepancies between the percentage employed compared with more traditional employees (monitor); and it will check whether its target has been achieved at the end of the 2-year period specified in the aim (evaluate).

Most authors on diversity believe that, if the management of it is to be successful, it must be tied into the company's strategic aims (Kandola and Fullerton, 1998; Herriot and Pemberton, 1995).

Herriot and Pemberton, in their review of diversity initiatives, have a slightly different classification from that of Dass and Parker. They classify diversity approaches gastronomically as follows: vindaloo, nouvelle cuisine and Sunday lunch.

Vindaloo

 Companies that follow the vindaloo approach to diversity management tend to operate by the process of assimilation. In such companies the recruitment and selection processes operate to attract and retain individuals who are 'like' existing members of the organization. People who do not 'fit in' with existing members are likely to leave. As a consequence, the organization comes to consist of people who are highly similar in beliefs, attitudes and behaviours. Like a real vindaloo, although the ingredients are different at the start, once they've been boiled up together they all end up tasting the same.

The problem with the vindaloo approach is that it ignores the fact that real differences do exist between people and so makes it difficult for certain groups to gain a legitimate foothold.

Nouvelle cuisine

Nouvelle cuisine is characterized by companies that are very keen to have members of certain minorities in prominent positions. Such companies may have a small number of minority-group members in key roles in the organization but, in making such a transparent (albeit genuine) attempt to encourage this, they can attract criticisms of 'tokenism': placing members of minorities within the organization to deflect attention away from the fact that, on the whole, minorities are not well represented. Herriot and Pemberton have labelled this approach nouvelle cuisine because it is focused (or appears to be focused) largely on presenting the *appearance* of being committed to diversity, whilst in reality paying lip service to it.

Sunday lunch

Sunday lunch is similar to the systemic approach described by Dass and Parker (1999). In the Sunday lunch approach differences are valued for themselves and each set of differences is seen as complementary to each other. All differences contribute to the organization's goals and differences are encouraged through organizational policies. Like a real Sunday lunch such an approach recognizes that the value of difference comes from the way each part of the lunch contributes to the complete experience of the meal.

Implicit in both Herriot and Pemberton's and Dass and Parker's work is the notion that diversity is something that needs to be truly valued by an organization if it is managed effectively. Before we go on to think about how an organization might set about encouraging its employees to value diversity consider the scenario in Reflection Box 8.3.

8.5 A model for managing diversity

The following model, shown in Figure 8.2, is taken from Kandola and Fullerton (1998). Their aim is to show how organizations can move

Reflection Box 8.3 Don't blame me, blame my customers!

A small business based in the North-East of England sells information-technology services and wanted to recruit a skilled salesperson to open up a difficult local market. The company employed three staff, all in administrative roles, and was overseen by the company owner and managing director. A recruitment advertisement was placed in a local paper. There were more than 50 applicants which the managing director reduced to a shortlist of five on the basis of their previous relevant work experience.

The shortlisted candidates were invited for interview. Two were outstanding at interview, one of whom was a young Asian man, a graduate with a good degree, but who had been able only to secure sales jobs since graduating 3 years before. The managing director discussed the two candidates with his team in order to make a decision about which one to select. Although the team felt the Asian was probably the better candidate, the managing director decided not to give him the post because, he argued, a lot of his customers probably were racist and he couldn't afford to lose business.

To what extent do approaches to diversity management take account of the broader social context within which companies are located? What, if anything, could be done to account for these contexts?

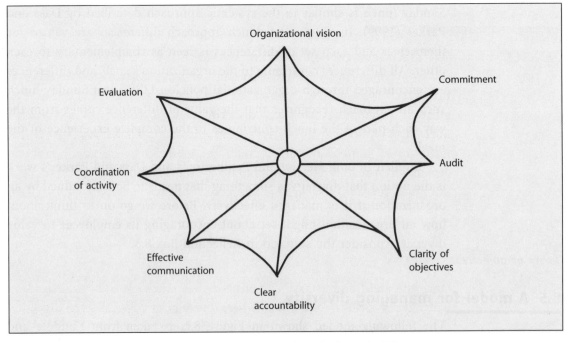

Figure 8.2   The strategy web [adapted from Kandola and Fullerton (1998)].

towards the Sunday lunch (Herriot and Pemberton) or the systemic (Dass and Parker) method of diversity management. The model is presented as a web to emphasize the point that each spoke of the web is connected to each and every other. Let's start at the top and work round.

Organizational vision

The recommendation here is that organizations should make a clear statement about why diversity is considered to be important and on the ways in which diversity is linked to their business objectives. The vision should emphasize that managing diversity is the responsibility of all employees and that the strategy is concerned with developing every individual's potential.

Top-management commitment

Senior managers should make sure that their own commitment to diversity is made clear to all employees, either by fronting the diversity campaign or by attending diversity training sessions, to communicate to staff the importance of the diversity initiative.

Auditing and assessment of needs

The organization should examine its culture and the systems and procedures in operation and the make-up of their human resources. For instance, in examining culture a company may wish to assess the attitudes of employees towards diversity. Among its systems and procedures it might look at its current selection and appraisal systems. And the make-up of human resources could be achieved by an organizational census in which relevant biographical details would be gathered and examined for signs of discrimination (see minority monitoring in Section 8.3).

Clarity of objectives

Once the audit and assessment of needs has taken place an organization will have a clearer idea about where the blocks to successful diversity management may lie. They may, for instance, establish that there is something wrong with their selection procedure. Or they may find that employees do not understand what diversity means or why they should be concerned about it. Whatever the audit uncovers, it is important that the organization sets out a clearly defined strategy for tackling issues and a timetable for their resolution. However, Kandola and Fullerton point out that such objectives should not be seen as 'targets set in stone' but rather as benchmarks against which the organization's progress can be checked (but which might be changed as more is learned through the process).

Clear accountability

Once the strategies identified through the audit and setting of objectives have been established, accountability for ensuring they are implemented has to be decided. Kandola and Fullerton recommend that accountability should not reside solely in the human-resource department but should be devolved within the whole organization. Reward systems might be modified to encompass this, such that managers are rewarded for meeting the objectives set within the various diversity strategies. However, it must be remembered that managers need to do more than increase the numbers of people from minority groups; they must also be responsible for their retention and development. Any reward system needs to account for this to avoid what Kandola and Fullerton call the revolving door: plenty of minority members come in, but go straight out again when they realize they are there simply to make up numbers.

Effective communication

There are three important aspects of communication:

1   the vision, importance and goals of the diversity strategy have to be communicated to all employees;
2   the various strategies to be used to manage diversity need to be explained so that people know what the strategies are supposed to achieve and why they have been introduced in the first place;
3   feedback from all concerned to monitor the effectiveness of the diversity strategies and to identify stumbling blocks to their successful implementation.

Communicating in this way will not only help to foster ownership of the diversity initiative but will also enable the diversity strategy to be modified where appropriate. Training is seen as one of the key practices for these sorts of communication, though Kandola and Fullerton are cautious about training because they believe some of the content of training courses might serve to reinforce stereotypes rather than break them down. Training, in their view, should be used to facilitate learning rather than to encourage particular ways of thinking.

Co-ordination of activity

Individuals, or groups of individuals, need to be given specific responsibility for coordinating the various parts of the diversity initiative, for deciding what needs to be communicated to whom and for providing the organization with the 'big picture'. Such people, who might have specially designated jobs (diversity director, perhaps), are needed to ensure that the diversity strategy is on course and that all those involved are fully aware of the total set of activities, how they are related and what progress is being made.

Evaluation

Evaluation of the diversity strategy must be done against the set objectives. It should also be ongoing and used as a learning device. Evaluation feedback should be given to all organization members as soon as possible so that the initiative is seen to be having tangible effects.

8.6 Managing diversity: a conclusion and critique

Most authors interested in diversity agree that if organizations truly want to foster a diverse workforce they should incorporate it into their strategic plans rather than implement it piecemeal. Dass and Parker (1999) suggest that if companies are not serious about diversity, attempting to adopt the sort of strategy outlined by Kandola and Fullerton is most unlikely to bear fruit. Dass and Parker (1999) suggest that championing diversity in conditions in which there are few external pressures to increase it can alarm shareholders and stiffen internal resistance when the diversity programme fails to achieve its promises.

So, how can organizations be persuaded to take diversity seriously? It is probably unwise to suggest that organizations have something to gain in a business sense from increasing workforce diversity. Suggesting that diversity 'adds value' really makes it more difficult to persuade organizations to take the issue seriously, because the evidence that diversity delivers what some authors promise is simply not there.

Comer and Soliman (1996) found that very few companies that have implemented a diversity initiative have actually evaluated it. As they suggest, this is possibly because the programmes have not delivered the promises made for them. And, as Dale (1998) argues, some diversity programmes have been introduced for fashion's sake rather than for business or ethical reasons.

How straightforward is it to implement a strategy such as that suggested by Kandola and Fullerton? Creating a vision and securing top-management commitment are probably the easiest goals to achieve. However, in many organizations there is a great deal of cynicism about mission statements and messages about commitment from senior management because, as Dale (1998) points out, the workforce perceive initiatives such as diversity as just another 'management fad'.

Assessing and auditing the current situation is a lot less straightforward than the strategy model implies. Gathering reliable evidence about attitudes to issues such as diversity and persuading people to say what they really think is notoriously difficult.

Political correctness may encourage people to espouse one particular set of attitudes. Also, individuals may not perceive that there is anything wrong and may not believe that any blocks to diversity exist, no matter what statistics might suggest. Marshall (1984), for example, found that despite the fact that female managers were far less likely to be promoted than their male counterparts many claimed never to have experienced sexism or other forms of discrimination.

Clear accountability and effective communication are also more problematic than the model implies. Like many of the approaches to diversity management in the literature, it is assumed that the majority of the organization's members will be interested in and concerned about diversity. Such assumptions are based on a **unitarist** view of organizations; that is, that people in an organization basically want and believe in the same things. As we discussed in Chapter 7, most organizations are in fact **pluralist**: different people want and believe in different things. If this is true, achieving clear accountability and effective communication will not be straightforward because some people simply will not be interested. As Kandola and Fullerton suggest an important tool in this regard is the

---

Reflection Box 8.4 Encouraging managers to change their values through reward systems

A police force was concerned about the amount of human-resource problems that appeared to be created by welfare issues. They found that sickness absence and premature retirements were related to poor treatment handed out by senior officers. In an attempt to change the situation training programmes were introduced that encouraged senior officers to think more deeply about the welfare needs of their staff and how to cope with welfare problems. (A typical problem might be an officer who was under pressure because of debt.)

Convinced that training alone would not succeed in producing the behavioural changes required, success at passing promotion panels was linked to senior officers' ability to successfully answer questions relating to welfare matters. Two years following the introduction of these procedures there appeared to be no discernible change in the behaviour of senior officers nor in levels of absenteeism or premature retirements.

How could an organization set about making more rigorous linkages between values and rewards?

---

reward system in the organization. However, this must be carefully thought through (see Reflection Box 8.4).

On the whole, therefore, while models like that offered by Kandola and Fullerton are to be applauded for attempting to address the issue in a strategic way, they are probably too prescriptive and naive in their assumptions.

8.7 Summary

We began this chapter by defining diversity, noting that it is concerned with *all* the ways in which individuals differ from one another. Having described some of the research that shows the ways in which minority groups can be disadvantaged, we moved on to examine the literature on the reasons for these disadvantages, specifically in relation to the workplace.

We examined the notion that the career progression of women can be impeded by 'invisible barriers' that are located in organizational culture. Research has suggested that when men numerically dominate an organization the culture comes to reflect male ways of thinking and behaving. It has been suggested that this prevents women from being able to participate fully in both the formal and informal aspects of organizational life, with the consequence that they may be perceived as less competent than their male counterparts.

Another body of literature suggests that the differential career progression of women relative to men can be traced back to socialization processes. The argument here is that boys and girls are raised with different expectations about appropriate ways to behave and feel. This encourages men and women into different jobs. These socialization effects are reinforced by workplace processes. For instance, women may be perceived as being 'good at relationships' and filtered into roles that involve interpersonal skills. Men and women may be stereotyped as possessing certain characteristics which in turn are perceived to be important prerequisites for some jobs. Research suggests that management characteristics are often perceived to be more typical of men as a group than of women.

We then looked at the issue from the other side of the fence: what difficulties do organizations face in trying to attract and recruit minorities. We noted that company image or reputation can be a factor here. Another emerging body of research suggests that some occupations are embodied: they involve the need to 'look the part'. Certain minorities may be deterred from applying for certain jobs because they cannot see themselves performing that role; they are the 'wrong body'.

The chapter moved on to consider a range of practices that organizations can introduce to both attract more minorities and prevent discrimination against them during selection. We argued that even if an organization succeeds in increasing minorities within the workforce it still needs to consider how to manage diversity. We looked at the literature that has examined different approaches to diversity management, noting that the majority of research appeared to agree that successful initiatives were those that tied diversity to the achievement of organizational goals. We then presented a model aimed at helping organizations to take a strategic approach to diversity management.

We concluded the chapter by suggesting that diversity-management models were somewhat naive in the assumptions they make about the nature of organizations and the people within them.

Questions

Self-test questions

1 List the sources of workforce diversity.
2 In what ways are minorities disadvantaged in the workplace?
3 What does the term 'glass ceiling' mean?
4 In what ways might organizational culture impede the career progression of women?
5 In what ways does socialization affect the self-perceptions of men and women?
6 Describe how organizations reinforce societal expectations about appropriate roles for men and women.
7 What does the term 'dual commitment' mean?
8 Define the concept of embodiment and illustrate how it affects career aspirations.
9 Describe the practices that organizations can use to attract minorities.
10 Describe the practices organizations can use to prevent discrimination against minorities during the selection process.
11 Why do organizations need to be concerned with managing as well as increasing workforce diversity?
12 Outline three approaches to diversity management.
13 Detail the features of the managing-diversity strategy web.
14 Explain some of the limitations of the strategy-web approach.

Discussion questions

1 If a lack of workforce diversity is not creating any particular performance problems for organizations, why should they be concerned about it?
2 Is it feasible or appropriate to talk about an organizational culture as reflecting male ways of thinking and behaving?
3 Changing societal norms will eventually filter through to organizational practices and the position of minorities will improve accordingly. We should wait until then rather than worrying about their position now. Discuss.
4 How can an organization realistically assess the attitudes of its employees towards diversity issues, given that most people genuinely do not believe themselves to be racist or sexist?

5   Which theories or concepts covered in this chapter best explain the problems described in **Case Study 6 'Take your mother not your lover'?**

Answer to Reflection Box 8.2: The surgeon is the boy's mother.

References and bibliography

Bhavnani, R. (1994) *Black Women in the Labour Market*. Manchester: EOC.

Bourdieu, P. (1984) *Distinction: A Social Critique of the Judgement of Taste* (translated by Nice, R.), Cambridge, MA: Harvard University Press.

Breugal, I. (1989) Sex and race in the labour market, *Feminist Review*, **32**, 49–68.

Brown J., Maidment, A. and Bull, R. (1992) Appropriate skill-task matching or gender bias in deployment of male and female officers?, *Policing and Society*, **2**, 1–16.

Cassell, J. (1996) The woman in the surgeon's body: Understanding difference, *American Anthropologist*, **98**(1), 41–53.

Comer, D. R. and Soliman, C. E. (1996) Organizational efforts to manage diversity: do they really work? *Journal of Management Issues*, **8**(4), 470–484.

Cook, M. (1998) *Personnel Selection* (third edition), Chichester: Wiley.

Cooper, C. L. and Lewis, S. (1998) *How to Manage Your Career, Family and Life*, London: Kogan Page.

Crompton, R. and Jones, M. (1984) *White-collar Proletariat*, London: Macmillan.

Dale, K. (1998) Managing diversity: Human resource for transforming the workplace (book review), *Industrial Relations Journal*, **29**(1), 92–93.

Dass, P. and Parker, B. (1999) Strategies for managing human resource diversity: from resistance to learning, *The Academy of Management Executive*, **13**(2), 68–84.

Deaux, K. (1976) Sex: A perspective on the attribution process. In Harvey, J. H., Ickes, W. and Kidd, R. (eds) *New Dimensions in Attribution Research*, Volume 1, Hillsdale, NJ: Erlbaum.

Department of Employment (1988) *Labour Force Survey*, London: HMSO.

Dickens, L. (1997) Gender, race and employment equality in Britain: Inadequate strategies and the role of industrial relations actors, *Industrial Relations Journal*, **28**(4), 282–290.

Eagly, A. H. and Johnson, B. T. (1990) Gender and leadership style: A meta-analysis, *Psychological Bulletin*, **108**, 233–256.

Grant, J. (1988) Women as managers: What they can offer to organizations, *Organizational Dynamics*, **16**(3), 56–63.

Graves, L. M. and Powell, G. N. (1996) Sex similarity, quality of the employment interview and recruiters' evaluations of actual applicants, *Journal of Occupational and Organizational Psychology*, **69**(3), 243–262.

Hackett, G. and Betz, N. (1981) A self-efficacy approach to the career development of women, *Journal of Vocational Behavior*, **18**, 326–339.

Herriot, P. (1989) (ed.) *Assessment and Selection in Organisations*, Chichester: Wiley.

Herriot, P. and Pemberton, C. (1995) *Competitive Advantage Through Diversity: Organizational Learning Through Difference*, London: Sage.

Hitt, M. A. and Barr, S. H. (1989) Managerial selection decision models: Examination of configural cue processing, *Journal of Applied Psychology*, **74**, 53–61.

Holzer, H. and Neumark, D. (1999) Are affirmative action hires less qualified? Evidence from employer-employee data on new hires, *Journal of Labor Economics*, **17**(3), 534–575.

Kandola, B. and Keane, C. (1998) But they just don't apply. . . . Paper presented to *British Psychological Society Occupational Psychology Conference, January, Eastbourne*.

Kandola, R. and Fullerton J. (1998) *Diversity in Action: Managing the Mosaic* (second edition), London: IPD.

Kanter, R. M. (1977) *Men and Women of the Corporation*, New York: Basic Books.

Kerfoot, D. and Knights, D. (1996) The best is yet to come? The quest for embodiment in managerial work. In Collinson, D. and Hearn, J. (eds) *Men As Managers, Managers As Men: Critical Perspectives on Men, Masculinities and Managements*, London: Sage.

Labour Market Trends (1996) Women in the labour market. Results from the *Spring Labour Force Survey, March*.

Maitland, A. (1998) Pick up where you left off. *The Financial Times*, 26 November, p. 15.

Marshall, J. (1984) *Women Managers: Travellers in a Male World*, Chichester: Wiley.

Morash, M. and Greene, J. R. (1986) Evaluating women on patrol: A critique of contemporary wisdom, *Evaluation Review*, **10**(2), 230–255.

Osland, J. S., Monteze, M. S. and Hunter, L. (1998) A comparative study of managerial styles among female executives in Nicaragua and Costa Rica, *International Studies of Management and Organization*, **28**(2), 54–65.

Polachek, S. (1976) Occupational segregation: An alternative hypothesis, *Journal of Contemporary Business*, **5**, 1–12.

Reskin, B. and Hartmann, H. (eds) (1986) *Women's Work, Men's Work*, Washington, DC: National Academy Press.

Rice, F. (1994) How to make diversity pay, *Fortune*, 8 August, p. 78.

Riley, P. A. (1983) A structurationist account of political culture, *Administrative Science Quarterly*, **28**, 414–437.

Robinson, J. G. and McIllwee, J. S. (1991) Men, women, and the culture of engineering, *The Sociological Quarterly*, **32**(3), 403–421.

Rosener, J. (1990) Ways women lead, *Harvard Business Review*, **68**(6), 119–145.

Rosenthal, P., Guest, D. and Peccei, R. (1996) Gender differences in managers' causal explanations for their work performance: A study in two organizations, *Journal of Occupational and Organizational Psychology*, **69**(2), 145–152.

Schein, V. E. (1973) The relationship between sex role stereotypes and requisite management characteristics, *Journal of Applied Psychology*, **57**, 95–100.

Schein, V. E. (1975) The relationship between sex role stereotypes and requisite management characteristics among female managers, *Journal of Applied Psychology*, **60**, 340–344.

Sheppard, D. (1989) Organizations, power and sexuality: The image and self-image of women managers. In Hearn, J., Sheppard, D., Tancred-Sherrif, P. and Burrell, G. (eds) *The Sexuality of Organization*, London: Sage.

Wise, J. (1988) British banks give women more time to bring up baby, *American Banker*, 16 May, p. 20.

Yoder, J. D. (1991) Rethinking tokenism: Looking beyond numbers, *Gender and Society*, **5**(2), 178–192.

9

Organizational and management development

Contents

Objectives

By the end of this chapter you should be able to:

- appreciate how organizations change and develop over time
- describe the main techniques of organizational development
- evaluate the concept of knowledge management as applied to organizations
- be aware of the significance of management development to the organizational development process

9.1 Introduction

As the competitive environment becomes tougher, organizations can respond by becoming more able and expert in the areas that are **business critical** for them (in other words, their survival depends on it) and devoting fewer resources to areas of lower business value. These critical areas are the ones that define the organization's structure and skills mix. To change them means judgements have to be made about what the future holds and how best to respond to it. This process is what we call organizational development (OD). With the churning business environment that many organizations are now facing, the need for almost continuous OD has become more pressing.

A simple definition of OD is to say it is *a means of changing the organization in any way that makes it better able to meet its agreed objectives.* In practical terms this means using different technological approaches, retraining or replacing staff and a whole range of other interventions that enable the organization to perform better.

More complicated definitions can be found in French and Bell (1995), where the authors claim that:

> OD is a top management-supported long-range effort to improve an organisation's problem solving and renewal processes, particularly through a more effective and collaborative diagnosis and management of organisation culture.

Another definition is provided by Porras and Robertson (1992), for whom OD is:

> A set of behavioural science-based theories, values, strategies and techniques aimed at the planned change of the organisational work setting for the purpose of enhancing individual development and improving organisational performance, through the alteration of organisational members' on-the-job behaviours.

The crucial element in these definitions is that they emphasize the significance of the social sciences. There are many ways of changing organizations, such as introducing new accounting systems, new appraisal schemes or physical layout changes. *None* of these is really OD, although they may well lead to increases in performance. It is the concern with **knowledge-based solutions** to issues of organizational performance that gives OD its particular characteristics and importance. Such changes in the organization

knowledge base (what the organization holds in its collective memory) usually mean redefining relationships between groups, individuals or areas. What are the characteristics of successful OD?

- OD is a *long-term process*. It has to do with *complex and lasting change*. As a result there must be a clear link between the strategic planning process and OD to ensure that strategic decisions actually work at the operational level.
- OD *must* have the support of top management, who are usually the chief **power brokers** and **change agents** in any organization. So, any attempts to make significant impact without them is doomed to failure.
- OD effects change through a learning process. As employees learn about what is now required by the OD process, new ideas, beliefs and attitudes emerge which change both the behaviour and the culture of the organization. So, employees at the end of the development chain need to be involved in the generation of new answers to old problems and new answers to new problems. They should similarly be included in setting new targets, developing change objectives, considering solutions and evaluating the new state against the old.

According to Harvey and Brown (1996) a central tenet of OD should be that everyone who is likely to be involved in the changes should have an opportunity to contribute to them. According to Rothwell *et al.* (1995) 'Organisational effectiveness and humanistic values meet as employee ownership increases in change processes and outcomes.'

Research by Porras and Hoffer (1986), who asked 42 leading OD specialists what it was that they achieved from successful assignments, revealed:

- more open communications;
- more collaborative relationships;
- more willingness to take responsibility;
- maintenance of a shared vision;
- more effective problem solving;
- more respect and support shown for colleagues;
- more effective interaction with other members of the organization;
- more inquisitiveness to ensure that things were being done right;
- more openness to experiment with new ways of doing things.

According to Burke (1987) there are at least five major challenges that OD specialists are likely to face in the future:

- A move in many major corporations from growth to consolidation. If the demands for performance improvement remain it follows that many organizations will be expected to yield more from less as the revenue increases from pure growth are denied them. The resulting increases in **organizational stressors** (things that cause difficulties within the organization) are likely to provide much work for the OD consultant as new approaches are required to provide internally driven growth.

- Organizations that found it tough to move at only moderate speeds will now have to move much faster. Advances in communications technology have now created a 24-hour market place that requires decisions to be made on business movements much more quickly. Organizational structures and relationships that might have been based on a different more sedate era cannot be allowed to hold back the adoption and exploitation of new opportunities.

- Organizational complexity and diversity are continuing to increase. Legislative controls now exist over a whole range of actions (e.g. employment) which were previously within the domain of the organization. Diversity among employees also poses questions for those organizations seeking to operate on a global basis. A corporate culture biased towards certain ethnic or moral beliefs may not hold fast in other areas of the business world.

- Managers will be seeking ever faster and more effective interventions. Under pressure to perform, most managers may feel unable to wait for the results of a strategic OD intervention to 'kick in' after 3 or 4 years, even though behavioural and cultural change which most effective OD is all about may need the benefit of time to emerge.

- **Organizational stakeholders** (anyone with an interest in what the organization does or does not do and how they do it) have shown a renewed awareness of ethical issues as pressure groups flex their muscles in areas such as ecology and the environment. The rights of individuals as employees as well as customers are being given increasing weight both legislatively and by means of investigative media reporting.

> ### Reflection Box 9.1 What does the ideal organization look like?
>
> In order to be effective organizations need to be responsive, flexible and forward-thinking. They have to be able to manage things right internally through excellent communication and involvement of employees in decision-making processes and externally by being able to monitor what is going on in their market place and knowing how to react effectively.
>
> Think about some businesses you are familiar with. What stops them from achieving excellence in all of these areas?
>
> Find out what you can about the objectives of your educational institution and consider how you would recommend they develop to meet them. What resources are essential? How will the necessary resources be acquired and secured? How should they be managed? And how will the institution ensure that all the stakeholders are given a chance to contribute?

9.2 Models of organizational development

Models of organizational development and change are simply representations of the steps to be followed in carrying out an OD intervention. Models are often based on research of past practices so they cannot always accurately predict new ones. But they do give a framework for discussion and bring a better understanding of what needs to be done and when.

The organization life-cycle model

Smither *et al.* (1996) believe that over time most organizations become larger and more complicated. For them it is possible to speak of a typical **organizational life cycle** in which the organization goes through a number of stages from birth to decline. Figure 9.1 shows the typical life cycle.

In each phase of the cycle a different style of management is required. In the **birth** phase the organization needs **entrepreneurial flair** to seize opportunities. It can survive with a fairly informal structure. Things can get done by everyone 'mucking in' together without having to obey strict hierarchies or rulebooks. As the organization grows, direct owner control is usually replaced by a group of managers.

As the complexity of the organization grows a management cadre must be in place to oversee existing and future actions. Moving into the **growth**

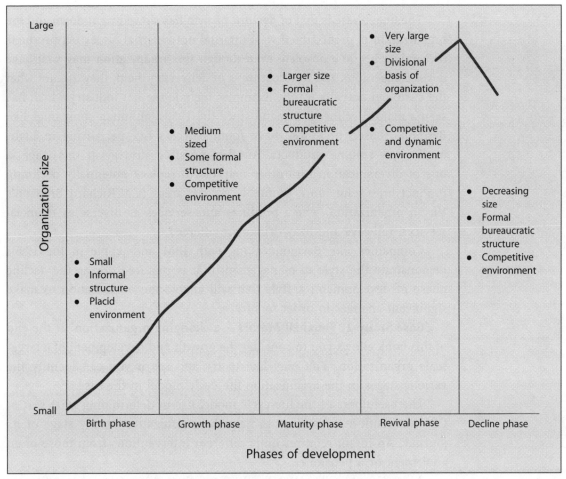

Figure 9.1   The organizational life cycle [adapted from Smither *et al.* (1996)].

phase is where increased specialization within the organization often leads to functional division and the subsequent redistribution of managerial responsibilities from senior to middle management.

During the **maturity** phase of the cycle, growth will begin to slow down and the management task now focuses on getting more out of established relationships. Often during this phase the organization itself slows down its internal processes and decisions start to take longer to get through the increased layers of **bureaucracy** that have been built up to support the growth of the earlier phase.

If the organization becomes so ineffective that restructuring, innovation or major renewal is required, the next phase of the life cycle, **revival,** could see the return to growth and even rapid expansion if the strategic vision to take the company forward is right.

The final phase is that of **decline**, growth has slowed right down and the organization is preoccupied with internal not external issues. As products or services become obsolete even though the organization may well have devised ingenious and low-cost ways of delivering them, they are not what the customer actually wants. Examples include the hat industry which has seen a major decline in demand since the 1950s, although companies like Bermona, based in Luton, have found success by specialising in high-quality low-volume products. Another possible strategy at this stage is one of diversification into other markets to replace potentially declining product lines with more profitable growth areas (e.g. Richard Branson's Virgin organization, where products and services as diverse as financial services, railways and fizzy drinks are offered).

Companies like Bermona along with IBM and Apple in the 1990s demonstrate the style of management that is required during the decline phase of development: a style that will enable the organization to make significant changes in order to survive.

Case Study 2 'Vauxhall Motors – a changing organization' at the end of this book allows you to consider the growth and development of a large-scale organization. You may like to try and see if you can identify the various stages in the organization life-cycle model in the case.

The usefulness of the life-cycle model lies in determining what sort of OD intervention is required to help the organization at any stage of its journey. An infant requires quite different interventions from those of an adolescent or a pensioner.

According to Ellis (1996), who investigated an OD intervention to introduce a more business-focused way of working into Royal Mail in the early 1990s, the importance of the culture of the organization was crucially linked. Royal Mail's attempts to gear up for an expected privatization was found to run counter to the accepted way of working in the organization and achieved very little.

Harvey and Brown's change model

Major changes often face large-scale resistance that originate in the cultural norms of an organization. Barriers can be so high that the OD intervention fails (as in the case of Royal Mail) and improvements in organizational performance are lost. It is important to know the level of resistance likely to arise and what lies behind it. The model of change developed by Harvey and Brown (1996) is a useful way to predict resistance (Figure 9.2).

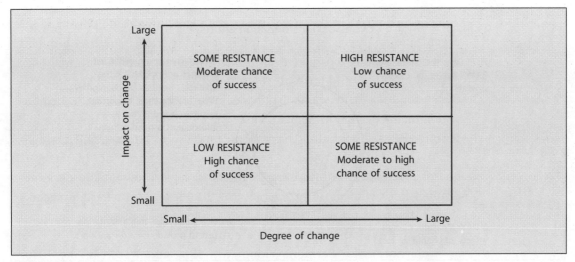

Figure 9.2   The Harvey and Brown change model [from Harvey and Brown (1996)].

As the model shows, the easiest interventions are those in which the change is viewed to be small and have little impact on the culture. However, in practice, by their very nature, most OD interventions will not lie in this quadrant. They are much more likely to be in the two quadrants on the right where the change is large and the impact on culture is either moderate or large.

Shewart's PDCA cycle

The excellent performance of Japanese organizations – such as Toyota and Honda – which practise continual quality improvement has reawakened interest in another change model – Shewart's Plan, Do, Check, Action (or PDCA) model (Figure 9.3). This model which dates back to 1924 was used widely by W. Edwards Demming who is recognized as one of the founders of the quality-improvement movement. The model is of particular interest to those concerned with OD as it can be applied to the phases occurring within a typical intervention. In other words, at each stage of the OD process you can use the PDCA model to guide what has to be done.

9.3 Organizational development and knowledge management

The first point to make about organizational knowledge management is that while some of the concepts and derivations of the term might be relatively new the need to manage knowledge is not. Ives (1998) traces

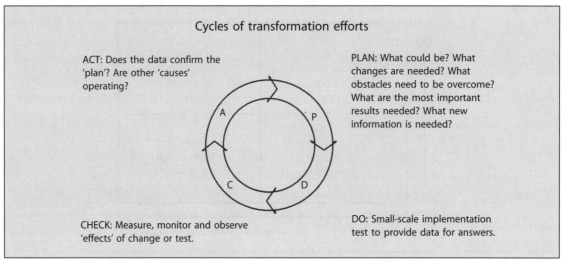

Cycles of transformation efforts

ACT: Does the data confirm the 'plan'? Are other 'causes' operating?

PLAN: What could be? What changes are needed? What obstacles need to be overcome? What are the most important results needed? What new information is needed?

CHECK: Measure, monitor and observe 'effects' of change or test.

DO: Small-scale implementation test to provide data for answers.

Figure 9.3   Shewart's PDCA model.

the historical context back to the ancient Sumerian civilization where cuneiform archives survived to inform future generations of the acquired knowledge of the time. Modern management practice from its Taylorist roots at the beginning of the industrial century has in large part focused on standardization of knowledge or its requirements so that the application of accepted principles can be replicated and where possible improved by the subsequent manager or implementers.

Ritzer (1996) identified the modern version of this concept calling it MacDonaldization of society whereby every application of human behaviour (business related or not) could be reduced into essential small knowledge chunks so that potentially more people could participate albeit in a reduced or restricted way.

It is undoubtedly true that the microchip has allowed organizations to develop the potential to distribute and integrate knowledge much more effectively than ever before, but this has also presented a tremendous challenge to OD. Knowledge-management experts such as Prusak (1997) and Sveiby (1997) acknowledge that the challenge facing most business organizations in the era of information overload is to identify ways of identifying what knowledge is needed, who should have it, when they should have it and what should they do with it.

Allee (1997) takes knowledge management to mean "attending to processes for creating, sustaining, applying, sharing and renewing knowledge to enhance organisational performance and create value".

Knowledge management can often encompass mapping and identifying intellectual assets within the organization, generating knowledge for competitive advantage and making corporate information accessible.

In short, it seems that knowledge management is about increasing the use of the intellectual capital of organizations for competitive advantage.

Critics of the concept of the **learning-organization** concept argue that it merely presents a case for learning for its own sake. They argue that while it might be an effective stimulant to employees' development and creativity, it is not necessarily aligned to organization strategy, imperatives or opportunities. **Organizational learning** in its broadest sense differs conceptually from the learning-organization idea on precisely this point. For organizational learning to be effective it must be tied closely to predetermined strategic objectives, strategic imperatives and timely interventions.

There is a clear difference between those organizations that possess a culture, structure and strategy that allows learning to take place (the learning-organization concept) and one in which learning is treated as a fundamental part of the business process (organizational learning). Organizational learning emphasizes the organization more than the learning. Learning in this context is conducted for a predetermined business purpose.

A definition of organizational learning (in contrast to the learning organization) can be found in Probst and Buchel (1997). For them organizational learning is the process by which an organization's knowledge-and-value base changes, leading to improved problem-solving ability and capacity for action.

The impact of technology on the development of knowledge management also needs to be monitored and managed. Studies on technological breakthroughs such as **groupware** (a software package that allows work groups to work with and share common data) suggest that they do not necessarily change attitudes about sharing information. For example, Vandenbosch and Henderson (1997) found no discernible difference in the effectiveness of communication groups after the installation of Lotus Notes. Nahapiet and Ghoshal (1998) wrote "the availability of electronic knowledge exchange does not automatically induce a willingness to share information and build new intellectual capital".

Scarborough *et al.* (1999) claim that the limits of technology determine the need for a consciously strategic approach to knowledge management. In the absence of such an approach the imposition of technology is likely to have a random impact at best. This view is supported by Baker *et al.* (1999),

---

Reflection Box 9.2 Knowledge management: passing fad or significant concept?

According to a KPMG Knowledge Management Research Report (1998) only 2 per cent of respondents (100 leading UK companies) believe that knowledge management would disappear when the next organizational-development fad came along. This represents a major change since a similar question was asked by the Information Systems Research Centre of Cranfield University School of Management in 1997 and almost one-third of respondents thought it would be a passing fad.

The KPMG report further stated that 10 per cent of organizations in the survey believed that knowledge management was transforming the way their organization did business. 43 per cent of the survey claimed that their organization already had a knowledge-management initiative in place.

There is little doubting the sudden upsurge of interest in the field of organizational-knowledge management. In 1996 there were eight major conferences around the world on the subject. Many have said we are moving from a post-industrial to a knowledge-based economy (e.g. Drucker, 1993a; Sveiby, 1997) and a recent survey by the *Journal of Knowledge Management* revealed that 92 per cent of responding executives believed that they worked in knowledge-intensive organizations (Chase, 1997).

Do you see a long-term future for the concept of knowledge management or do you believe it will die quickly after everyone has tried to understand and use it?

---

and Alavi and Leidner (1997), who suggest that technology could actually restrict learning. They liken the organization to a modern-day *Tower of Babel* in which there is much information but little understanding.

The typical knowledge-management view that the only really sustainable source of competitive advantage is what an organization knows, how it can utilize its knowledge and how fast it can learn something new makes it essential that any planned OD measures take account of these crucial issues.

9.4 Management development

Before we look at the ways organizations develop their managers, we need to get a firm grasp on a slippery topic: What do we mean by management and managers? (Reflection Box 9.3.)

Reflection Box 9.3   What is management?

How would you define management? Can you put together a definition that covers all the aspects of management but is not too wide ranging to mean everything we do is actually management?

Many authors have attempted to define precisely what is meant by management but, unfortunately, no firm conclusion has yet been reached. According to Easterby-Smith (1997) "There is little consensus amongst academics about the nature of management and managerial work."

While we can give accurate definitions and descriptions of what management does, it doesn't really help us to find out what management *is*. Definitions that concentrate on management as a decision-making activity also run into difficulties when one considers that we all make decisions constantly, but that does not mean we are acting in a managerial capacity. For example, when you decide what to have for breakfast are you making a managerial decision or carrying out a managerial activity?

In a similar way a number of definitions of management concentrate on the fact that managers must take responsibility for the actions of themselves and others. Once again the use of a universally applicable concept, 'responsibility', does little to clarify what management actually is. While a mother has responsibility for her children is she managing them? Is a car driver who has responsibility for the vehicle he or she is driving managing the car? Clearly the use of the idea of responsibility as a metaphor for management still leaves room for confusion.

Hales (1993) suggests that a categorizing of the managerial process is useful as it classifies five conceptually distinct yet intertwined elements. For Hales managing work in general means:

1   deciding and planning what is to be done, and how;
2   allocating time and effort to what is to be done;
3   motivating, or generating, the effort to do it;
4   coordinating and combining disparate efforts;
5   controlling what is done to ensure that it conforms to what was intended.

This formulation is close to Fayol's (1949) 'classic' and often-repeated conception of management as forecasting or planning, organizing, commanding, co-ordinating and controlling, but it diverges slightly. Fayol's analysis is enduring but it has been further updated by the work of Koontz *et al.* (1984). Mintzberg (1977) and Stewart (1967) both sought to refute the Fayol postulate by claiming that research into what managers actually do does not now support his original analysis.

As a result of the failure to establish a conclusive definition of management some researchers and writers (most notably Jaques, 1997) have come to the conclusion that the discipline of management is intellectually bankrupt.

Eccles and Nohira (1992) suggest that managers must display a high tolerance for uncertainty and ambiguity. They must be willing to act without sometimes fully knowing the consequences of their actions. Indeed, many of the actions taken by a skilled manager are intended to actively uncover additional information that can be used to guide further actions.

The observation of managers in action carried out for this book reveals an echo of Mintzberg's (1977) observations, that even though they may describe their work in rational terms, managers spend very little of their time explicitly engaged in planning, organizing, staffing, directing, coordinating, reporting and budgeting. These activities, as Hannaway (1989) found in her study of managers at work, "do not in fact describe what managers do. At best they describe vague objectives for managers which they are constantly trying to accomplish in a far more messy and hectic stream of ongoing activity".

Managers also spend little time by themselves. They rarely spend time alone drawing up plans or brooding over critical decisions. Instead, they spend most of their time interacting with others, both inside and outside the organization, including casual interactions in hallways, phone conversations, one-on-one meetings and larger group meetings. Indeed, managers probably spend about two-thirds of their time with others. As Mintzberg has pointed out "Unlike other workers, the manager does not leave the telephone or the meeting to get back to work. Rather, these contacts *are* his work."

The picture of management presented so far may strike you as unconventional or unflattering. While acknowledging that rational choice is still the most desirable way for managers to act, our experience suggests that this is an unattainable fiction given the situations that managers commonly face. The limitations of rational-choice models of managerial action will be brought into sharp focus by considering the following example suggested by Winograd and Flores (1986). In addressing the problem of creating computer systems that work the way effective managers do, they ask you to imagine chairing a meeting of 15 or so people at which an important and controversial issue is to be decided. Winograd and Flores outline several interesting conditions that arise in this common managerial situation, among which are:

- problems rarely come to managers in well-defined ways;
- most of the time the problems managers must solve are poorly defined and have 'fuzzy' boundaries.

Keen and Scott-Morton (1978) frame the matter nicely "Most, if not all, of ... managers' key decisions tend to be 'fuzzy' problems, not well understood by them or the organization, and their personal judgment is essential." Indeed, managers spend a great deal of their time just trying to better understand the nature of the problem they are confronted with. For instance, a manager may have an irate employee vent her frustration over one thing and later discover that the real problem was something quite different.

These features help us to understand broadly what it is we are considering when we look at developing management and managers. Further contextual issues have to be allowed for in the analysis of how best to develop the organization's managerial capacity. The first of these concerns the type and style of the organization.

The management skills required in a car-manufacturing plant will be quite different from those needed to manage a fast-food outlet, so these organizations will need to develop their managers in very different ways.

Given the diversity of managerial activity, it should come as no surprise that the approaches taken by organizations to develop their managers differ greatly. The more commonly used programmed-development techniques include **in-company courses** and **sponsorships** to undertake advanced management courses at outside bodies such as **business schools.** Less frequent use is made of **self-study programmes** tied into performance reviews and appraisal systems. For senior managers, or **top teams,** many organizations may turn to more intense one-to-one coaching sessions.

Other schemes might involve a programme of job moves or project responsibilities to allow the developing manager to learn more about their role experientially. Much of what constitutes management development is based on improving the 'people skills' side of management, in particular relationship building and the crucial ability to influence others.

The 'harder' technical managerial skills of problem solving, budgeting and scheduling are important, but many organizations are recognizing that the real essence of good management centres on the '**soft skills**' (dealing with people and all their attendant problems) and are constructing development programmes which emphasize them.

There could also be a tension between what the organization sees as necessary development for its managers and what the manager him or herself wants to do to develop. The two sets of needs are not always congruent and may lead to conflict between the two parties.

The competencies in Table 9.1 are typical of those used by large organizations to guide management development and illustrate the increased significance placed on soft skills alongside technical ability. Examples of the development techniques used to improve the performance and ability of managers are featured in Figure 9.4.

You will see from Figure 9.4 that management development covers a very broad area, ranging from the basic toolkit of 'managerial survival skills' needed to do the job to more sophisticated strategy-development sessions.

The development of an organization's management resources is the crucial means of support taking the organization forward and implementing strategic or operational initiatives. The approach taken by many organizations is that the development of managers should be a feature of their working life. In other words, learning and developing has to become an accepted part of the manager's job. Simply knowing tomorrow what you already know today is not enough.

9.5 Summary

In this chapter we have introduced the notion of what organizational development is. We have seen how the development of any organization can only come about through the development of its people, usually accomplished by carefully thought-out learning programmes.

You have also become aware of the organizational life cycle through which most organizations progress from birth, growth to maturity and eventually death.

We have also looked at a model of change that takes into account the vital issue of organizational culture. We learned that attempts to change

Table 9.1 *Typical competency framework for senior executives.*

Technical knowledge	Demonstrates subject knowledge and keeps up to date with matters relating to own field. Committed to continuous learning and enhancing technical expertise.
Leading business	
Strategic vision	Displays breadth of thought and understanding of strategy. Has a vision for the future, develops strategy based on long-term value creation.
Initiating change	Recognizes the need for change and the constant demand for improvement. Is flexible and adaptable in approach. Challenges, where appropriate, traditional assumptions, working methods and value destroyers. Identifies fresh approaches to create value and generates original ideas for products, services and ways of working.
Aligning organization	
Analysis and judgement	Seeks relevant information for solving problems and making decisions. Draws accurate, logical and objective inferences from information available. Undertakes critical evaluation of evidence.
Management planning	Is able to consider the bigger picture and keep overall strategy in mind. Develops clear plans to achieve objectives in alignment with business priorities. Anticipates problems and difficulties and is flexible in revising contingencies accordingly. Effectively uses and encourages performance management to manage own objectives and the performance of others.
Organizing people and tasks	
Leadership	Defines clear objectives in line with strategy, aligning and motivating people to achieve them. Leads by example demonstrating high standards of personal integrity. Is able to display a range of leadership styles as appropriate. Is willing to be firm when necessary.
Technical and professional	
Commercial orientation	Demonstrates a focused concern for identifying value drivers and understanding what creates and what destroys value. Understands the financial implications of actions taken not only for own area but also organization wide.
Individual specific	
Persuasive communication	Verbal communication is clear, confident and succinct. Written communication is clear and succinct. Tailor's style and content to different situations and audiences. Persuades and influences others in a way that wins their commitment to a decision of course of action.
Building and maintaining relationships	Interacts with others in a sensitive manner and builds rapport. Is an effective listener and seeks to understand and show respect for the views and values of other people and other cultures. Builds and maintains networks and positive working relationships both inside and outside. Is diplomatic and politically astute.
Drive and resilience	Demonstrates energy, enthusiasm and commitment. Is motivated by the achievement of results and seeks to accomplish challenging goals. Strives continually to deliver value to the business. Stays calm and self-controlled under pressure. Perseveres and remains positive even when setbacks occur.
Culture specific	
Customer focus	Seeks to understand, meet and exceed external and internal customer needs. Creates, builds and maintains profitable long-term customer relationships based on providing a consistently rewarding experience. Encourages others to value the customer and deliver excellent service.
Promoting teamwork	Cooperates and works well with others in the pursuit of business aims. Enables and supports a sense of team spirit, encouraging an environment of open communication and the sharing of information. Actively looks for synergies and fosters cooperation across other business units and/or functions.

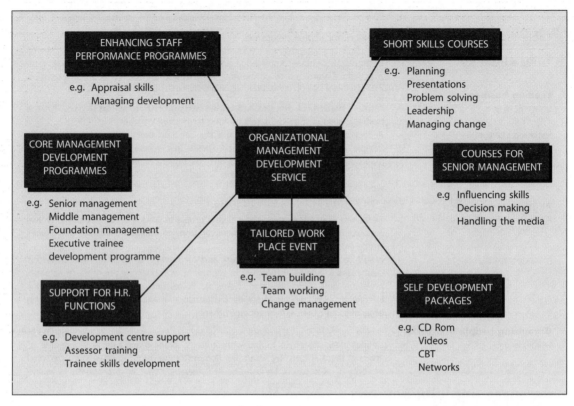

Figure 9.4   Facilitating management development.

organizations that are not grounded in its culture are doomed to failure. Resistance to change will be augmented only if we ask people to act in ways perceived to be counter-cultural because we will be asking them to reject accepted beliefs, values and organizational rules.

We saw that organizational value is tied up in intellectual capital or organizational knowledge and is not simply the physical assets of the business.

The section on management development highlighted the difficulties faced by organizational researchers and OD practitioners in identifying precisely how to define management.

In developing the organization, we saw that any steps that can be taken to develop the capability of managers to manage will be a key input. We recognized that investment in management development can range from precisely scheduled learning to experiential placement or secondments. One of the key requirements of any management-development programme is its focus on teaching managers how to deal with people who may have diverse needs and abilities.

Questions

Self-test questions

1   What is meant by the term organizational development?
2   Explain one model of how organizations are thought to change and develop over time.
3   How is the concept of knowledge management crucial to organizational development?
4   Why is management development and training thought to be a central part of organizational development?

Discussion questions

1   As some organizations have been around for over 100 years why do they still need to develop?
2   What activities do you think make up the typical day of a manager?
3   What skills do you think a good manager needs to have?
4   How can effective knowledge management lead to organizational development?

References and bibliography

Alavi, M. and Leidner, D. (1997) *Knowledge Management Systems: Emerging Views and Practices from the Field*, INSEAD Working Paper Series 97/97/TM, Fontainebleau, France.

Allee, V. (1997) 12 principles of knowledge management, *Training and Development*, **51**(11), 71–4.

Baker, B., Leidner, D. and Galliers, R. (1999) *Strategic Information Management: Challenges and Strategies in Managing Information Systems*, Oxford: Butterworth-Heinemann.

Burke, W. (1987) *Organisation Development: A Normative View*, Reading, MA: Addison Wesley.

Chase, R. (1997) The knowledge based organisation: An international survey, *Journal of Knowledge Management*, **1**(1), 38–49.

Drucker, P. (1993a) *Managing for the Future*, Oxford: Butterworth-Heinemann.

Drucker, P. (1993b) *Post-Capitalist Society*, Oxford: Butterworth-Heinemann.

Easterby-Smith, M. (1997) Disciplines of organisational learning: Contributions and critiques, *Human Relations*, **50**(9), 1085–1113.

Eccles, R. and Nohira, N. (1992) *Beyond the Hype, Rediscovering the Essence of Management*, Boston, MA: Harvard Business School Press.

Ellis, S. (1996) An investigation into strategic change management at Royal Mail, M.Phil thesis, University of Luton.

Fayol, H. (1949) *General and Industrial Management* (translated by Storrs, C.), London: Pitman.

French, W. and Bell, C. (1995) *Organisational Development: Behavioural Science Interventions for Organisation Improvements* (fifth edition), Englewood Cliffs, NJ: Prentice Hall International.

Hales, C. (1993) *Managing through Organisation*, London: Routledge.

Hannaway, J. (1989) *Managers Managing; The Workings of an Administrative System*, London: Open University Press.

Harvey, D. and Brown, D. (1996) *An Experiential Approach to Organisational Development*, New Jersey: Prentice Hall.

Ives, W. (1998) *Knowledge Management is an Emerging Area with a Long History*, Anderson Consulting.

Jaques, E (1997) *Video Series on Managers and Management*, London: BBC Publications.

KPMG Management Consulting (1998) Knowledge Management Research Report, KPMG website: **http://www.kpmg.co.uk**

Keen, P. and Scott-Morton, M. (1978) *Decision Support Systems, an Organisation Perspective*, Reading, MA: Addison Wesley.

Koontz, E., O'Donnel, C. and Weirich, H. (1984) *Management* (eighth edition), Tokyo: McGraw-Hill.

Mintzberg, H. (1997) The manager's job; Folklore and fact, *Harvard Business Review*, **53**, July–August, 49–61.

Nahapiet, J. and Ghoshal, S. (1998) Social capital, intellectual capital and the organisational advantage, *Academy of Management Review*, **23**(2), 242–266.

Porras, J. and Robertson, P. (1992) Organisation development: Theory, practice and research. In Dunnette M. and Hough L. (eds) *Handbook of Industrial and Organisational Psychology*, Volume 3 (second edition), Palo Alto, CA: Consulting Psychologist Press.

Porras, J. and Hoffer, S. (1986) Common behaviour changes in successful organisation development, *Journal of Applied Behavioural Science*, **22**, 477–494.

Probst, G. and Buchel, B. (1997) *Organisational Learning*, New York: Prentice Hall.

Prusak, L. (1997) *Knowledge in Organisations*, Oxford: Butterworth-Heinemann.

Ritzer, G. (1996) *The McDonaldisation of Society*, Newbury Park, CA: Pine Forge Press.

Rothwell, W., Sullivan, R. and McClean, G. (1995) *Practising Organisational Development*, San Diego, CA: Pfeiffer and Company.

Scarborough, H., Swan, J. and Preston, J. (1999) *Knowledge Management: A Literature Review*, London: IPD Publishing.

Smither, R., Houston, J. and McIntire, S. (1996) *Organisation Development, Strategies for Changing Environments*, New York: Harper Collins.

Stewart, R. (1967) *Managers and their Jobs*, London: Macmillan.

Stewart, T. (1997) *Intellectual Capital: The New Wealth of Organizations*, London: Doubleday.

Sveiby, K. (1997) *The New Organizational Wealth: Managing and Measuring Intangible Assets*, Berrett Koehler.

Vandenbosch, B. and Henderson, J. C. (1997) Understanding strategic learning. Paper given at the *1997 Academy of Management Meeting, Boston, MA*.

Winograd, T. and Flores, F. (1986) *Understanding Computers and Cognition*, Reading, MA: Addison Wesley.

Case studies

Contents

Guide to analysing a case study

As a first step you should make a precis of the contents of the case study. The following questions should help you do this:

- What is this case study about?
- What are the main issues highlighted?
- What seems to be causing the 'problems' in the case?
- What further information might you need to help you understand the causes of the problems?

The next step is to try to relate the theoretical material covered in the textbook to the issues and problems you have identified. You might use the following types of questions to help you:

- Is this an issue or problem that is mainly concerned with individuals, groups or the organization itself, or is this something that concerns all three categories?
- Which theories and concepts covered by the book might help you explain what is going on?
- How do these theories or concepts explain what is going on?

Using theories or concepts to explain issues within a case study requires you to be systematic. You need to break the concept down into components and apply these to the relevant points of the case. So, for instance, if you want to use the concept of organizational culture to analyse **Case Study 6 Take your mother not your lover**, it would be useful to:

- define what organizational culture actually is;
- identify ways to think about culture (e.g. Schein's typology);
- apply each dimension of the typology to the case – for example: What sort of beliefs seem to dominate in terms of the nature of human nature? Are there specific examples from the case that you can use to illustrate your point?
- What does the theory or concept not explain?
- Are there alternative theories available that can fill such gaps?

Finally, you might complete your analysis by thinking about how to resolve the main issues highlighted in the case study. Again, the following questions will be helpful:

- What needs to be done to resolve the case study?
- In what ways do these resolutions relate to the theoretical analysis of the case?

Case Study 1

Building a flexible organization: British Gypsum

The Background

British Gypsum is part of BPB Industries Group and is concerned with mining and manufacturing gypsum products. For many years the company enjoyed a near monopoly position in the UK plasterboard market, but since 1988 it has faced competition from Redland and Knauf, a German company, with the result that its market share fell from 96% in 1987 to 60% in 1994. In addition the UK building industry was just emerging from a major period of recession, and overcapacity is now the norm in the plasterboard industry. The company has six sites employing 1,750 people now compared with 3,500 in 1989. Pre-1989 industrial relations in the company developed along the lines experienced by many typical UK organizations:

- high relative manning levels in certain areas;
- numerous job grades with 10 hourly paid grades;
- sectioned bonus schemes which were difficult to control and administer (e.g. one site operated eight different bonus schemes);
- reluctant flexibility existed as management time was tied up with sorting out disputes over the variety of bonuses and grading decisions;
- overtime mentality ruled at shop floor and supervisor level;
- 'them and us' attitudes typified relationship between hourly paid employees and staff.

The drivers for change

Competitive forces meant that the company had to refocus its efforts on being the lowest cost producer. It set itself the objective of improving productivity, reducing unit costs and maximizing company profitability and competitiveness. The key to the changes was a new negotiated employment package which was named the New Deal. The objectives of the New Deal were:

- achieve a more efficient use of working time;
- maximize flexibility between jobs encouraging individuals to use their knowledge and skills to the fullest;
- provide a new payment structure giving high regular payments and harmonization of conditions with the staff side.

In detail the New Deal used the following flexibilization tools:

- an annual hours contract, incorporating a system of bank hours;
- the elimination of overtime;
- review and standardization of shift patterns;
- fewer grades;

- flexible working and training;
- pay calculated on an annual basis;
- improved sick pay.

The changes were conditional on an agreed reduction of the workforce of 15 per cent achieved by voluntary means.

The implementation process
Negotiations were carried out quickly with two groups – process employees and craft employees – negotiating separately. Regular briefings took place for all employees throughout to ensure that communication was fully achieved. In addition, local management held question-and-answer sessions. The financial side of the new package was carefully planned so that the majority of employees stood to benefit in pay terms. In addition, a 'sweetener' was offered which included:

- lump sum of £150;
- interest free loan of £200 to assist the transition from weekly to monthly pay;
- phasing in of pay dates over 6 months;
- all outstanding holiday pay paid up.

A ballot agreement (58 per cent in favour) led to preparatory training for management and for clerical and hourly paid employees who had to learn new skills to properly implement the new scheme. The whole process took 18 months from negotiation to implementation. In hindsight the company thinks it went too quickly and should have allocated more than the 6 months allowed for training between presentation of the negotiated agreement and implementation. Post-implementation management guidelines were issued regularly by the employee-relations manager to ensure consistency of implementation at all locations. Review meetings were held to help solve any difficult implementation problems. These can be referred from local to national level if required and, as a result, minor modifications to the agreement have been made.

The flexibility scheme
All employees except management grades are now part of the annualized hours agreement. Each employee is contracted to work a total number of hours per year, not per week. At British Gypsum the figures are 1,776 (based on a 39-hour week) for non-continuous shift workers and 1,871 for continuous shift workers. These figures arrived via the following calculations:

Continuous shift workers		Non-continuous shift workers	
Basic weekly hours 41		Basic weekly hours 39	
Annual hours 41 × 52.2	2140	Annual hours 39 × 52.2	2035
minus holidays 41 × 5	205	minus holidays 39 × 5	195
and public holidays 8 × 8	64	and public holidays 8 × 8	64
Annual working hours	1871	Annual working hours	1776

These hours are then rostered throughout the year in a shift pattern and any hours outside the rostered time are counted as leisure time. All employees are also required to work 170 hours additional 'bank hours' (negotiated down from 208). These hours are not rostered and are paid for as part of the annual salary irrespective of whether they are used or not. They provide cover for sickness, training, short-term peaks, plant breakdowns or other essential housekeeping tasks. The company is committed to minimizing the use of banked hours. They are shared out evenly and employees get at least 24 hours' notice. If an employee does not attend for banked hours he/she is liable to disciplinary action.

The payment system

Employees receive salary paid in 12 equal amounts throughout the year made up of the following elements:

- core payment;
- occupational grade allowance;
- flexibility and training allowance;
- disturbance allowance;
- bonus payment.

In order to implement the new system regrading had to be carried out to move from seven to three process grades and from three to one craft grade, making transfers and flexibility much simpler. In addition, departmental bonus schemes were replaced by a site scheme relating to the performance of all departments.

Difficulties in operating the new flexibility scheme

The main problem concerned absenteeism because the new sick-pay arrangements initially gave all hourly paid employees full pay for sickness absences. This had to be reviewed as abuse of the system was detected. Absence increased from 4–5 per cent average to 9–10 per cent. The result was a reintroduction of the 'waiting day' concept for individuals who had poor attendance records. As a result the absenteeism average fell back to 3 per cent. Other areas of difficulty included the redundancy package which was designed to give the longest serving employees the best deal. Unfortunately, these employees had the key skills and experience that the company required. The knock-on effect of this was a reduction in performance as replacement staff were trained. In addition, the plant accident rate increased as more inexperienced staff used the machinery.

The company points out that the improvements in productivity did not occur immediately. A 6-month delay was experienced before significant productivity improvements were achieved.

The benefits of flexible operations

For the company:

- reduced unit costs, mainly through reductions in staffing;
- elimination of voluntary overtime which has released management time and changed work attitudes;
- an improved ability to manage change by fostering an atmosphere of teamworking and cooperation;
- better planning and utilization of available time and resources;
- simplified pay structure;
- easier administration – through monthly cashless pay systems;
- an open style of management;
- increased flexibility of skills and labour;
- improved teamworking;
- better organized training.

For the employee:

- increased leisure time;
- better structured and planned working time;
- higher basic pay;
- stable income;
- staff conditions for all, so removing traditional barriers;
- increased job security;
- increased job satisfaction through training and involvement;
- increased skills/employability.

Conclusion

The package introduced by British Gypsum is recognized as a leading-edge intervention in flexible working agreements in the manufacturing sector. It enabled the company to face up to the business challenges of the 1990s. Plans for further developments of flexibility within the company include multi-skilling across trades and improved training.

[Based on IPD Research Publication, *Flexibility and Europe* (1997).]

Questions

1 What were the pressures for change facing British Gypsum outlined in the case?
2 What organizational advantages did the move towards greater flexibility promise?
3 What positive and negative aspects of flexible working are identified in the case?

Case Study 2

Vauxhall Motors – a changing organization

Vauxhall Motors, best known for producing contemporary high-volume car models such as the Vectra, Tigra, Astra and Omega, provides an excellent example for following many of the debates about organizational behaviour outlined in this book. Vauxhall cars have changed over time. In a similar way, the organizational practices that have brought about more and more efficient production are also constantly evolving.

Brief company history

The company now known as Vauxhall Motors started life back in 1903 and moved to its Luton home in 1905. The company is a wholly-owned subsidiary of the American giant General Motors and has a second production plant at Ellesmere Port on Merseyside, which opened in the 1960s. Around 10,000 people are currently employed in direct production of motor vehicles by Vauxhall and at least as many again get employment indirectly by supplying and servicing the plants. In addition, Luton is now the home of Vauxhall's European Headquarters and is responsible for much of the strategic planning, design and purchasing functions across many geographical borders.

All this is a far cry from the original ambition of the founder of the company, Alexander Wilson. Wilson was a marine engineer, not a businessman, which led to many problems over such things as cash flow and business planning, illustrating at once the need for organization and management expertise alongside that of the entrepreneur. It was not until 1931 that the company became involved with commercial vehicles, before this the company concentrated mainly on marine engineering and engines for paddle steamers and River Thames tugs; only a handful of cars were produced for wealthy or important private customers. The first Vauxhall car, a very basic design by today's standards, cost £136 and the company sold about 40 of them.

The factory site first used in 1905 in Luton was a small shed (which survived at the heart of the existing plant until the mid-1980s). In the 1990s Vauxhall initiated a £50-million plan to revamp its Luton plant. Many redundant buildings were demolished and 55 acres of land were sold off to non-car-related activities, reflecting how technological advances had reduced the space needed for production.

In 1912 output of vehicles rose to the dizzy heights of 300 per year as the company began to adapt to a range of customers from Royal Family members to the armed forces. By the late 1920s the production-line process was established at the plant, allowing production to rise to 1,400 cars and bringing with it new methods of working (and living) for the 1,800 people then employed.

In 1925 the company was taken over by General Motors Corporation of the USA. The price paid was $2.5 million, making Vauxhall the first manufacturing plant owned by GM but located outside North America. This tie-up allowed Vauxhall to grow apace and by 1933 the company was completing 10,000 vehicles per year and in 1934 20,000, all with a labour force of around 6,000. During the war years the company's development was understandably interrupted but by 1957 Vauxhall was employing 22,000 people and a new commercial vehicle plant in Dunstable. Further expansion was undertaken and a completely new plant was commissioned at Ellesmere Port on Merseyside.

Growth and development of newer and more advanced engineering continued for the company until the late-1970s, after which the organization began to run into difficulties. Major restructuring took place in the face of economic downswings and poor trading results. The commercial vehicles division at Dunstable was converted into a separate company and by 1983 this part of the operation was reported to be losing money to the tune of £52 million per year.

Modern times

The recession of the early 1990s, in addition to an increasingly hostile trading environment founded largely on global competition, placed Vauxhall under increasing pressure to maintain performance and market share. In addition, technological leaps made the production of cars possible at a much faster pace than ever before and with far fewer employees. One of the major challenges facing this and other car-production companies now is that the worldwide over-capacity. Vauxhall now has the capacity to produce around 36 cars per hour at each of its UK plants and employs around 5,000 workers at each one. Noticeably, the company has expanded its non-production-based activities such as marketing, global purchasing, financing and leasing contracts and continues to play an important role in both the local and European economy. As an organization the company has gone through many stages of initial unplanned growth, rapid expansion, takeover, restructuring, contraction, diversification and now consolidation.

In many ways the developments outlined at Vauxhall reflect the way that many other organizations have changed over the years. The pictures of the two cars at the beginning of the case illustrate the tremendous development that the company has achieved over less than 100 years of operation. Just as the different levels of sophistication and complexity of the cars makes them almost unrecognizable as even distant relatives, the magnitude of change in organizational theory, practices and policies experienced over the same period has been equally dramatic.

[Adapted from *The Griffin Story* (1990) Public Affairs Department, Vauxhall Motors Limited, Luton, England.]

Questions

1 How does the development of the Vauxhall organization over the years reflect developments in organizational behaviour?
2 As an organization grows, what are the different challenges to be faced in ensuring that all the people employed are pulling in the same direction?
3 How can an organization that plays a global role ensure that it takes account of local issues?
4 What are the advantages of size that organizations such as General Motors can exploit. Can you think of any negative features of being so big?

Case Study 3

Positive aspects of teamworking: total employee involvement at Smith and Nephew

Background

Smith and Nephew plc is leading worldwide health-care business whose principal activities are in the manufacture and sale of wound casting and bandages. They produce textiles which are used in bandages and medical dressings. The company operates in more than 35 countries and their turnover in 1997 exceeded £1 billion. At the Brierfield site in Lancashire they employ about 650 people.

The arrival of a new MD at Smith and Nephew in Brierfield became a catalyst for a change in the way teams and team leaders were used by the organization.

Why did the MD introduce new teamworking ideas?

The team focus was to become the driving force behind the company's campaign for improved quality and efficiency. To achieve high-performance teams the new MD believed that excellent leadership was a key requirement. Competitive cost pressures meant that those selected for team leadership would not be paid more and they would still spend 90 per cent of their working time on the shop floor doing routine production duties.

How were the team leaders developed?

A project team was set up to construct a profile of the responsibilities of a team leader. Once this was established the company looked for suitable internal candidates and about 30 employees were invited to take on the leadership role. Those identified were then subjected to an intensive leadership-development programme. This training, which was carried out in the employees' own time, was universally praised by those involved.

Total employee involvement

The 'Total Employee Involvement' scheme gave the new team leaders a set of clear responsibilities for the daily monitoring and evaluation of the team's performance and output. Team leaders were also expected to monitor and take action over sickness absenteeism within the team. The overall well-being of the team was made the clear responsibility of the team leader. Simple acts such as obtaining cold drinks for team members on hot days was a way of demonstrating that the team leader could support the team through difficult periods and not just carry out a policing role.

Although the company had a number of employees who brought a positive attitude to the changes, problems were encountered over getting sufficient volunteers for the demanding team-leadership role. This is easily understandable when the job is described by the production manager as 'Come in early, stay late, come back in your own time and get no extra payment whatsoever.' Before long the company realized that it had to provide a way of rewarding team leaders, most probably through a flat-rate pay supplement, but without increasing the overall labour cost. Thus, the initiative of teamworking was expected to pay for itself by harnessing cost and efficiency gains which could then be passed on to the team leaders.

Questions

1 Does the case confuse the terms of leadership and management? What do you think is the difference between the two?
2 How might the team-leadership project lead to efficiency gains and thereby not add to costs?
3 How realistic do you feel the concept of total employee involvement is in organizations that you have worked for?

Case Study 4

More positive aspects of teamworking: NatWest rings the changes at a call centre

Background

The march of technology and the cost efficiencies linked to it have led many financial-service organizations and many other organizations in the UK and elsewhere to investigate and set up a call centre to service client needs. The NatWest version at Theale, near Reading, a greenfield site, was set up as the bank's pilot centre in September 1994. The centre has operated on a 24-hour basis since March 1995. By 1997 the centre employed about 400 staff and is still growing. Many of the employees work part-time and sickness absenteeism is high (about 7 per cent) although this is in line with the experience of other call centres. Until late-1995 staff turnover was also high, peaking at around the 25 per cent per year mark.

Teams and team management

The call-centre telephone teams not only provide the chance to manage individual perform-ance but also offer a focus for staff in what is otherwise a fairly routine and pressurized environment. Operations in which technology dominates so strongly can often cause a degree of isolation. Customers become faceless 'problems' and relationship building is a real difficulty. Each team comprises up to 15 people and is named after a famous high achiever, chosen by the team themselves. Typical ones are Dickens, Nelson, Cromwell and Nightingale. Team members are encouraged to socialize and there is an element of competition between the teams. Each month the team with the highest sales or quality rating receives an incentive reward. Each team has a manager and a deputy, which are added responsibilities taken on by team members on a voluntary basis. Some of the newer teams also have coaches to help the team leader ensure that each member is keeping up with developments.

Rewards

Team and individual performance are closely monitored. Some elements of the team members' work can be judged on a daily basis by using technology to record the time spent per call or down time (the time spent not working on answering calls). Salaries of team members and managers are determined by individual performance, market rates, and affordability, plus a bonus payable three times per year.

Organizational problems

The setting up of a greenfield call centre entirely outside the existing experience of the organ-ization led to a number of problems. Some of these (a 5-month delay in going operational was one) were attributed to technological shortcomings which were eventually ironed out once the service settled down and more appropriate software and systems were introduced. Other problems were more to do with organizational personnel policies and procedures, which were produced centrally and meant to cover the whole of the organization.

The call centre initially employed staff on standard NatWest terms and conditions of employment and these were not appropriate for workers in a call-centre environment. Working hours and pay rates were both changed significantly to allow for greater flexibility and premium pay required to attract and retain staff. At the same time, more specific measures of performance quality and productivity were introduced. After much negotiation and full involvement of the relevant trade unions, new conditions of employment were introduced in 1996, after which the ability to recruit and retain staff was greatly enhanced.

Consequences and results

Customer surveys regularly monitor the effectiveness of the call centre. In addition, 'dummy customers' conduct internal audits of the service. Performance to date is judged to be very satisfactory. Employee satisfaction is also high and many employees believe they have good career prospects and a variety of work through involvement with team projects.

Questions

1 What aspects of organizational behaviour are illustrated by the high labour turnover experienced at the call centre before the initiative?
2 How does the introduction of teams change the nature of the job?
3 Why did the call-centre staff need significantly different terms and conditions of employment?

Case Study 5

Hot Groups

A Hot Group is the name given to a lively high-achieving dedicated group, usually small, whose members are given an exciting and challenging task. Hot Groups while they last captivate their members and they can achieve difficult goals swiftly. The vast majority of Hot Groups do not arise in a planned and ordered manner. More frequently they emerge by accident. By examining what Hot Groups do and the circumstances in which past Hot Groups were created, managers might be able to prepare in advance the conditions for the formation of further Hot Groups.

Characteristics of a Hot Group

- **Total preoccupation** Members of Hot Groups focus on the task to the exclusion of all other distractions. They talk about it constantly and see any setback as a temporary stumble on the road to eventual success. Participants in Hot Groups achieve this level of preoccupation because they see the task as immensely significant both personally and organizationally. The task must be uplifting, stretching and intellectually stimulating.

- **Intellectual intensity, integrity and exchange** Members of Hot Groups have to use their mental powers to the full. Intellectual energy stems from the Hot Groups' relief of inhibition that often characterizes less effective groups. Some of their ideas might appear from the outside to be extreme but Hot Groups push organizational and individual capacity to, and often beyond, their normally accepted limits. Noise and seemingly unorganized discussion is more the rule than the exception.

- **Emotional intensity** Hot-Group members are infatuated with the challenge of the task. They will sacrifice many interests and commitments outside the group in order to achieve success. Hot-Group members will volunteer for extra duties if they further the goals of the group. Hot groups are too dynamic and challenging for the phenomenon of groupthink to occur. Unquestioning conformity, which is the prerequisite of groupthink, cannot survive in an atmosphere of creativity and debate.

- **Fluid structure and small size** Hot Groups have ever-changing structures and outsiders or investigators may not be able to define any coherent form. The size of the groups may range from three to no more than 25–30. Hot Groups by their very nature have to be temporary and relatively short lived. They come together to solve a problem or create something new. Once that problem is no longer an issue for the organization the group has done its job and will disband. Hot Groups, unlike other organizational groupings, are not concerned with preserving their own longevity.

When do Hot Groups occur?

Very special conditions are required to grow a Hot Group, which is why they are relatively rare.

It is probably easier to list the organizational factors that will *restrict* the growth of typical Hot Groups:

- rigid organizational structures;
- ageing and over-bureaucratic procedures and policies;
- non-customer-focused operations;
- rigid and non-negotiable organizational objectives and 'missions';
- poor information flows;
- lack of trust and openness in communications;
- non-supportive organizational culture;
- poor HR focus in the organization;
- lack of external threat or crisis;
- fear of change and new technology.

Anarchy at Apple Computers: the most famous example of a Hot Group

In the early 1970s the Apple Computer Company displayed many of the characteristics of a Hot Group. All the employees in this emerging technological area were under 30 and the culture of the entire company was exciting, urgent, flamboyant and defiant. They had the energy to take on the computer industry giant IBM and a belief in the values their product embodied. Apple had an open culture which reflected its origins in the technology-rich Californian Silicon Valley. Apple's flagship product, the Macintosh, was developed by a small Hot Group. The group consisted of people from all over the company. Led by the aggressive and charismatic Steve Jobs, the group was spurred on to build a small computer which would bring the positive benefits of computers to the masses. While IBM concentrated on the needs of big business, Apple could justify its position as a crusader (by bringing computing resources 'to the masses') giving the Hot Group a noble reason for bringing the product to market.

Negative features of Hot Groups

Hot Groups are not pleased when their concentration is disturbed by, for example, having to deal with more mundane everyday organizational issues or bureaucratic procedures. Members of the group may also develop an air of isolation from, or a sense of superiority over, the rest of the organization. If any group is freed from the normal constraints of the organization for a special project, others may well feel resentment. Hot Groups do not readily welcome newcomers, who might easily disrupt the established dynamics, unless they can bring a skill that the group obviously needs. Finally, individuals can 'burn out' because they are so intensely wound up in the group task that they refuse to take a break or relax. All of these difficulties mean that the leader of the group must be alive to the human issues and understand and manage the problems that might occur.

***

Questions

1   What positive features of groups and teams are exhibited by Hot Groups?
2   How can organizations help to create and sustain Hot Groups?
3   How would you feel about being a member of a Hot Group?

Case Study 6

Take your mother not your lover

Introduction

Jenny was the first woman sales representative to be employed by Puffin Insurance, a pseudonym for a major UK insurance company. Her appointment to the sales force in the late 1980s was something of a radical change of policy for the company and a significant break with the past. The job of sales representative in Puffin had always been considered a 'man's job'. Indeed, this stereotyped assumption has been pervasive within the UK insurance industry throughout the twentieth century. Frequently it has been assumed that men are best suited for the 'breadwinner' function of sales, while women are ideally employed in the 'homemaker' support role of clerical work in the office. These assumptions have tended to inform selection practices in the industry.

For many years Jenny had worked in the sales-support function but she had increasingly made it known that she wished to pursue a career in sales. She had in-depth knowledge of Puffin's products and had developed very good relationships with the company's clients. As a consequence of her performance record she was promoted to sales representative after applying for a vacant position. Her appointment also reflected Puffin's recently stated public commitment to being an equal-opportunities employer. It therefore provided tangible evidence that the company was making progress in that area.

Invitation to the sales convention

During her first year as a salesperson Jenny was so successful that she sold the highest number of policies in the entire sales force. Like many other insurance companies, it was the policy at Puffin to organize an annual sales convention, attended by the most successful salespeople, which culminated in an award ceremony for the highest achievers. Seeking to secure an invitation to this all-expenses-paid annual meeting was an important motivation for all members of the Puffin sales team. The venue for this elite gathering was invariably somewhere exotic. Its sun-drenched location and the sumptuous facilities of the hotel were heavily emphasized in the company recruitment literature for salespeople and in the monthly newsletters distributed to sales staff.

In this particular year the convention was sheduled to be held in Barbados. All of the high-achieving sales representatives and their wives or partners were invited to attend. This was the first convention where a woman sales representative had been invited. When Jenny received her invitation she advised the organizer that she would be bringing her partner Brian, who worked in a lower graded post within the sales-support function. Yet Jenny's stated intentions began a chain of events which brought her into conflict, not only with the sales manager, but also with the other salesmen.

The sales manager arranged a meeting with Jenny specifically do dissuade her from inviting Brian to Barbados. He raised various objections. First, he implied that as she was unmarried it would be 'more appropriate' if she took her mother, rather than Brian, to Barbados. He explained that it might be 'threatening' for some of the wives of the sales representatives to see Jenny at the meeting with a partner who was a member of the sales-support team. He explained that this relationship could give the wives 'cause for concern' in relation to their husbands. The implication was that being unmarried Jenny might be perceived as promiscuous by the other wives. This in turn could make them concerned, for example, about her presence as the only woman on the many company-sponsored training courses for sales representatives.

Second, he stated that many of the salesmen were unhappy about a member of the sales-support staff (who they considered to be junior to themselves) benefiting from a company-sponsored holiday in Barbados. Such rewards were not available to Brian in his support position and he had done nothing in his own work to warrant his presence at the convention.

Third, the sales manager explained that there were various social excursions arranged for the wives during the convention. He felt sure that, as the only man, Brian would feel very uncomfortable participating in these excursions. Fourth, the manager stated that during the prize-giving ceremony, flowers and chocolates would be presented to the wives of the highly successful sales representatives as an acknowledgement of their outstanding contribution and support throughout the year. Of course it would be inappropriate to present Brian with flowers, he elaborated. Hence the manager concluded that Brian was likely to feel excluded and isolated for most of the vacation. It was therefore unwise and indeed unfair to take him.

Jenny rejected the manager's arguments. She believed that the company was trying to influence and regulate an aspect of her personal life which had nothing to do with the management or the other sales-force members. She pointed out that the invitation was for herself and her partner and reassured the manager that there was no reason for him to be concerned since Brian would simply look after himself if he did not wish to participate in the excursions. Jenny added that she had no wish to take her mother, whom she knew would have very little in common with the people on the trip.

The sales manager was unhappy with Jenny's reply and, over the next 3 weeks, he tried on three more occasions to convince her to change her mind about taking Brian. Jenny refused to reconsider her decision.

The sales convention

When Jenny and her partner arrived in Barbados they found the atmosphere very strained. Throughout the week's stay the salesmen were decidedly cool towards the two of them. The prize-giving ceremony for the top sales representative was held during the dinner on the final evening of the visit. Although the alcohol flowed freely after the ceremony was completed, the evening became increasingly difficult for Jenny and Brian. As the drink began to take its toll on her male colleagues, various ambiguous and suggestive remarks were made to Jenny concerning her sleeping arrangements. Brian decided that as the evening was deteriorating he would go to bed.

Having just received her award Jenny felt that she should remain at the dinner a little longer. However, as the evening progressed she became more and more uncomfortable. The wives of the salesmen ignored her and even her boss remarked that Brian would be waiting for her to join him upstairs. When the evening finally ended Jenny was extremely upset about the immature way her colleagues had behaved.

The aftermath

On her return to work back in the UK Jenny discovered that two of the married salesmen who had attended the Barbados convention had been accompanied by their girlfriends rather than their wives and that one of the girlfriends was a secretary in the company. Jenny presumed that the wives of these particular salesmen were unaware that they had been invited to the sales convention or that their husbands had preferred to take their girlfriends.

Jenny became extremely annoyed and complained about the way that she had been treated both by her colleagues and her boss. The manager replied that she was overreacting and that she was too sensitive about the situation. He pointed out that, prior to the convention, he had offered 'constructive advice' which she had chosen to ignore.

The experience of the Barbados convention revealed to Jenny the deep-seated and contradictory character of the highly masculine assumptions embedded both in the occupational culture of the sales force and in the management practices of Puffin Insurance.

Within 2 years of this experience Jenny resigned from the company, hoping to find a more supportive working environment elsewhere. Puffin had lost one of its most effective and knowledgeable employees.

(Margaret Collinson is a tutor and David Collinson a lecturer in organizational behaviour at Warwick Business School, University of Warwick.

Questions

1   Why did the manager take this view with his most successful sales representative?
2   If you had been the sales manager how would you have responded to the tensions between Jenny and the other sales representatives?
3   What does this case suggest about sex discrimination and gender inequality in employment?
4   What does the case reveal about the management of men's and women's sexuality in organizations?

Suggested answers to self-test questions

Contents

Chapter 1

1. List all the contacts you make with organizations in your day-to-day life.

There is a wide range of possible candidates here but a typical response should include contacts with all the utility services such as light, power and water. Also in the list should be T.V. and Radio companies if they are used for entertainment or information. The respondent might also read a newspaper so must include the organizations that create, distribute and sell it.

Organizations that provide transport to and from college or work might also be on the list, as will providers of meals or food during the day. Marketing messages can be seen on posters or billboards so the organizations that design and place them should also feature alongside the organization mentioned in the advert/publicity. Any shopping that is done during the day involves organizations that create, transport and retail the goods or services bought. Other organizations might be involved depending on what the person does during the day or evening.

2. Why are people the organization's best asset and their biggest potential liability?

People are the organization's biggest asset as they represent the capacity for innovation, creativity and they have the skills for combining all the other resources in the organization in the best possible way. The reason they are also the biggest liability is that through their actions or omissions, people can either make or break the organization. In addition respondents might cite the belief that for most organizations the wage bill is often the largest single expenditure item.

3. What are the three traditional levels of complexity used in the study of organizational behaviour?

The three traditional levels of complexity into which much of the study of OB is often classified are: **Individual**, i.e. what individuals do, how they react and behave in an organizational setting; **Group**, i.e. how people operate in teams or groups within organizations; and **Whole Organization**, where we consider the way organizations as whole entities, change and develop.

4. How far do you think that virtual organizations will be able to use technology to replace the functions that traditional organizations perform?

The response here needs to consider what aspects of organizations need to be physically located in the same place and which can be delivered in a technologically enhanced way. In service organizations it is likely that far less physical limitations are present compared to heavy manufacturing where plant and equipment has to be used. Where personal services such as hairdressing or tailoring are concerned moving the point of business from shops to clients has already occurred in a small scale.

In these and other examples where internet provision is growing rapidly, virtual organizations are already replacing many of the activities previously carried out by traditional organizations. Geographical boundaries are no barrier to virtual organizations, but work remains to be done to encourage consumer confidence in organizations that are hard to track down if things go wrong.

5. How does the use of indirect measures assist in identifying and estimating subjective phenomena?

Indirect measures of subjective things like emotion, motivation levels and attitudes aim to give an indication of the true readings which can be observed but not actually measured in themselves. Because of this reliance on accurate representation is necessary.

Someone might behave in a way that we normally interpret as being highly motivated but this interpretation could easily be mistaken, the individual concerned may not after all be highly motivated, but highly frustrated with the job and trying to make up for this by working in an apparently highly motivated way. In addition we often need to know the underlying causes of the behaviour and using indirect measures is less likely to throw any light on this. Just because somebody acts in a certain way, or displays a certain emotion, we still need to know the reasons why they are feeling like that.

In summary indirect measures are not ideal but they may be the only indication we can get, from which to interpret the implications of human behaviour. It would be wise to check interpretation at each stage and look for triangulation with a number of other indicators to ensure greater accuracy of understanding.

Chapter 2

1. Describe three key differences between nomothetic and idiographic approaches to the study of personality

Nomothetic approaches assume that every individual possesses the same personality traits, though in different quantities. Thus an extrovert differs from an introvert simply in terms of the quantity of extroversion s/he possesses. Conversely, idiographic approaches assume that personality is *unique* to each individual and that it is probably meaningless to attempt to compare individuals.

Nomothetic approaches assume that personality can be *measured* and used for purposes of *comparison*. From this perspective it would be possible to compare two individuals in order to judge which of the two possessed the 'right' characteristics for a job. Idiographic approaches suggest that it would be difficult to make such comparisons, because we cannot assume that two 'extroverts' possess similar characteristics.

Nomothetic approaches assume that individuals *do not change* their behaviour much across time or situations. This means it is possible to predict human behaviour. Idiographic approaches tend to be based on more *dynamic* assumptions about personality, believing that it may change or develop over time and situations.

2. What are the benefits of approaches that assume it is possible to measure personality?

It is useful to be able to *systematically and objectively* compare people in some work situations, such as selection.

If we assume that human behaviour can be *predicted*, then it may save organizations both time and money if personality measurement enables a better prediction of fit between a person and a job.

Organizations may better *justify* their selection deacons if they use personality measurement to form part of the basis for these decisions. Personality measurement, unlike some interviewing techniques, is said to be an *objective* measure of behaviour.

3. How does role theory differ from the theory of personal constructs?

Role theory views the source of our behaviour as residing in the *interaction* that takes place between the individual and others in his or her environment. Personal construct psychology views the source of our behaviour as residing in our own unique *perceptions* of the world.

Role theory is explicitly concerned with *behaviour*. Personal construct psychology is more concerned with *perceptions*.

Personal construct psychology is concerned with the way we see ourselves and focuses mainly on the *content* of our self-view. Role theory is concerned with the *processes* that mediate the acquisition of different roles and in specifying the factors that facilitate effective role learning or role taking (e.g. rewards).

4. What is an attitude?

An attitude is concerned with the way we think about objects in the social world. Most social psychologists agree that attitudes have three components – affective, cognitive and behavioural. This means that any given attitude we might have comprises an element of feeling (e.g. liking animals), an element of thinking (e.g believing animals to be important and in need of protection) and an element of behaviour (e.g. joining the RSPCA).

5. Explain why not all attitude-discrepant behaviours result in cognitive dissonance

It is broadly agreed that cognitive dissonance is most likely to occur when: (i) the individual believes they have freely committed to a certain course of action and when (ii) the individual has knowledge of the consequences of that action. Thus, for example, if I decided to buy a car and felt very pleased with my purchase, believing it to be both reliable and cost-effective, I would experience dissonance if a friend told me they had bought the same car for half the price. Cognitive dissonance theory predicts that I would be motivated to change my attitude about the car to bring it in line with my behaviour. Thus, in this case I might exaggerate some of the nicer features of my car to make my purchasing decision more understandable. However, if I bought the car because I had been persuaded to do so by a car salesman, or without knowing much about cars, I would probably experience less dissonance on receiving my friend's news, perhaps in these cases demanding my money back from the vendor of the car.

6. *Why are organizations keen to understand the processes that lead to job satisfaction and organizational commitment?*

It is generally assumed that people who are committed to their organization and who are satisfied with their job are more likely to put extra effort into their work, without needing much in the way of external motivators, such as pay or other rewards. Clearly, if organizations can understand how to motivate people intrinsically, then this would not only save them a lot of money, but perhaps facilitate their business performance through having highly productive employees. With more and more businesses operating in the service sector of the economy, the need to have highly motivated employees assumes more and more importance, because quite often the employee is the service. The demand for quality in the manufacturing sector also means that businesses need employees who are prepared to put extra effort and care into their work.

Chapter 3

1. What is the difference between content theories and process theories of motivation?

Content theories of motivation are concerned with identifying *what* motivates people, such as, for example, needs (Maslow) or rewards (Herzberg). Conversely, process theories of motivation are concerned with explaining *how* motivated behaviour occurs. For example, Vroom suggests that our judgements about the likelihood of improving our performance and the extent to which that will result in a valued outcome combine to influence the degree of effort we will put into any given activity. Conversely, Adams suggests that motivation proceeds from the process of comparing what we do and receive in comparison with people in similar circumstances to our own.

2. Differentiate between intrinsic and extrinsic motivators, providing two examples of each

Intrinsic motivators are those factors that cause motivated behaviour and which are located inside the person. Two examples might be need for self-actualization and need for friendship. Extrinsic motivators are those factors that cause motivation that are located outside the person. Two examples might be pay and the work environment.

3. List the key principles of scientific management

i. All jobs can be analysed and specified in terms of the activities and actions that comprise their content and outcomes.

ii. Some jobs can be redesigned so that outcomes can be achieved more efficiently by, for example, cutting out actions or activities that do not contribute to the job outcome.

iii. Jobs in the same class (e.g. production-line tasks) can be standardized so that the job becomes independent of any individual worker. The activities are specified to a precise degree.

iv. Individuals need only learn the job tasks and are not required or expected to innovate or develop their jobs.

v. Individuals can be encouraged to become more productive by offering financial incentives.

4. What is 360° appraisal and why might this system be preferable to traditional boss/subordinate appraisal?

360° appraisal is a form of performance management. Traditionally, organizations monitored job performance through boss/subordinate appraisal: the line manager gave their subordinates feedback about their job performance over the preceding year, using specific criteria (e.g. productivity, communication skills). 360° appraisal involves receiving feedback on job performance by a number of people who are in contact with the employees. Such people might include peers or colleagues, customers, members of other departments with whom the employee has dealings and the boss or line manager.

This form of appraisal is gaining in popularity for a number of reasons. First, as the name suggests it is a more rounded view of performance than traditional appraisals and thus is possibly more objective and fair. Second, as organizations develop ever-flatter hierarchies, the boss-subordinate ratio may be so great as to render traditional appraisal inappropriate. In such circumstances the line manager may not know the employee or may have little knowledge about the employee's job content. Third, the greater amount of feedback means that employees are more likely to accept it as valid and, as a consequence, be more prepared to adjust their performance in order to improve it.

5. Describe the Job Characteristics Model and its main predictions

The Job Characteristics Model attempts to specify those aspects of a job that will lead to improved performance and job satisfaction. The model suggests that individuals who experience their jobs as meaningful, who believe themselves to be responsible for the outcomes of their work and who are given feedback about their job performance are those most likely to be highly motivated and job satisfied, with the consequence that they will be productive and unlikely to be absent. The model predicts that jobs that contain variety (skill variety) that are perceived to have some importance in societal terms (task significance), and that the employee perceives to be a meaningful part of a whole process (task identity), are those that result in the experience of meaningfulness. Jobs that allow the individual to have some discretion or say in the way that the job is completed (autonomy) or carried out will be those most likely to result in the experience of responsibility for the job outcomes. Finally, the extent to which feedback is available to the employee, either from the job itself or from colleagues, bosses or customers, is vital to the experience of motivation.

6. Describe three changes in the work context that have occurred in the past 30 years

One of the major changes that has occurred is the economic shift from manufacturing to service industries. This has resulted in quite different sets of demands that employers have of employees. Organizations are now more concerned with personality and behaviour than previously, because in the service industry both are vital to effective business performance.

It is now more common for people to be employed on temporary short-term contracts, rather than permanent long-term contracts. This means that people are potentially more job insecure than ever before. The benefit for organizations is that they are not 'saddled' with employees who are not as productive as they could be. The disadvantage is that employees may lack commitment or loyalty to the business, being unconcerned with service or product quality.

It is also more common for people to have several career changes in their working lives, rather than training for specific skill or profession that is used throughout the working life of the individual.

Chapter 4

*1. **Explain the meaning of the following terms as they relate to group working: Group
cohesiveness; Formal groups and Informal group***

Responses

Group cohesiveness is the term used to describe the way members of a
group or team will stick together if times get tough. Cohesion is increased
by many team development programmes and often develops over time.
Negative events that affect the group like changes in personnel, changes
in roles or location can reduce cohesiveness. If group cohesion becomes
too strong the group might begin to set an agenda and prioritize issues and
activities that meet its own objectives and not those of the organization.

Formal groups are those found in organizational descriptions or charts.
Informal groups are more likely to emerge around social or unofficial
activities. Formal groups often have written procedures and scheduled
events which take care of group activities. Informal groups will be more
fluid and tend to tackle issues as they arise without resorting to a structure
or a procedure. One could argue that informality is more conducive to
creativity and speed of solutions, while formal groups will be more
effective in ensuring rules are complied with and procedures are followed.

Team roles is the term used by authors such as Belbin and Margerison
and McCann to describe the various activities that have to be completed in
effective groups. These roles include things like orchestrating the group,
planning activities, doing things, supporting other members and evaluating
what has gone on (among others). Research points to different people
having a preference for operating in different roles. So long as all the
roles are covered by the members collectively, group effectiveness will be
high. Where people have to perform roles that are outside their preferred
range they are likely to experience frustration and difficulty in performing
to a high level. In putting together new teams or investigating why teams
are not performing to a high level, consideration of the roles and who is
completing them often supplies valuable insights.

*2. **According to Belbin, what are the main roles that need to be present to create effective
work-groups?***

The Belbin team roles are:

- Implementer

- Co-ordinator
- Shaper
- Plant
- Resource-investigator
- Monitor-evaluator
- Team-worker
- Completer-finisher

3. What could cause the misalignment of group or team goals with organizational ones?

Group or team goals could be misaligned with those of the organization because the group members are not aware of what the organization's goals are. Alternatively the goals and objectives of the organization might have changed significantly and the group is still working to old established ones.

A more serious situation occurs when the group deliberately operates with a different set of objectives because they believe the official organizational ones to be wrong. It could be that the group is operating closer to customers or has information from suppliers that other parts of the organization does not have access to. If this situation is allowed to continue the organization will have to consider whether to force the group to change its objectives or agree that they were right after all. Where this situation occurs and the organization refuses to change its position, the group may consider moving away from the organization and setting up on its own, many organizations started in this way.

4. What are the main negative aspects of team-working?

Teams and teamworking does not always provide the best way for the organization to achieve its objectives. Teams often take longer to make decisions than individuals so for situations where speed is essential, individual action might be preferable. Teams might also be unable to organize themselves well and may prefer to use collective responsibility rather than seeking to take responsibility individually for results or errors.

Teams may exert undue influence on individual members and insist on adherence to group norms at the expense of individual creativity, although this must be balanced against the likelihood of increased interaction in teams which should lead to more creative solutions.

5. What are the four stages of the Tuckman model of group development?

- Forming – when the group first gets together
- Storming – when the group sorts out roles and responsibilities
- Norming – when group rules are established
- Performing – when the group actually begins to achieve results

6. What are the pros and cons of Self-managed work-teams?

Pros	Cons
Prioritizing can be achieved by those having to do the tasks.	Need a higher level of skills in the team.
Teams can achieve 'ownership' of issues.	Organization needs to be able to trust the team to deliver.
Succession planning and recruitment to the team can be carried out by the members.	
Disciplinary and reward issues can be dealt with by the team.	Risk that the team will adopt objectives that are not what the organization needs.
Motivation is likely to be higher.	
Less management time will be required.	

What are the main factors likely to raise or lower the effectiveness of work-groups?

7. Physical environment

A group's physical environment affects interaction within the group. Even items as apparently trivial as the layout of the work-room will affect who interacts with whom. Circular tables are likely to encourage more participation, with interchangeable leadership, while teams that work predominantly in isolated cubicles and only come together for the occasional group meeting will be less interactive.

Social environment

Compatibility of group members in both needs and personality may lead to higher group productivity. Individuals who have a high need for dominance, for example, are more compatible with people who can play a subordinate role. The level of group conflict will inevitably increase where the members are not compatible.

Numbers in group

Typically, productivity is lower in large groups than in small ones. Group-size has several effects, including the degree of participation possible, and the strength of bonds between members. Large groups have more resources to call upon, but these will be balanced by the difficulties of getting agreement between large numbers of people on a course of action.

Nature of task

Two characteristics of group tasks have a major impact on how effective that group will be. If the task requires a high degree of co-operation, (e.g. a hospital surgical team), small groups will generally be more effective than large ones. It is easier to manage the co-operation and co-ordination of smaller numbers. The second factor concerns the degree of complexity of the task.

Chapter 5

1. What is leadership and how does it differ from management?

Leadership is where the organization gets its vision and direction from. Leaders also have to get other employees to buy into the vision and direction in order to mobilize support. The final job of the leader is to motivate and inspire staff to produce their best efforts.

Management, in contrast, is focused much more on activities that control what is going on in the organization. Managers work to plans, deal with budgets and concentrate on making activities as efficient as possible. A manager can require others to work often by virtue of their positional power. Leaders often work more through influence and personality relying far less on the power of their position.

To summarize, while leadership sets the direction and tries to inspire performance, managers seek to ensure that the operations that are required to satisfy the leadership are carried out to a maximum quality with the minimum resources.

2. Where does leadership power come from and how can it be lost?

In the chapter you will see the following sources of leadership power listed:

- **Legitimate power:** power coming from a formal position in the organization and from the authority attached to it.
- **Reward power:** stemming from the leader's ability to bestow rewards, financial or otherwise.
- **Coercive power:** the power to punish or recommend punishment.
- **Expert power:** resulting from the leader's knowledge or skill regarding the tasks performed by followers.
- **Referent power:** coming from the leader's personality characteristics that command identification and respect.
- **Elected power:** power derived from votes of interested parties, such as trade-union representatives.
- **Resource power:** the power to allow use of exclusive resources, such as land or capital.

3. What are the different leadership styles that can be used?

Most classifications describe a spectrum of leadership style from dictatorial, where the leader does not see the need to discuss any aspect of the policies and procedures decided, s/he just insists that his or her employees do what s/he says, through to democratic. At the other end of the spectrum is the democratic style of leadership where widespread consultation and assessment of a variety of opinions lead to the final decision. In between are the consultative style where the leader canvasses opinion from senior members of the organization before making a decision and participative where organization members other than the leader are given the opportunity to take the decision in accordance within a predetermined set of principles.

4. What skills and abilities will the leader of the future need?

In the chapter you will find the claim that in the future leaders may require different skills in order to cope with the changing demand on organizations to be more flexible, quicker to react to market changes and more reliant on developing the organization's knowledge base.

These future skills are described as:

- **Orchestrating:** seeking to influence and direct the organization from afar.
- **Acting as a focal point for organizational learning:** developing systems and procedures that will allow the fostering and capture of organizational knowledge.
- **Facilitating 'different types of thinking'** about business problems or product and service innovations.

Chapter 6

1. List the main features of bureaucracy

      i. hierarchical ordering of positions; that is, levels of power and authority;

      ii. authority: the power to enforce sanctions and rewards;

      iii. regulation of activities: all jobs should be described in terms of the tasks and activities of which they are composed. The way different jobs relate to each other should be clearly stated;

      iv. impersonal rules: any job will have certain rules and regulations that have to be followed. These rules and regulations are part of the job, not of the person doing the job;

      v. appointments based on qualifications: jobs should be filled by people who have the appropriate skills and abilities.

2. To what sorts of environmental conditions is a bureaucratic structure most suited?

Bureacratic structures are most suited to environments that are stable and relatively certain; that is, where there are unlikely to be major changes to which the organization might need to rapidly adapt.

3. List the main features of an organic organization and describe the environment to which it is most suited

      i. fewer levels of hierarchy;

      ii. knowledge and skills are the basis for authority and power;

      iii. communication is networked rather than linear;

      iv. few rules and loosely defined roles.

Organic organizations are most suited to environments that are highly uncertain and turbulent. The organic organization is able to adapt to major changes and it can respond rapidly to changes as they occur.

4. What are contingency theories?

Contingency theories of organization are concerned with understanding conditions both inside and outside the organization that mediate structure. Contingency theories attempt to specify the links between strategy and structure. For example, Chandler (1962) argued that as the economic environment changed – decline or evolution of certain product markets and technologies – organizations had to develop strategies to enable them to survive. For example, a company who make soft drinks might need to develop a strategy to produce different types of drink or even a completely different product as the demand for its original product fluctuates. When this happens, the company will need to consider its structure. For instance, in the example we are using the company may need to split into divisions if it develops new products and may need to think about ways of both marketing its new product as well as gathering relevant market information to enable it to compete.

5. Describe any four organizational subsystems

Strategic subsystem: proactive or defensive
This is concerned with how the organization approaches its strategic planning. Some organizations tend to react to changes as they occur. For example, a business might discover its market share is being reduced by a competitor and may take steps to counteract this, such as an aggressive marketing campaign. Conversely, the organization might take a very proactive stance in its planning, anticipating changes as they occur. For example, many companies developed their own websites in anticipation of the explosion of the Internet.

Technological subsystem: complex or routine
Technology in this sense refers to the methods used to achieve the organization's chief task. This can obviously involve information technology, but also embraces human skills and knowledge. Some technologies are highly complex, changing rapidly as new research becomes available. Medical science is one example here. Other technologies are more straightforward and tend not to change much over the years. A master furniture craftsman might be one such example.

Structural subsystem: mechanistic or organic
This is concerned with how the organization is structured. Is it highly bureaucratic with many rules and tightly specified roles, or is it more organic with a relatively flat hierarchy and much functional flexibility?

Managerial subsystem: autocratic or democratic
This is concerned with the general behaviour and methods of management. An autocratic subsystem will be characterized by command and control

management activities, where the emphasis is on surveillance, monitoring and the correction of poor performance. Conversely, a democratic subsystem will be characterized by consultation, considerable autonomy and discretion afforded to employees and the opportunity for everyone to influence strategy and goals.

6. What does the term congruence with reference to the systems approach to organizational analysis mean?

The systems approach to organizational analysis assumes that, like any organic system, all subsystems need to be working harmoniously to ensure the health of the whole system. Thus, for example, if the human heart starts to dysfunction, it will be incongruent with other subsystems which are co-dependent with it. So, for instance, the skeletal system will suffer because not enough oxygen and other nutrients are being transported to it. Similarly, organizational subsystems are co-dependent. So, a subsystem that is working in opposition to any others will create problems. For instance, if an organization is structured bureaucratically, but has a democratic managerial subsystem, this might cause problems because the structures and mechanisms that will be needed to facilitate effective consultation are unlikely to be in place.

7. List the strengths and weaknesses of both the systems and structure approaches to organizational analysis

Strengths of structural organizational analysis
  i. draws attention to the importance of the business environment;
 ii. helps an organization identify what needs to change to facilitate adaptation to environmental changes;
iii. provides a clear visual picture of the organization's functions.

Limitations
  i. plays down the behavioural elements of organizational life. Reducing hierarchical levels will not guarantee an 'organic' response;
 ii. plays down issues of power and conflict. Most organizations have some form of hierarchy, no matter how 'flat'. This means that there are always power relations in organizations that result in conflict and dissatisfaction.

Strengths of the systems approach to organizational analysis

i. draws attention to the sub-components of an organization and to an understanding of how they relate to each other and the broader business environment;

ii. focuses on the sites where subsystems may be in conflict with each other, enabling an understanding of where problems may be occurring.

Limitations

i. very rational in its assumptions. For example, while it can help us identify that the managerial subsystem is incongruent with the structural subsystem, it provides little insight into why this might be the case;

ii. assumes that organizational subsystems should work harmoniously. However, it is clearly the case that conflict and lack of harmony can sometimes facilitate organizational learning and development.

8. List some of the key features of a flexible firm

i. numerical flexibility: organizations employ a minimum number of core staff, usually on permanent or long-term contracts and a large number of peripheral staff who are brought in at key times, on short-term contracts to cope with fluctuations in demand.

ii. functional flexibility: employees are employed to perform a range of skills, which may include some supervisory duties. There is no demarcation and employees are deployed to tasks as dictated by production or service demands;

iii. outsourcing: organizations place many peripheral functions, such as cleaning, catering and recruiting, in the hands of external contractors. The organization is able to ensure that these functions are carried out cost effectively by encouraging tenders for contracts.

9. Briefly describe the features of a complex system and explain why these are useful to consider in an organizational analysis

i. emergent order: complex systems are not designed deliberately. The function of the system emerges as an inherent property of the system;

ii. radical unpredictability: complex systems cannot be analysed into discrete components that enable predictive models of their behaviour to be developed. Complex systems behave in unpredictable ways and it is not possible to identify all the variables that influence their behaviour;

iii. chaos: complex systems do not behave in regulated ways. Rather, they behave in erratic ways that at face value make little sense. However, the irregularities in the system appear to be the source of its survival and development.

Complexity theory is useful for analysing organizations because they show many of the elements of complex systems. Once this is accepted, the traditional assumptions of prediction and control can be discarded and instead the focus is on learning and development. Thus, for instance, rather than being concerned with what might happen if a manager is not present to supervise a group of workers, the focus is on allowing the group to self-direct and develop their own ideas and methods of working.

Chapter 7

1. Describe what is meant by unitarist and pluralist views of organization

A unitarist view of organizations sees them as composed of people who are essentially similar in their goals and values. From this perspective organizational members are seen to be in broad agreement about what the organization is like and what it should be doing. Conversely, a pluralist perspective sees organizations as composed of diverse groups, are unlikely to be in agreement at all times, and who are also likely to have competing interests and goals.

2. How can organizational culture be defined?

Organizational culture is concerned with the behavioural elements of organizational life. Specifically, it attempts to identify values, beliefs and attitudes that are shared by members of an organization and which serve as 'guides to action'.

3. What is the difference between functionalist and interpretive approaches to organizational culture?

Functionalist approaches view organizational culture as something that an organization possesses that can be both managed and changed. These approaches tend to see the founder of the organization as key to the formation of the attitudes and beliefs that come to be shared by organizational members. In contrast, interpretive approaches view culture as something an organization is. From this perspective culture is a subjective experience comprising the resources that organizational members use to make sense of their working experiences. Culture is seen as neither manageable, nor amenable to change, but as something that is both reproduced and transformed through organizational practices and societal norms.

4. Describe two of the dimensions along which culture can be analysed according to Schein's typology

The nature of human activity (beliefs about what the core activity of the business should be)
Organizational members have beliefs about what the organization's principal purpose should be. While there is likely to be some consensus,

there will also be differences. For instance, in hospitals many of the staff may believe that the principal purpose should be to make people well and to educate people as to how to maintain and improve their general health. However, hospital managers may believe that the core activity should be ensuring that the resources available are allocated appropriately and that departments should learn to stick within budgets.

The nature of human nature (beliefs about what people are like)
Organizations tend to develop theories about certain groups with whom they come into contact. For instance, in many organizations there are strong ideas about the importance of reliability in colleagues. However, companies may also develop ideas about the typical customer, or the typical consumer. Such beliefs can have a strong influence on the way employees behave. For instance, if a company believes that a typical customer does not really know much about the product or service they are buying, this may lead them to attempt to 'bend' the truth about the product or service.

5. What are the chief disadvantages of a cultural analysis?

    i. explicitly concerned with the behaviour of employees and in developing an in-depth understanding of the factors that influence behaviour;

    ii. systematic and rigorous analytic tool that helps identify why a specific organizational change process is faltering or being resisted;

    iii. useful for examining contradictions between what the organization says it wants to achieve and how it actually behaves. For example, expressing ideals about customer satisfaction while employing few mechanisms to actually monitor the extent of it.

6. Name two features of a typical definition of power

    i. the idea that power is a possession; that is, that power resides in a person and is a characteristic of that person;

    ii. the idea that power has an effect on the behaviour of others. A person with power is assumed to have the ability to persuade other people to do his or her will.

7. List Pfeffer's bases of organizational power

       i. providing resources;
       ii. coping with uncertainty;
       iii. being irreplaceable;
       iv. affecting decision processes;
       v. being central.

8. Explain why the possession of power alone will not guarantee its expression

Sometimes groups or individuals may not recognize that they possess power. For instance, some employees may not realize that the knowledge they possess has given them the power of being irreplaceable. If a group or person does not realize they possess power, then they are unlikely to express it. Possessing power and recognizing that possession are insufficient conditions for guaranteeing its expression. To mobilize power individuals need to believe that there is an attainable reward to be had. For example, a group of employees who realize they are irreplaceable are only likely to mobilize power to gain some advantage – say, resources. Conversely, a group may recognize its power and have a reward in mind that would justify its mobilization, but may be dissuaded from mobilizing their power because of perceived sanctions – say, fear of redundancy.

9. What is meant by a stakeholder analysis and what is its value?

A stakeholder analysis involves drawing a map of all the groups that are likely to have an interest in any given organizational decision. Thus, for instance, if a mobile-phone company wanted to build a new mast in a particular town, it would need to consider all the people who are likely to be for and against the development. Individuals likely to be in favour of the development would be mobile-phone owners and the company itself, while opposition might come from local residents and competitors. The value of such an analysis is that it draws attention to the specific differences of interest that exist both within and outside the organization and encourages a greater consideration of decisions and options.

10. What might cause conflict in an organization and what steps can be taken to manage it?

   i. Intraorganizational conflict: occurs between functions or departments, often over resource or responsibility disputes
   ii. Intragroup conflict: members of the same group or team disagree
   iii. Intergroup conflict: one part of the organization has a dispute with another
   iv. Interpersonal conflict: between a customer and a salesperson, for example
   v. Intrapersonal conflict: occurs within an individual because of a threat to personal values or beliefs, or a feeling of unfairness.

Two of the most common conflict management strategies are negotiation and mediation. Both strategies explicitly recognize that the interests of the conflicting parties are unlikely to be brought into line, and thus the focus is on achieving a mutually acceptable solution with compromise on both sides. Negotiation involves developing a compromise solution to a problem that is acceptable to all. For instance, a mobile phone company may lose a bid to erect its mast in a field near a residential estate, but might secure permission to buy another piece of land. Mediation involves a third party that develops a solution that is likely to be acceptable by both parties. For example, a dispute between a trade union and a company might be resolved by a third party mediator who arrives at a solution that meeets the demands of neither party, but prevents escalation of the conflict.

Chapter 8

1. List the sources of workforce diversity

      i. gender;
     ii. race;
   iii. disability;
   iv. religion;
    v. sexuality;
   vi. work style;
  vii. skills;
 viii. knowledge;
   ix. personality;
    x. values and attitudes.

2. In what ways are minorities disadvantaged in the workplace?

Research suggests that members of minority groups tend to be both vertically and horizontally segregated in the workplace; that is, they tend not to be well represented in the upper or senior levels of the hierarchy and tend to be over-represented in low-status, low-skill roles. In addition, in the economy generally minorities fill most of the lowest paid, lowest status occupations and tend to be over-represented in temporary short-term, part-time jobs.

3. What does the term 'glass ceiling' mean?

The phrase 'the glass ceiling' was coined to illustrate that, for many minorities, promotion opportunities are visible and potentially attainable. However, barriers operate to exclude them from promotion. These barriers tend to be subtle and difficult to identify.

4. In what ways might organizational culture impede the career progression of women?

Where men numerically dominate in an organization, it has been suggested that the culture will come to reflect 'masculine' ways of thinking and behaving. Studies suggest that these forms of cultural masculinity impede the career progress of women by:

   i. rendering access to informal social networks problematic, since these tend to reflect male interests such as sport;

ii. making it difficult for women to be perceived as 'fitting in' because the working vocabulary reflects masculine interests (e.g. the use of military metaphors);

iii. making it difficult for women to be perceived as competent by emphasizing the importance of those aspects of the job most commonly associated with masculinity (e.g. technical versus social skills);

iv. making it difficult for women to experience inclusion because of the difficulties they have managing their own gender and its associated visibility.

5. In what ways does socialization affect the self-perceptions of men and women?

Socialization is the process through which individuals learn to conform with society's expectations. Different expectations exist with regards to what is perceived as appropriate behaviour for men and women. Women are expected to be good at relationships and more importantly to define themselves mainly through domestic concerns, such as the home and family. In contrast, men are expected to be the breadwinners, though this is probably changing somewhat. Men are expected to define themselves more through work than through home and to be interested in career progression.

These expectations appear to influence men and women's self-perceptions. Women tend to be less confident than men with regards to their own abilities and tend to perceive themselves as better at jobs requiring interpersonal rather than technical skills.

6. Describe how organizations reinforce societal expectations about appropriate roles for men and women

Organizations may reinforce societal expectations in the following ways:

i. deploying men and women in roles that mirror cultural definitions of femininity and masculinity;

ii. making stereotyped judgements about men and women during selection interviews;

iii. encouraging practices that are difficult for women to engage in, such as long working hours. This promotes the stereotyped assumption that women are less committed to their jobs than are their male counterparts.

7. What does the term 'dual commitment' mean?

Dual commitment refers to working parents (usually women) who are committed both to their job or profession and to their domestic responsibilities.

8. Define the concept of embodiment and illustrate how it affects career aspirations

Embodiment is a concept that suggests that our identity is greater than our self-concepts or self-views. It is inscribed in the ways we walk, talk, move, sit and look. Individuals tend to embody characteristics of particular social groups and are readily identifiable because of this. For example, research suggests that people are very good at differentiating between different social classes based on body posture alone and also that certain professions or occupations become embodied so that being a surgeon, for example, is more than the acquisition of medical knowledge and surgical skills. It also embraces posture and appearance. It is argued that some occupations are so embodied that members of some social categories are unable to perceive themselves in those roles. Surgery is one example, policing may be another.

9. Describe the practices that organizations can use to attract minorities

Positive discrimination
This is concerned with stacking the deck in favour of a particular minority group. Organizations can achieve this in a number of ways:

   i. advertising in minority media (e.g. gay and ethnic newspapers);
  ii. asking for candidates from particular minorities in the job advert;
 iii. shortlisting minorities only.

Flexible working practices
These sorts of practice are different from those commonly called flexible working practices (short-term temporary jobs). In terms of managing diversity, flexible working practices involve the introduction of working schedules that enable groups like mothers, and some religions, to accommodate their non-work commitments. Such practices include flexitime (allowing flexibility in starting and finishing times), annualized hours (allowing individuals to work when they can), homeworking, job-share, part-time working and the introduction of in-house crèches.

10. *Describe the practices organizations can use to prevent discrimination against minorities during the selection process*

    i. equal-opportunities policies: written statements that specify how the organization intends to reduce discrimination and which provide details of what individuals can do if they suspect they have been the victim of discrimination;

    ii. selection training: raising awareness of how stereotyped judgements can be taken for granted and how such judgements can operate to discriminate;

    iii. training people to use specific, objective and fair selection techniques, such as structured interviews;

    iv. minority monitoring: keeping tabs on both the number of minorities applying to various roles and departments and the number succeeding in their applications.

11. *Why do organizations need to be concerned with managing as well as increasing workforce diversity?*

Organizations might manage to increase diversity through any of the practices discussed above. However, to ensure that minorities receive fair treatment once employed, organizations need to monitor what happens to minorities in terms of career progression, career opportunities, treatment and turnover.

12. *Outline three approaches to diversity management*

    i. episodic approaches: the organization stages 'one-off' managing-diversity initiatives, such as a training event on equal opportunities or a seminar on racial prejudice;

    ii. free-standing approaches: the organization has a planned and continuous programme of diversity-management initiatives, but these are not evaluated or monitored against any strategic goals or standard;

    iii. systemic approaches: the organization's diversity-management initiatives are closely related to organizational strategy and goals. This means that the outcomes of such initiatives are evaluated against agreed criteria.

13. Detail the features of the managing-diversity strategy web

    i. organizational vision: organizations should make a clear statement about why diversity is considered to be important and on the ways in which diversity is linked to their business objectives;

    ii. top management commitment;

    iii. auditing and assessment of needs: the organization should examine its culture, and the systems and procedures in operation, and the make-up of their human resources;

    iv. clarity of objectives: the organization sets out a clearly defined strategy for tackling diversity issues and a timetable for their resolution;

    v. clear accountability: setting out who is responsible for ensuring the achievement of objectives and encouraging accountability through the organization's reward system;

    vi. effective communication: fostering ownership for diversity through various media including training, consultation meetings, use of steering groups and policy committees;

    vii. coordination of activity: individuals, or groups of individuals, need to be given specific responsibility for coordinating the various parts of the diversity initiative, for deciding what needs to be communicated to whom and for providing the organization with the 'big picture';

    viii. evaluation: evaluation of the diversity strategy must be done against the set objectives.

14. Explain some of the limitations of the strategy-web approach

    i. takes a unitarist view of organizations;

    ii. assumes that people will be honest in expressing their views about diversity issues;

    iii. managing diversity may be perceived as another 'management fad'.

    iv. 'sells' diversity as a business enhancer. Little evidence to support this view.

Chapter 9

1. What is meant by the term organizational development?

Organizational development (OD) is the term given to all the activities carried out with the intention of improving the organization's ability to meet its objectives. Typically OD often involves change in organization policies, training and developing employees and introduction of new technology. The best organizations see development as an ongoing activity and not a one-off event. This means that resources and time have to be devoted to the needs of development. When we see examples of restructuring or major change over a short period in an organization, we could argue that there has been insufficient attention paid to development in previous years. necessitating a catch up which is often painful and distressing for organization members.

2. Explain one model of how organizations are thought to change and develop over time

The text explains the Smither, Houston and McIntire (1996) model of OD where it is possible to speak of a typical life cycle in which the organization goes through a number of stages from birth to decline. The first phase is known as the birth phase; as the organization grows, direct owner control is usually replaced by a group of managers. This is the second phase known as the growth phase, where increased specialization within the organization often leads to functional division and the subsequent redistribution of managerial responsibilities. Next comes the maturity phase of the cycle, where growth will begin to slow down and the management task now becomes one of getting more efficiency out of established relationships. If the organization becomes so ineffective that restructuring, innovation or major renewal is required, the next phase of the life cycle – revival – could see the return to growth and even rapid expansion if the strategic vision to take the company forward is right. The final phase is that of decline, growth has slowed right down and the organization is preoccupied with internal not external issues.

3. How is the concept of knowledge management crucial to organizational development?

Knowledge management represents a key challenge to organizations in the age where knowledge and information is a crucial resource. Many organizations are looking for methods of mining the know-how and expertise that they already have, so that better and faster solutions to customer and organizational problems can be found. Many of the solutions look to Intranet or Internet technology to improve accessibility to knowledge for organization members. Another consideration should be the way the organization values and rewards knowledge and knowledge sharing. Where the culture of the organization dictates that information is treated as power and kept a closely guarded secret, the benefits of knowledge management will be hard to realize. If a culture of sharing knowledge and building on it is predominant, overall organizational effectiveness will be improved.

4. *Why is management development and training thought to be a central part of organizational development?*

Management development is a central part of OD because the things that managers do naturally dictate the way the organization changes, improves or stagnates. In effect, managers are responsible for implementation and resourcing of any changes that the owners feel is required. The quality of management within the organization will dictate how effectively any changes can be introduced so investment in developing the abilities of managers will have considerable payoffs.

Seeing managers as responsible for change and development as well as the day-to-day running of the business of the organization is placing more pressure on them. As a result, it is only reasonable to offer training and development support to organization managers. The traditional set of managerial skills required for maintaining and controlling the organization are very different from that set which is required for designing, implementing and evaluating changes. Many managers will need to be given assistance to be able to deal with the pressures of change and development alongside their existing role.

Recently, developments in the way we train managers have been able to offer more advice, guidance and skill-development exercises to existing managers. Major changes have occurred recently in management training. Where traditionally the acquisition of a specific knowledge base was the main activity, modern development programmes also include behavioural and psychological training in the process.

Index

Key terms are colour-highlighted